T0271674

The Lives & Deaths
of the
Princesses *of* Hesse

FRANCES WELCH

The Lives & Deaths *of the* Princesses *of* Hesse

The curious destinies of
Queen Victoria's granddaughters

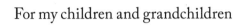

For my children and grandchildren

The letters of Princess Irène and several others are reproduced with the kind permission of the Hemmelmark Archives © Donata Herzogin zu Mecklenburg von Solodkoff.

First published in Great Britain in 2024 by Short Books, an imprint of
Octopus Publishing Group Ltd
Carmelite House
50 Victoria Embankment
London EC4Y 0DZ
www.octopusbooks.co.uk

An Hachette UK Company
www.hachette.co.uk

The authorized representative in the EEA is Hachette Ireland,
8 Castlecourt Centre, Dublin 15, D15 XTP3, Ireland (email: info@hbgi.ie)

Text copyright © Frances Welch 2024
Royal Collection Trust/© His Majesty King Charles III 2022

ISBN 978-1-78072-521-5

A CIP catalogue record for this book is available from the British Library.

Printed and bound in the United Kingdom

10 9 8 7 6 5 4

This FSC® label means that materials used for the product have been responsibly sourced

AUTHOR'S NOTE

Regarding dates, I have generally stuck to our Gregorian calendar. Occasional quotes from the Tsar's diary, however, remain in the old Julian Calendar, which is 12 or 13 days behind.

The Hesse sisters' letters to each other, mostly written in English, are frequently ungrammatical, with odd spellings and German word order and phrasing. To retain their full flavour, they are reproduced verbatim; to avoid interrupting the flow, I have used 'sic' sparingly. The sisters' anachronistic expressions remain in place, though some will jar with modern sensibilities.

'Did the Tsarina, surrounded by snow
in her gloomy Romanov palaces, dream
of Hesse? What terrible dooms and
destinies the family have had!'
Sir Henry 'Chips' Channon,
Monday October 6 1952,
Wolfsgarten.

PREFACE

'It is rapidly getting too late. Those
horrid words – too late.'
Irène

Weeks before the Russian Revolution, in February 1917, the Tsarina
Alexandra was installed, as usual, in her garish, mauve boudoir.

Nearly three years into the Great War, the Russian Army was struggling.
The British Government had sent a mission headed by General Sir Henry
Wilson to establish Russia's specific military needs. There was talk in Britain
of upheavals at the heart of the Imperial Court.

Upon his arrival at the Imperial Family's Alexander Palace, outside St
Petersburg, Sir Henry was struck instead by the lack of upheavals: 'We were
received in a charming suite of rooms with court officers in quaint uniforms
& some servants in marvellous Catherine [the great] clothes and feathers
in bonnets . . .'

The Tsarina had specially requested a meeting with Sir Henry and he was
duly escorted down a long corridor to her boudoir. As the pair exchanged
stiff greetings, he noted that she was surrounded by an unlikely array of
flowers, pictures and bric-a-brac.

The session began badly, perhaps not helped by the glacial temperature
of the room: the Tsarina always maintained that her lilacs thrived in a chill.
She had been keen to see the General because she remembered him from
her childhood days in Germany. As a 19-year-old student, Sir Henry had
spent a year learning German in Darmstadt, regularly visiting 'Alix', and

her three elder sisters who lived nearby. During the tennis parties, he had partnered all four girls, but Alix, 'Princess Sunshine' as she was known, had become his particular favourite, giggling as he fondly berated her for her indolence and lack of application on the court.

To Sir Henry, however, the 44-year-old Tsarina now seemed rather forbidding and remote, as though she were anxious to wind up the reunion as soon as possible. Registering her altered appearance, the General was struck by her profound melancholy: 'She has a beautiful face, but very, very sad. She is tall and graceful, divides her hair simply at one side and it is done up at the back. The hair is powdered with grey.'

Still, the bluff General was not to be put off, and the atmosphere was immediately transformed when he began harking back to the happy times the pair had shared 34 years before in Hesse-Darmstadt. He later described the breakthrough: 'She was very pleasant and nice to me. I reminded her of our tennis parties in the old days . . . She was so delighted with the reminiscences and remembered some of the names I'd forgotten . . . When I said I was going to leave her as she must be tired of seeing strangers and making conversation, she nearly laughed and kept me on for a long while.'

*

Alix and her sisters – the daughters of Louis IV, Grand Duke of Hesse, and Queen Victoria's second daughter, Alice – had grown up at the relatively informal Hesse Court in Darmstadt. Throughout their lives, they enjoyed repeated get-togethers at their 'dear old home', their affection undiminished by a series of traumatic blows, not least the early loss of their mother, Princess Alice, to diphtheria.

The girls had strong ties with Britain. With their mother, they regularly travelled back and forth for holidays with Queen Victoria at Balmoral and Osborne House. And after her death in 1878, the girls were eagerly adopted by their grandmama. Through their teenage years, she increasingly assumed a Mrs Bennet role as she agonised over their marriage prospects, assembling lists of suitable aristocrats, only to find herself repeatedly thwarted.

In 1883, at the time of young Henry Wilson's visit to Darmstadt, the Queen's matchmaking machinations were at an anxious peak. The eldest Hesse princess, Victoria, then 20 years old, was the sharpest and most capable of the sisters and the one to whom the others went with their worries. At that point she was engaged to Prince Louis Battenberg, an eminently sensible choice. However, the Queen was put out because the Prince had not featured on her lists; meanwhile, some of their relations felt that Victoria's fiancé was not quite smart or rich enough.

Eighteen-year-old Ella was the beauty of the four. Henry, who reportedly set his cap at her at the time, described her as the loveliest girl he had ever seen. She combined her arresting looks with poise and a decorous manner; she was accustomed to being in Grandmama's good books. But that year, she had fallen for an equally statuesque Russian grand duke, and Queen Victoria was horrified. She had not got over the Crimean War, which pitted the Russians against the British. She dismissed their people as savage, and disapproved particularly of the hulking Tsar Alexander III, who played the tuba and bent forks in knots at table.

She summoned Ella to England, intent on putting her off Russia and Russians for ever. She succeeded in persuading her to break off the relationship, only for the towering Grand Duke Serge to return to Darmstadt weeks later and win her back. By that autumn, the couple were formally engaged and the defeated Queen was furious: 'She refused Serge three weeks ago and now she takes him and forgets all!'

The third Princess, Irène, then aged 17, was the slowest and least striking of the four. Feeling herself outshone, Irène grew ever more diffident. But if Grandmama presumed that Irène, at least, would do her bidding, she was wrong. Four years after Ella's unsuitable engagement, the Queen was dismayed to hear that Irène was now engaged to the future Kaiser Wilhelm's younger brother, Prince Henry.

The Prussian Princes were first cousins to the Hesse sisters: their mother was Queen Victoria's eldest daughter, Vicky. The Queen disliked the idea of matches between first cousins, but she also had reservations about the boys themselves. In contrast to their more modest Hesse cousins, the Princes were full of the pomp of the Berlin Court. The Queen was shocked by their brazen lack of respect for their English mother. She had been very put out years earlier to hear 'Willie's' boasts of an improbable love match between him and Ella, who was at that point aged only 11. She made every effort to keep Irène and Prince Henry apart. But in the end, their match might have been something of a relief: the Queen had, by then, heard wind of Irène's attachment to a second Grand Duke, and raged: 'I shall never forgive it, if she is also to go to that horrid, corrupt country.'

As the Queen struggled with the marriage choices of the eldest three Hesse sisters, her bitterest blow was yet to fall. She had the highest hopes for Alix, her favourite little granddaughter, who almost matched Ella in looks and was as merry as her eldest sister, Victoria. These all came crashing down, in 1894, 11 years after the young Henry's Darmstadt sojourn, when Alix accepted a proposal from the Russian Tsarevich, Nicholas. The Queen declared herself 'thunderstruck', despairing to Victoria: 'Çela me revolte to feel that she has been taken possession of and carried away by those Russians.'

*

Fortunately, Queen Victoria did not live to see her direst fears regarding 'those Russians' and their 'horrid corrupt country' realised. She died in January 1901, and was spared the various tragedies of her beloved Hesse granddaughters as they became caught up in the maelstrom of early 20th-century Europe.

Russia began its descent into violent political turmoil and the ferment became such that Grand Duchess Ella and Tsarina Alexandra were both in danger from revolutionaries. The four sisters' easy comings and goings were brought to a halt as Ella warned against visits. The Tsarina barely left Russia for fear of terrorists.

The outbreak of war, in 1914, put a further strain on relations. Irène, in Germany, found her country ranged against those of her three sisters in Russia and Britain. Communication and travel became almost impossible. Britain was technically allied with Russia, but efforts to maintain links were continually thwarted by the chaos of war and ongoing revolutionary agitation. Letters to Irène, in Germany, frequently had to be sent via neutral Sweden.

During his visit to St Petersburg in 1917, General Sir Henry Wilson reported a troubled reference made by the Tsarina to her sisters: 'She said her lot was harder than most people's because she had relations and friends in England, Russia and Germany.'

Both he and Alix would have been aware of her predicament in Russia. She and Ella were ever more unpopular, labelled 'the German witches'. The Tsarina was justly accused of interfering in matters of state. Sir Henry may have wished she had retained more of the indolence that had blighted her tennis game.

He knew the extent of the resentment and disillusion among the war-weary Russian soldiers; and that the blame for the inefficiencies of the Government was laid squarely on her shoulders. For all his tender thoughts, he acknowledged her culpability, lamenting at the time: '. . . A murderous pity that the Emperor is so weak & so under the Empress's thumb; for, according to all the accounts I get he & the Empress are heading straight for ruin.'

He had heard senior Russian officials breezily weighing up several options, not least 'the advisability of murdering the Tsar and the Empress – or the Empress alone'.

Recalling the macabre threats against the Tsarina, together with the curiously serene atmosphere at the Alexander Palace, Sir Henry's tone was one of bafflement, describing the situation as 'an extraordinary state of affairs'.

The General had succeeded in charming the famously frosty Tsarina. But he struggled to equate her with his merry, rose-cheeked Princess Sunshine. He never forgot her change of mood whenever the conversation strayed from Darmstadt to the Hesse sisters' current situation: she became emotional, her eyes filling with tears. 'There is a strange air of fatality about her. One feels somehow that she is living under the shadow of some terrible tragedy.'

He was not the only one to feel a sense of impending doom. After her last visit to Alix and Ella, in Russia, Irène had been particularly overwrought: 'It is rapidly getting too late. Those horrid words – too late.'

1

'As handsome, clever and engaging
Children as it is possible to see.'
Queen Victoria

The four sisters' yearning for their Heimat was exacerbated by the turbulence of their adult lives. As they lived through wars and revolution, memories of their relatively peaceful childhoods in Darmstadt were increasingly cherished.

Alongside the tennis parties, Sir Henry Wilson treasured reminiscences of idyllic rides in the pine woods. The British Ambassador to Russia, Sir George Buchanan, was stationed at Darmstadt before being transferred to St Petersburg, and his daughter, Meriel, gave a rapturous description of the surroundings of one of the royal houses, Heiligenberg: 'There were glorious beech woods where violets and lilies of the valley grew in profusion. There were green fields of cowslips and buttercups, there were great pine forests that were full of sandy rides where one could gallop on one's horses for miles.'

The expansive sweep and charm of the countryside around Darmstadt was not reflected in its society. The Princesses' mother, Alice, had grown up consorting with Tennyson and Carlyle. In her adopted country, she did her best to maintain her cultural education, playing piano with Brahms – denounced by her daughter Victoria as 'an uncouth shy man' – and immersed herself in philosophy. But it was never enough. She complained of the 'narrow stifling atmosphere' of Darmstadt, and set tongues wagging with her determination to branch out. One local aristocrat sniffed: 'It interested me also to hear people speaking of the complete absence of court usages in her house, and of her intercourse with people of the middle class who were "not eligible" for presentation.'

Alice's breaking of social norms was not born of ignorance. She was well versed in society mores and, aged 19, had been taught to '*cercler*' – circulate gracefully – by means of addressing bits of furniture while remaining in step. Her problem was that she found the natives of Darmstadt monosyllabic, answering every pleasantry with a brief *Ja* or *Nein*.

She was happiest devoting her time and energy to setting up and supporting charities. But while she would instruct her children: 'Life is for work, not only for pleasure', their father, the boisterous Prince Louis, preferred treats. He spent full days out hunting, breaking only for large meals, followed by the loosening of corsets and a siesta.

At Victoria's christening, Prince Alexander of Hesse described Louis disparagingly: '[He] wears a Norfolk jacket, short breeches and multi-coloured garters . . . is very fond of sherry and horses, reads as little as possible and never writes at all. He is the Queen's confidant and is popular in England.'

Indeed, so popular was he with the Queen that she had been uncharacteristically amenable when asked for her consent to the couple's marriage. 'Certainly,' she said, while carrying on with her crochet.

Brimful of portraits of British monarchs, hanging alongside sketches of Windsor and Balmoral, the Grand Ducal Neues Palais in Darmstadt had an Anglophile flavour which was not universally liked, with some referring to it as a 'Victorian Piccadilly Mansion', entirely unsuited to its surroundings.

The eldest of Princess Alice's daughters, Victoria, was born at Windsor Castle in 1863. Her birth was deemed especially auspicious. Firstly, because her birth date, April 5th, was meant to be lucky. Victoria later wrote wryly that she was 'meant to be able to see fairies and find hidden treasure – neither of which I've done'.

Secondly, Victoria was the first of the Queen's granddaughters to be named after her. Perhaps most importantly, though, she was born in the same room as her mother, and indeed all the Queen's children, in Lancaster Tower, overlooking the Long Walk. For all her occasional radical inclinations, Alice had agreed to replicate her own birth, to the point of wearing the same outfit her mother had worn.

The Queen's eldest daughter, Vicky, recognised the new baby's special status. Vicky had, by then, given birth, in Berlin, to three children of her own, including the future Kaiser, Willie, and his brother Henry. She was full of rueful speculation. 'What a darling it must be. It will become your favourite of all your grandchildren now, I do not doubt, as you were present when it came into the world.' The Queen was inclined to agree: 'Of course I shall take great interest in our dear little granddaughter born at . . . Windsor in the very bed in which you were all born.'

Years later, Princess Alice assured the Queen: 'The child born under your roof and care is of course your particular one and later, if you wish to keep her at any time when we have been paying you a visit, we shall gladly leave her.'

The young Princess Victoria would, as it turned out, end up spending much of her adult life in England. She would become the Hesse granddaughter closest to the Queen.

Alice's second daughter, Ella, was born in Germany, arriving just over 18 months later, on November 1st 1864, at a hunting lodge, Bessungen, in Darmstadt. Alice wrote an over-optimistic note to the Queen regarding the new baby's name: 'Of course she must be called Elizabeth, only entre nous Ella.'

There was some consternation about Ella's sex and the Queen, candid as ever, commiserated: 'I am sorry it is again a girl.' But Alice was not to be cast

Queen Victoria and her granddaughter, Princess Victoria, 1864.

down: 'The little daughter was a disappointment for us, which passed . . . We console ourselves with the idea that the little pair will look very pretty together.' A year later, Alice was well and truly reconciled, insisting: 'I would not change them for boys if I could.'

Alice breastfed her daughters, a practice the Queen judged 'animalistic', pointedly naming one of her cows Princess Alice. The Queen may have been interested to hear that, by June 1865, Ella had two teeth, and presumably relieved to hear that she had been weaned.

Little Victoria had been called 'passionate' by her mother. Ella was turning out to be as forceful. In a letter to her husband, Alice wrote: 'During breakfast with me, Ella saw how I dipped my cookie in my coffee and said: "Oh mother so it's impossible" because I do not allow it to be done. She is so funny . . . not so easy to manage.'

The Queen would doubtless have been less amused to hear of her Hesse granddaughters, still barely out of the nursery, being introduced to their six Russian cousins. The meetings between the young Princesses and the six Grand Dukes were orchestrated by the Hesse-born Tsarina Maria (wife of Emperor Alexander II) and took place at her childhood home, the idyllic Heiligenberg estate.

Grandmama was disquieted to hear that little Victoria had already caught the eye of the six-year-old Grand Duke Serge. Years later, she would be enraged by Serge's father's blithe suggestion of a double union: Serge could marry Victoria, while his fourth son, Alexei, could marry Ella.

Shortly after the birth of Ella, threats loomed of a Prussian invasion. The two little girls were sent away from Darmstadt to Britain, to stay with their grandmama. Family loyalties were confusingly divided, with the Queen supporting her daughter Vicky's Prussians against Alice's Hessians, then supporting the Austrians.

But divided loyalties had no bearing upon the Queen's raptures over her two little Hesse granddaughters. The girls' three-month stay in England was a huge success. As the Queen wrote in her diary: 'Took leave with much regret of darling little Victoria and Ella, who are such little loves. They have been quite like my own during these last two months & are really as handsome, clever and engaging Children as it is possible to see.'

She was not blind, however, to Ella's trickier characteristics, referring to her at one point as 'obstinate and peevish'. Though aged only 47, the Queen may have fallen victim to little Ella's prejudice against old ladies. Princess Alice complained to her mother that Ella was 'civil to all strangers – excepting to my mother-in-law or to old ladies. It is too tiresome'.

Three-year-old Victoria handled herself with more diplomacy. In a note to her, the fond Queen effused: 'After having seen you almost every day for more than three months & every day for six weeks & living in the same house – we shall miss you very much.'

The two little girls returned to Darmstadt to find they had a new sister. Born on July 11th 1866, the baby was named Irène, meaning peace, in a nod to the recent end of hostilities. There was little fuss about the sex of this third daughter, the conflict probably putting such worries into perspective. Alice enthused to the Queen: 'Firstly I have to thank the Almighty for having preserved my own sweet and adored husband and for the blessing of having had him by me, so dear, so precious, during my confinement . . . Baby is well and very pretty.'

In fact, Irène would always be seen as less pretty than her sisters. The Queen wrote candidly to her daughter Vicky, describing a two-month visit from Alice and her young family: 'Alice's eldest daughters are indeed quite lovely and Victoria most engaging. Irène is very plain.'

Alice may have found Darmstadt society wanting, but she adored motherhood, deriving endless pleasure from her daughters: dressing their dolls, singing and playing the piano even when, as she put it, little fingers 'thrust themselves under hers on the keyboard to make music like big people'. She taught them to paint; Ella, particularly, loved drawing.

But her delight did not deter her from recruiting a strict British nanny. Thirty-six-year-old Mary Ann Orchard, or 'Orchie', arrived around the time of Irène's birth. She woke, washed and dressed the three little girls before giving them Bible lessons. Orchie was a stickler for the truth, dishing out several ingenious punishments for lying: 'a pinch of rhubarb powder on the tongue . . . then, with the younger lot, a pinch of quinine,' recalled Victoria.

Orchie's regime featured elaborate celebrations of her own birthday. 'Orchie's birthday was a great fete,' enthused Victoria. 'Several days before it she stirred her own cake after an English recipe, at which performance we always managed to be present.'

Remaining at Darmstadt for nearly 30 years, Orchie would tend all four Princesses, before following the youngest, Alix, to St Petersburg. At the Russian Court, she persisted in calling the Tsarina 'my baby', while her distinguished former charge apparently stood by, smiling agreeably. Perhaps it was fortunate that Orchie died in 1906, never knowing the terrible fate of two of the Princesses in Russia.

The Hesse sisters formed a happy trio. 'I want my dear grandmama to see my dear little sisters. Irène is always good. I love her so much & Ella too,' cooed Victoria to the Queen.

All three were in England for Irène's second birthday. The Queen was enraptured, well over Ella's peevishness and Irène's plainness: 'Dear little Irène's 2nd birthday. Ella is splendid as ever & very dear. They . . . can walk alone now . . . & are very happy together.' At dinner, she gushed, the 'dear little girls always come to dessert . . . they come up [to my sitting room] . . . to wish me good night.'

By the age of three, Ella's beauty was already being noticed. The Duke of Connaught declared her the prettiest of the sisters. Their aunt, Marie of Edinburgh, later wrote that Ella's features were 'all exquisite beyond words, it almost brought tears to your eyes.'

The three-little-maids' idyll ended with the birth of their brother, Ernest, known as Ernie, in 1868. Victoria noted and objected to the extra cannonfire that greeted the long-awaited son. Two years later, the birth of the girls' second brother, Friedrich, or 'Frittie', would be greeted with the same controversial fanfare.

From July 1870 to January 1871, Darmstadt was again embroiled in hostilities: this time the Franco-Prussian War. With her strong charitable instincts, Alice readily tended wounded soldiers. Years later her daughters, Ella and Alix, would do the same in Russia.

Two invalids were installed at the family's Neues Palais. Victoria, then aged just seven, retained vivid memories of one particular officer with a shattered leg. He 'liked to show us bits of bone he kept in a pill box'.

She later added dramatic descriptions of war-time activities: 'Grandmama, Queen Victoria, had given us a small pony and two Shetland ponies . . . A coachman drove them, walking alongside, while the nurse followed behind . . . After (the) outbreak of war we were escorted by a gendarme besides, as gipsies and the riff-raff of the big towns were flooding the region.'

In one effusive thank-you note to the Queen for birthday presents, Victoria made a plaintive reference to their father's military commitments: 'Thank you very much for the nice paint box and the pearls, they both gave me very much pleasure. Dear Mama gave me also a pearl, a dear little canary-bird and a doll . . . Dear Papa has gone away yesterday and we are very sorry but we hope that he and his soldiers will return soon.'

With the restoration of peace, the three sisters resumed their spartan routine with Orchie. At 6.00am sharp they were up, even in winter. Lessons began at 7.00, by candlelight if necessary. There was a break for cake, milk and fruit. Lunch at 2.00 was followed later by 'tee'. Chocolate was allowed only after Friday Communion.

The sisters all spoke English and German. Victoria was reading German by the age of six and English by the age of seven.

Alongside their lessons, the Princesses were obliged to acquire domestic skills. Their elevated status would not exclude them from laying and lighting fires and making cakes; they must all be handy with a broom and duster. As Alice insisted: 'I bring my children up as simply and with as few wants as I can.'

Years later, her daughter Alix would follow the same practices at the Alexander Palace with the five Imperial children.

*

Differences were emerging between the two elder sisters. Victoria was a tomboy, inclined to climb trees and ruin her clothes. Hair ribbons were a particular bugbear: if the girls lost more than one metre in a month, they would have to replace the ribbon out of their pocket money. Victoria later admitted: 'Needless to say, it was I who lost most of them! Ella even in the most exciting moments taking some care of her clothes and appearance.'

Victoria was imaginative, conjuring up fantasies of monsters in hidden staircases; Ella preferred to devote herself to art, music and tending dolls. Victoria shone in lessons; Ella was bored by printed words and sums made her cry.

While the two elder sisters struggled with their contrasting challenges, Irène was inclined to be obliging. Years before, Princess Alice had described the placid Irène to one of her brothers: 'Irène rolls about the floor over & over, like a ball & enjoys the noise and fun of her sisters.' The Queen echoed Alice: 'Dear Irène is such a dear, good child, so unselfish & good tempers [sic] & always pleased & very sensible & so affectionate.'

In 1871, the Hesse family came to Britain for a prolonged visit. There were stays at Sandringham, Balmoral and Buckingham Palace. The Queen's eldest son, Bertie, the future Edward VII, was, at that point, ill with typhoid. But this did nothing to dampen the atmosphere among the little cousins. Victoria's memory of Windsor Castle centred on an unsupervised table laden with biscuits 'which we used to pilfer'. The light-fingered children may have derived an additional thrill from the table's position, directly outside their fearsome Grandmama's room.

Victoria recalled Grandmama cooling her tea by pouring it from one cup to another. She had less entrancing memories of unappetising desserts:

bread and butter pudding without raisins and tapioca with lumps. 'I still remember [them] with a shudder of disgust,' she wrote later. Among popular distractions was a toy lion which, when wound up, devoured Russian soldiers whole.

Following their return to Darmstadt, the two elder daughters resumed their dutiful correspondence with the Queen. In November 1871, Ella had just turned seven: 'Dear Grandmama, I thank you very much for the beautiful birthday presents, I have looked at the Bible pictures, they are very nice. It is very foggy and we play in the corridor.'

In 1872, on June 6th, the fourth Princess, Alix, was born at the Neues Palais. The three older sisters, then aged nine, eight and five, would have been thrilled to have a baby sister, following the two brothers. Alice was enraptured by her pretty, cheerful new daughter, writing to the Queen: 'She is a sweet happy person, always smiling, with a deep dimple in one cheek, our "Sunny".'

In fact, just before Sunny's birth, Princess Alice had been rather unhappy, in the throes of a sort of spiritual quest. It was later suggested that she had passed her malaise on to her new baby. As a young girl, Alix would become obsessed by the supernatural, a preoccupation that was to blight her adult life.

Two months after Alix's birth, Victoria was obliged to write to the Queen, from another estate, Kranichstein, on behalf of her ailing mother: 'Mama . . . is laid up with a feverish attack and rheumatism so that she cannot write.'

The creation of a theatre for the children that Christmas may have raised their mother's spirits. In her younger days, Alice had experimented with amateur theatrics in Darmstadt. But her efforts to play coquettish widows had not gone down well within Darmstadt's narrow cultural confines.

Within a year of Alix's birth, the first of a series of terrible misfortunes struck the young Hesse family. In May 1873, Alice's fifth child, Frittie, died, aged just two. Three months previously, Princess Alice had made the chilling discovery that her second son was a haemophiliac after a cut to his ear bled for a full three days. Alice was all too aware of haemophilia: her brother Leopold was a sufferer, dying aged just 30.

Frittie died after falling from a first-floor window. The accident happened when Ernie, aged four, was playing with him in Alice's bedroom. Ernie had been waving at Frittie from an adjacent window. As Alice went to retrieve Ernie, Frittie climbed on to a chair and then on to the ledge. Alice was said to have been playing a series of piano pieces, including Chopin's Funeral March.

The Hesse children were forever haunted by haemophilia. Months after the death, Victoria wrote a poem for her mother: 'Oh weep not mother I beseach [sic] thee for Frittie is in heaven. In heaven where angels sing with glee and sins are all forgiven.' Little Alix, not yet one year old, must have felt the prevailing sorrow.

The window Frittie fell from was made into a stained-glass memorial, on which was engraved: 'Not lost, but only gone before . . . of such are the Kingdom of Heaven'. The grieving Orchie was not forgotten, with Alice thoughtfully compiling a book of photographs and pressed flowers: 'For dear Orchard, in remembrance of our darling Frittie.'

Following Frittie's death, Alice was overcome by '*douleur*', a kind of morbidity. 'I am good for next to nothing, I live on my sofa and see no-one,' she lamented to the Queen. To a visitor, she remarked, 'Of course I am gay sometimes, and sometimes I can be pleasant, I suppose, but I am rather a contemplative, serious being, one who looks into the depths of all water, whether it be clear or dark.'

Attempts by the bereft family to resume normal life featured a seaside holiday at the Belgian coastal town of Blankenberge. But such ventures had their pitfalls, as Princess Alice complained: 'I felt quite shy, for all the people sit round and look on.' Victoria recalled more beguiling elements;

she described horse-drawn bathing machines that 'bumped and rocked' as bathers entered the water and seeing 'little men made of lobster claws' for sale.

The family were staying at Mainau, on Lake Constance, digging on the shore, when seven-year-old Irène was accidentally hit by a playmate wielding a spade. Irène, already outshone by her three sisters, now found her nose knocked out of alignment. As Victoria pointed out, the blow, 'spoilt the shape of Irène's nose'.

Princess Alice's seventh child, May, was born in May 1874. Two-year-old Alix made a flamboyant debut at her baby sister's christening. She was pretty in pink and, according to her already rapturous grandmama, 'still improving in looks'. Alice noted that Alix was 'immensely admired'.

Thank-you notes from Darmstadt to the Queen continued unabated, with Ella writing in November: 'I thank you very much for writing to me and for the saddle and bridle . . . Mama says now I have a saddle Victoria and I may ride together.'

The Queen would have been gratified by Victoria's concern for her ailing mother. Aged 11, she was already 'thinking of others'. 'She [Mama] has had a bad sore throat for the last day or two and Sunny [Alix] had one too but as it is mostly lovely weather now I hope they will soon be well again . . . I hope I may be able to become what you wish for, I should very much like to be a comfort to Mama.'

The young Princesses accompanied their mother tirelessly on visits to various charitable institutions. She had spent much of her married life setting up charities: first the Princess Alice Women's Nursing Association – the Alice-Frauenverein für Krankenpflege – then a shop called the 'Alice' bazaar, where impoverished ladies made and sold their work. 'I went to Mama's little hospital to see the nurses' Christmas tree. One of them had lifted somebody too heavy & hurt her leg,' Ella informed the Queen.

The Queen would have had mixed feelings on hearing of a visit from the Princesses' Prussian cousins for Victoria's 12th birthday. The Prussian Court, in Berlin, was then presided over by the German Emperor Wilhelm I and would have been considered more important than its humbler Hesse counterpart.

Aged 16, Willie, the future Kaiser Wilhelm II, was all too aware of his superior status. Bossy and pompous, he would order his Hesse cousins to listen to him reading the Bible. His other offences included putting feet on sofas and throwing down tennis rackets in fury in the middle of matches.

It was during this visit in 1875 that Willie took his unwelcome shine to young Ella, writing love poetry to her and conjuring up visions of wedded bliss. As he rhapsodised to his mother: 'Ella, who is my special pet, is very much grown & is exeedingly [sic] beautiful; in fact she is the most beautiful girl I ever saw . . . We both love each other warmly . . . If God grants that I may live till then, I shall make her my bride once if you allow it.'

The object of Willie's dreams gave her own account of his stay to Grandmama. Though broadly positive, Ella made no mention of the couple loving each other warmly. 'Willie of Prussia has been here a few days,' she wrote baldly. 'We enjoyed his stay very much. On Sunday he read to us all a very nice book.' Victoria later said the book was Captain Frederick Marryat's *Midshipman Easy*, a swashbuckling tale, hardly suitable for the young Princesses.

What the Queen thought, three years on, when it seemed a wedding between Willie and Ella might really be on the cards, is unclear. Given her misgivings about the swaggering Willie, she would presumably have been unsettled by talk, in Berlin, of Ella as 'our future Empress'. In unpublished memoirs, the Kaiser admitted that his feelings for Ella had continued to grow.

Doubtless to the relief of the Queen as well as Ella, Willie eventually switched his attention to the woman he actually married: Auguste Victoria

'Dona' of Schleswig-Holstein. Later he insisted that it was his parents who had prevented his marriage to Ella. His mother, Vicky, may have been worried about the emergence of haemophilia in the Hesse family.

The tomboyish Victoria had gone along with Willie's *Midshipman Easy*, but she was all too aware of her cousin's flaws. She recalled him and one of her tutors posturing and preening during an argument. The pair 'outbid each other in emphasis and what I considered false pathos'.

Her distaste for Willie did not prevent her from embracing one of his bad habits. It was Willie who first introduced Victoria to smoking, a weakness she never shook off. The girls' governess, Miss Margaret Jackson, disapproved and Victoria found herself having to be circumspect: '[I] remember secretly smoking up chimneys and out of windows.' At one point an obliging companion lowered cigarettes from window to window on a string.

Years later, at Balmoral, Victoria's habit came in useful as the Queen asked her to smoke in order to keep midges at bay, with Grandmama enjoying a few puffs herself. Victoria would end up chain-smoking, a tendency she shared with two of her future brothers-in-law, Alix's Tsar Nicholas and Irène's Prince Henry. In a rather curious twist, she once claimed she was cutting down by breaking her cigarettes in half.

Ella's growing beauty continued to attract attention. A visiting British aristocrat, Sir George Arthur, attested: 'It is possible to say without hesitation or reservation that Princess Ella was the most lovely child one had ever looked upon.'

The Queen concurred, describing a visit from the Hesse children in 1875: 'The two eldest Victoria and Ella, a wonderfully pretty child, are with us here and bring life into the house with their childish merriment.'

Ella was soon rivalled by Alix. So taken was the Queen with Alix's appearance that she attempted to draw a portrait: 'Tried to make a sketch of the adorable splendid little Alix. She was very fidgety & said, "I don't like to be maked". She has the most beautiful colouring & large deep blue eyes.'

During that same visit to Balmoral, Ella referred to the Queen's fond manservant Mr Brown. 'We went today to the Mother of Brown . . .' she reported to her mother. 'Brown threw stones in the water and maid [sic] them jump 6 or 7 times.' Brown was already a controversial figure, his duties including brushing the Queen's skirt and polishing her shoes. Before meals at Balmoral, he would throw open the billiard room door and issue a bluff announcement: 'All what's here dines with the Queen.'

Weeks later, the Queen sent the girls trinkets thoughtfully constructed from their collections of stones. Victoria wrote appreciatively from Kranichstein: 'Dearest Grandmama, How good of you to send me such nice brooches and those buttons. We little thought when we were so sorry to leave our dear basket of stones at Balmoral that they would follow us in such pretty shapes. Thank you many times for them, we shall always think of you and dear Scotland when we wear them.'

Much of the sisters' news to Grandmama involved animals. The children had a lamb called Milly, as well as a wild boar and a fox 'which smelt abominably', according to Victoria. They also had goats, ducks and a hare named Tommy. Victoria recalled the sisters begging the kitchen for crusts for their various pets, the scraps mostly being eaten by Irène and their brother Ernie.

The Queen's present of a grey pony from Windsor proved especially popular. 'We got the grey pony & thank you so very many times for it . . . We have so long wished to have one & are quite delighted. . . . It went very well & it is so pretty,' gushed Ella. Victoria added on May 21st 1876: 'We go out riding very often now on the little grey pony you gave us. It is a dear little thing called "Ironsides" because of its grey colour . . .'

Alix's good looks were matched by her courage. The toddler did not hesitate when she saw a fight brewing between the family's pet boxer and a wild boar: 'Alicky [Alix] is so funny and so brave,' reported Ella. 'Once Mama's dog boxer was going to bite a wild boar & she tried to pull him back without being afraid of it, the dog was very badly wounded but is much better now.'

The Queen and her Hesse granddaughters now began furiously 'working' treasures for each other: 'Those hats you worked for us are so pretty and the poplin too,' enthused Ella to Grandmama.

And by May 1876, nine-year-old Irène was part of the 'work' team at Darmstadt. Ella sent the Queen effusive birthday greetings: 'I shall never forget how happy I was in Balmoral that day last year . . . Victoria, Irène and I have made a little mat for you.' A day later, Victoria was adding her voice, with a thoughtful allusion to the future Edward VII: 'We three have made a lamp mat for you & hope you will like it . . . We are all so pleased that dear Uncle Bertie has come back safely.'

The young Victoria's fond relations with Grandmama could not be faulted. By the age of 13, however, she was creating ructions with her parents. The worry was that she was becoming too unruly; she liked risk-taking, at one point racing in a carriage and tipping it over. On another occasion, she and Ella created havoc during rehearsals at the Darmstadt Court Theatre. Victoria initiated a series of pranks, with both sisters. 'Going down traps and producing terrible thunderstorms, startling the actors, who were rehearsing, by these unexpected effects,' as she reported.

Did Victoria wield too much power over her younger sisters? She later admitted she was bossy, but insisted she was no bossier than Ella. It was Ella, after all, who labelled herself 'Aunt Fuss'. Victoria recalled that the two elder sisters 'divided [the] younger children', each persuading their team to enact various fantasies. Victoria favoured knights and brigands, while Ella went for polite little girls and fairies.

Victoria led rumbustious games in ruined buildings: one party attacked while the other defended. These rougher games inevitably resulted in torn dresses as well as the lost ribbons. Victoria always remembered her mortification as her exasperated mother forced her to greet the Empress of Russia in a darned frock.

Princess Alice was alive to her eldest daughter's struggles. As she wrote to the Queen on Nov 26th 1876: 'I hear she has been good and desirous of doing what is right; and she has more to contend with than Ella, therefore double merit in any little thing she overcomes and any self-sacrifice she makes.'

It was decided that Victoria should study for a newly devised Oxford exam for girls. She would be obliged to spend less time climbing trees and more, as she put it, 'reading and drawing and suchlike maidenly pursuits'. The studies had unexpected effects. By the time she was 14, Victoria was confidently lecturing her royal relations on 'the advantages of socialism'.

Fortunately 'dear Grandmama' was mostly shielded from such rumblings. There was no break in the stream of effusive letters from Darmstadt. In October 1876, Victoria wrote: 'Many many thanks for having sent us some of that good shortbread. I did not write sooner because we were not quite certain who had sent it us . . .'

On November 3rd 1876, Ella was piping up: 'I thank you so many times for the beautiful necklace . . . I found the photograph of you so nice . . . everybody found it so pretty & like you.' She added commiserations: 'I am so sorry to hear about Mrs Brown's death. I remember so well the day we went to see her & the nice milk we had there & her dear little grandchildren.'

2

'Think of me as your mama.'
Queen Victoria

In June 1877, Victoria was again writing to the Queen on behalf of her languishing mother: 'She [Mama] has allowed me to have the pleasure of writing to you for her. Mama is very tired and looks very white.'

Princess Alice's failing health had been further compromised as she took on extra duties following the death of the head of the Hesse family, Grand Duke Louis III. By the time she visited England the following year, she had not yet recovered. The Queen fretted: 'At 3, Alice arrived with Louis, Ernie, Alicky and May. Poor Alice is looking dreadfully thin, so pale and thin. The children . . . are in the old nurseries, always a pleasure to me, as I love to hear the little feet & merry voices above.'

But Alice did not allow her physical weakness to get in the way of her good works. She was patroness of the Albion Home in Brighton and was intent on visiting a home for reformed prostitutes in Eastbourne.

While their mother focused on the less fortunate, her daughters immersed themselves in the high life. Victoria and Ella both stayed at Buckingham Palace, attending a garden party at Marlborough House, reuniting with their grand Wales cousins.

They visited the House of Lords, the Natural History Museum and the Royal Botanic Gardens at Kew, where they heard the story of a gardener who inadvertently killed a fly-catching plant by feeding it cheese. The voluble Victoria always enjoyed a tale. It may have been during this visit

Postcard from Queen Victoria to Irène, Christmas 1877: 'To dear Irène of Hesse from her very affec. Grandmama VRI'.

that the Queen began dryly referring to her chatty granddaughter as a 'gasbag'.

The Queen would have been pleased to hear of the girls' glamorous garden party. Despite her worries about first cousins, she may already have harboured dreams of matchmaking Bertie's sons with Princess Alice's daughters.

The winter of 1878 saw a devastating change in the lives of the Hesse family. In recent years, Victoria had registered, in some dismay, their mother's increasing spells of ill health. But nothing could have prepared any of them for the deadly bout of diphtheria that swept through the Neues Palais.

Victoria was the first to succumb. Her voice became hoarse as she read aloud from *Alice's Adventures in Wonderland*. Ella was moved out of their shared bedroom, to sleep with Irène. When Irène developed symptoms, Ella was sent to stay with her German grandmother. Ella was the only one of the four Princesses to avoid illness.

Alix, then aged six, sickened shortly after Victoria. Their mother kept Grandmama abreast of the worsening news; the Queen agonised in her diary: 'This is dreadful, My sweet precious Alicky so ill. The doctor saw at once that it was a severe case.' On November 13th, she added: 'Alice telegraphs: Alicky tolerable; am miserable, such fear for the sweet little one . . . Poor dear Alice and she so delicate herself.'

Three days later, it was little May, Alice's fifth daughter, who developed symptoms before rapidly deteriorating.

Princess May died on November 16th, at just four years old.

Ernie, aged nine, was in bed with the fever when his mother told him of May's death. He was so upset that his mother could not resist embracing him. Shortly after that, Princess Alice herself fell ill.

As soon as their mother succumbed, the Hesse children were separated from their parents, moving to the Schloss at Darmstadt. Ella now wrote to her sick mother, trying to maintain a breezy tone: 'Your loving child Ella, I write so bigly, so that you can read it easier as you are in bed.'

But Alice was going downhill. Victoria wrote to the Queen in despair: 'Dear Mama is so dreadfully ill & the news . . . is very bad, we are so anxious & miserable.'

Princess Alice died, aged 35, on December 14th. Victoria later lamented to Ernie: 'Always I have remembered those last words I ever heard her speak, when I saw her at the door of Papa's room, on her return from seeing Aunt Marie at the station: "Ich bin so müde" [I am so tired] . . . She had no strength left to resist the disease.'

Alice was later said to have received, from her own son, Ernie, the kiss of death.

The Queen, at Windsor Castle, wrote in anguish: 'Brown coming in with telegram from Ludwig [Louis] which I did not at first take in saying: "Poor Mama, poor me, my happiness gone, dear dear Alice. God's will be done."' She was momentarily distracted by the date of her daughter's death, which was the same as her husband Prince Albert's: 'This very anniversary seems almost incredible, and most mysterious.'

Reunited with her siblings, Ella described the blighted atmosphere to the Queen, lamenting that no one dared 'speak of what was uppermost in their thoughts. Poor Papa looked dreadfully miserable. It seems like a horrible dream – would that it were.' But she, like Victoria, was soon dutifully 'thinking of others'. 'Dearest Grandmama, I have no words to express what I feel for you and Papa. May God help us all to be a comfort to you both.'

Ella's Christmas letter to the Queen was very mature for a 14-year-old: 'We all wish you, dearest Grandmama, a happier New Year than this has been and that you may take comfort in the thought that dear Mama is happy at last. It has been said that death is a dark lattice that lets in a bright day & and may that comfort you – as it did poor Mama in thinking of little May.'

She even tackled some practicalities, including the macabre sending of 'some of dear Mama's hair', which, she added in a hasty 'PS', was having to be disinfected: 'Papa had himself intended to take it with him to England for you, but if you wish to have it before that time, please to let him know and he will send it at once.' She also sent the Queen a sprig of conifer from Alice's funeral wreath.

Christmas 1878 fell ten days after Alice's death; the grieving Hesse family made forlorn efforts to celebrate. They were not helped by regulations to prevent further infections, including the burning of toys. Victoria wrote about missing her mother: 'without her & little May it does not seem like home.'

The Queen wrote a sort of prayer for her bereaved grandchildren: 'This must have been a dreadful Christmas and what a New Year! That every blessing may be yours in this new and terribly altered year is the earnest prayer of your loving, devoted & sorrowing Grandmama.'

She warned them that their grief would get worse. Darker still was her inference that their dear mama died for them. As she wrote: 'You will feel day after day more & more the irreplaceable dreadful loss your darling Mama is to you! . . . Treasure her in your hearts as a saint . . . It is a great responsibility to become really worthy of her . . . to be unselfish, truthful, humble-minded, simple & try & do all you can for others as she did . . . who gave her precious life for you all!'

Ella assured her grandmother that she was determined to make 'Mama's life our example' – a promise she kept. Ella would devote her adult life to charity.

The Princesses' English governess, Miss Margaret Jackson, arrived at Darmstadt three months before Alice's death. Then in her forties, she had some unattractive quirks: Victoria later referred to an 'unfortunate manner', while the Queen dismissed her as crabbed-tempered. But Margaret, or 'Madgie', was to gain the four Princesses' undying affection, remaining in contact with them all for the rest of her life.

Madgie was taken to be a mistress of probity. She had worked for the Duchess of Connaught and her sister had been governess to the Duchess of Buccleuch's daughters. She had left one previous post solely because the family converted to Roman Catholicism.

But discrepancies in her personal records indicate a cavalier regard for truth. On the 'Ancestry' website, Margaret Hardcastle Jackson is listed as having been baptised on September 25th 1835, but other records list her as born on September 20th 1837. On her job application for governess at Darmstadt, she gave her birthplace as one of London's smartest areas,

Kensington. But records show that Madgie, daughter of the tanner, William Jackson, was actually baptised at Burton Leonard, York.

Perhaps as a result of such anomalies, Madgie was always averse to idle chatter. 'It was from Miss Jackson's dislike of gossip that we never took any interest in local tittle-tattle,' wrote Victoria. It is hard to imagine the inquisitive and chatty young Victoria eschewing tittle-tattle. But, years later, Alix confirmed to one of the maids at the Russian Court that gossip had, indeed, been '*verboten*' during her childhood. It was as well that Orchie never knew of Miss Jackson's quirks; she would have been reaching for the rhubarb and quinine.

Madgie insisted, rather primly, that her pupils converse on abstract subjects. She had a radical streak and was adamant that her privileged pupils develop social consciences. It may have been these po-faced attitudes that so riled Grandmama. Certainly, Miss Jackson seems to have devoted more time to the cause of women's education than to her own teaching. The historian, Robert K Massie, points out that at least one of her pupils, Alix, failed to receive a proper grounding in grammar, substituting dots, dashes and exclamation marks for formal punctuation.

Victoria, in later life, became a great supporter of Miss Jackson, proclaiming her, curiously, a strong British conservative. She recalled that Madgie 'carried on every rule and suggestion my mother had made. Only as a grown woman did I appreciate her full worth'.

But during that last visit to England with their mother, the pair had not seen eye to eye. The governess had disapproved of Victoria, aged 15, and Ella, 13, being rowed on an artificial lake by yet another young cousin, Prince Louis Battenberg. None of them could have known that the intentions of Battenberg, then 24, were entirely honourable and, indeed, that he and Victoria would, one day, be married.

*

Within weeks of Alice's death, the Hesse children visited the Queen at Osborne. Victoria felt, like Ella, that her primary duty was to cheer Grandmama. Before their arrival, she sent a consoling note: 'I know how sad it will be for you to see us arrive! But please take comfort that it is just what dear Mama would like best – to know us with You.'

Bertie, the future Edward VII, met the grieving family at Flushing and they travelled together to the Isle of Wight, on the *Victoria and Albert* yacht. The question was who found themselves consoling whom. Writing in her diary on January 21st, the Queen groaned: 'I . . . called the dear children, who were all crying, excepting dear little unconscious Alicky. It is terrible to see these blooming children, all in deep mourning.' Nonetheless, she marched them all to the local village to inquire after the vicar's wife, who had typhoid.

The Queen's attachment to the 'unconscious' little Alix deepened. She wrote that Alix 'looked very sweet in her long cloak. I feel a constant returning pang, in looking at this lovely child, thinking that her darling mother, who so doted on her, was no longer here on earth to watch over her'.

But the three elder Princesses were rather disparaging of their six-year-old sister. 'Alix will never know what we have known,' complained Ella; she 'understands nothing of our loss & is as merry as possible'.

In fact, Alix was, of course, affected by her mother's death. Several accounts indicate that she lost, for some time, her 'Sunnyness'. She was forever haunted by a memory of finding Orchie 'silently crying' in the nursery.

Alix would find herself in a curious firing line. Her exacting Aunt Vicky later insisted that her motherless status made her 'a little vain and conceited and affected at times'.

Life changed for the young princesses after their mother's death in all sorts of subtle ways. The family stopped, for example, visiting one of the girls' favourite Schlosses, Kranichstein. Victoria later wrote wistfully of the freedoms they had enjoyed on holidays at Kranichstein while their mother was still alive. It was there that they had first learnt to ride, on a pony called Dred, named after the eponymous hero of Harriet Beecher Stowe's novel: *Dred: A Tale of the Great Dismal Swamp*. She and her sisters would row on a boat, using a Japanese parasol as a sail.

Meriel Buchanan, daughter of the last British Ambassador to Imperial Russia, later described a haunting atmosphere at Kranichstein: 'The old great castle itself seemed to me like the enchanted palace of the Sleeping Beauty, its walls and battlements reflected in the waters of the lake, deserted, silent.' Visitors swore they'd seen Alice's face at the window – they heard a happy voice calling children in from play.

*

From the first, the Queen had taken a keen interest in her four Hesse granddaughters. Now she was intent on taking over their upbringing altogether. She did not underplay her attachment: 'How I love you darling children . . . You are so doubly dear as the children of my own darling child I have lost & loved so much.' And her instruction to Victoria was unequivocal: 'Think of me as your mama.'

Over the next few years, the Queen issued streams of directives. Victoria's chattering was among her first challenges. 'You must learn to be posée, not talk too much or too loud – but take your place as your beloved Father's eldest daughter deprived of your beloved mother,' she instructed. Later she sent a reminder: 'And at the dinners remember not to talk too much & especially not too loud & not across the table.'

More strictures followed as the Queen scolded: 'It is not ladylike to kill animals & go out shooting – & I hope that you will never do that. It might do you g[rea]t harm if that was known, as only fast ladies do such things.' She warned: 'Never make friendships: girls' friendships & intimacies are very bad and often lead to great mischief.' Finally, she must never forget her responsibilities: 'So much depends on you darling Victoria as the eldest.'

Victoria may not have taken much notice of Grandmama's instructions on hunting and female friendships; she certainly maintained her lifelong passion for chattering. But she was keenly aware of the importance of her role as a mother figure for her younger siblings. As she expressed it: 'My childhood ended with her [Princess Alice's] death for I became the eldest and most responsible of the orphaned children.'

The lurking Grand Dukes were an ongoing worry. Years before, the Queen had complained that the Princesses' mother was becoming obsessed with the visiting Romanovs. 'Aunt Marie, Uncle Sasha, Nixa, dear Sasha, Alexei, Misha etc. I own I think it is a little too much,' she had complained to her daughter Vicky.

In fact, by the time of Alice's death, only two of the six Grand Dukes remained unattached. The eldest had died over ten years before. The Queen would have been relieved as the second and third were safely married off and a fourth spoken for. But that still left Serge and Pavel.

Had the Queen heard Victoria's early dismissal of the Grand Dukes she might have felt less worried. Victoria, then aged 16, left a damning description: 'Very tall & lazy & never seem to know how to amuse themselves, they talk very little and don't seem to know what to say, so that after we have talked about the weather and the roads they generally are silent or talk among themselves.'

The Queen would not have found Victoria's additional report so comforting. Victoria had been enraged to hear the Grand Dukes being rude about various nationalities, '. . .even once about the English that it made one quite angry . . . They seem to think themselves perfect too'.

The Grand Dukes were probably influenced by their sister, Grand

Duchess Maria, who had married the Queen's son, Affie, six years before. She was the aunt who had been so bowled over by Ella's childhood beauty.

That marriage, which should have improved Anglo-Russian relations, did just the opposite, as the outspoken Maria railed against most aspects of English life. As her mother reported: 'Maria thinks London hideous, the air there appalling, the English food abominable, the late hours very tiring and the visits to Windsor and Osborne boring beyond belief.'

The Queen's grim warning to Victoria, at the time, was hardly necessary: 'I HOPE you will not get at all Russian.'

Nearly every autumn, the Princesses' father, Grand Duke Louis, took the Hesse children to Windsor or Osborne or, more often, Balmoral. Following one visit, Victoria received strict orders to ensure that her younger siblings were 'very punctual about their lessons – for I am sorry to say all 3 [Irène, Ernie and Alix] tried to evade them when they were here'. Victoria was suitably chastened: 'I am very sorry to hear that the others were lazy at Balmoral'. She went on to say that her sisters, presumably Irène and Alix, 'are very sorry to have vexed you about their lessons and wish me to tell you . . . that they will work hard now'.

When the family were not staying with the Queen, Victoria kept her grandmama up to date with all the sisters' activities, not least how they spent their ten marks a month pocket money. Any slack was enthusiastically taken up by Miss Jackson, who sent monthly reports detailing all the books they read and what they wore. Sewing patterns for dresses had to be approved by the Queen. Regarding their meals, Miss Jackson was happy to report that the Hesse household continued to favour British cuisine. At Christmas, Miss Jackson insisted on pink quince sausages, English plum pudding and mince pies sent from England. Every March, the Princesses tucked into Orchie's English birthday cake.

The combined efforts of Miss Jackson and Grandmama to nurture the four Princesses proved largely successful. But it soon became clear that Irène was falling behind. Aged 12 when her mother died, Irène had been forced to cope with her grief in addition to the onset of puberty. Orchie, who had tended Irène from birth, had begun to worry.

The Queen did not shirk her duties regarding puberty; she had guided her own five daughters through their teenage years, and had already informed Victoria and Ella that there would be a time each month when they should ride as little as possible.

It was the forthright Victoria who gave the Queen an alarming description of Irène's symptoms: 'She suffers at times from headaches and a feeling of weakness & giddiness now & then that makes Orchard rather fidgety and anxious.'

But when Orchie pronounced Irène delicate, insisting she follow a strict regime of early nights and no excitements, it was Victoria who rebelled. She was disinclined to agree with such tactics, now teaming up with Ella to 'liberate' their sister. As she boasted: 'We have begun . . . Irène's Emancipation but it is rather difficult at times.'

On the rare occasions when Irène ventured out, she was regarded as too mousey. Writing to the Queen of Irène's prospective visit to Balmoral, the chatty Victoria was gently critical of her reticent sister: 'I think you will find her improved, but she is very silent, partly from shyness, partly from the sense that she is slow, I mean in thinking. Ernie and Alicky are much quicker & I think she feels it.'

The bereaved sisters wasted little time before resuming their good works. Following their mama's example, all four were drawn to what the poet Robert Southey called 'the voice of woe'. Victoria and Ella eagerly reverted to their tasks at the Alice hospital, while little Alix informed the Queen that she was knitting mittens for poor people.

Their sympathy for the less fortunate did not, however, amount to egalitarianism. The summer after Alice's death, the children were holidaying in France, when poor Orchie made what Victoria regarded as a disrespectful gaffe. As they were playing on the beach, Orchie heard French nannies addressing their Princesses solely by their Christian names. Victoria wrote: 'Being somewhat of a snob I was rather horrified at dear old Orchie following their example, and dropping the "Princess" before our names.'

Though the Queen continued her attempts to stem Victoria's chattering, she could do nothing about her granddaughter's insatiable curiosity. At one point, Victoria informed Grandmama she had seen a mesmerist, an experience she found enthralling. Nor could she stop Victoria forming – and, of course, voicing – views. In November 1880, Victoria was focused on world news, writing to the Queen: 'You must be very vexed at the new disturbances that have broken out once more in the Cape.' She took a line on Home Rule for Ireland, later admitting that, aged 16, she bravely lectured 'Grossmama' on the subject. Almost a hundred years later, in 1979, Victoria's younger son, Louis Mountbatten, would be killed by the IRA.

The Queen's secretary, Henry Ponsonby, was chary of Victoria, describing her as 'bright and lively but full of strange ideas. She locks herself up with her mother's books and papers and has imbibed Kant'. Years later, Chips Channon described her in his diaries as erudite but 'over-educated'. Her son Louis referred baldly to her as a 'walking encyclopedia'.

Victoria was the most easily amused of the sisters. In June 1880, she described a ride with the Queen: 'Grandmama has been riding several times when we walked & her pony will stop at all the bushes to eat & once the wind blew her cloak over her parasol which she shut up, so she was all covered up in it; we laughed dreadfully.' She gave a brazen description of King Leopold II of Belgium, who had a 'nose nearly as long as Cyrano de Bergerac's'.

Though still so different in character, the two elder Hesse sisters, Victoria and Ella, remained very close, sharing a bedroom into adulthood. The pair staged theatrical entertainments for their grieving father, making use of the theatre created for them the year before Princess Alice's death.

In 1880, the Queen travelled to Darmstadt for the sisters' joint confirmations. She took Victoria's hand, while the sisters' German grandmother took Ella's. The Queen described her granddaughters as suitably awe-struck: 'Victoria and Ella, all in white, both looking nervous . . .' They were asked: 'Do you intend to continue steadfast in the confession of this church and suffer all, even death, rather than fall away from it?' Their reply was: 'I do so intend with the help of God.' Years later, Ella would not continue steadfast with the Lutherans, but follow her husband into the Russian Orthodox Church.

The following year, Victoria and Ella 'came out' together in Darmstadt. Victoria had objected to their father's plan to introduce them to the local gentry. Echoing her mother's reservations, she was dismissive: 'They are rather second rate & have often not very good manners.'

But Irène enthused to the Queen that Victoria got over her gripes. There may have been a touch of envy as she described Victoria's elan: 'Miss Jackson says everybody [was] most pleased with her nice manners and she did not seem at all shy.' Victoria, in her turn, praised Ella's social graces: 'How often has she gone to a party or a ball, amiable & kind to all whilst suffering from a raging headache, merely that others should not be disappointed.'

In the summer of 1881, Ella and Victoria returned to England. The ever-tactful Ella informed Grandmama that, though they were both excited about visiting Aunt Vicky in Berlin, they looked forward 'with much greater pleasure to our visit in England . . . You cannot think what pleasure it gives us'.

Of course, the Princesses would see their Prussian cousins in Berlin. But, fortunately for Ella, Willie was safely out of the way, months into his marriage to Dona. It was several years before Henry began making his bid for Irène.

During their English visit, the two Princesses met the Prime Minister, Benjamin Disraeli, at Windsor Castle and played lawn tennis at Marlborough House; Victoria enjoyed a dizzying dance with Uncle Bertie: 'I felt quite faint.' Ella painted a picture for Ernie back in Darmstadt: 'Scold me for not having written to my old boy & naughty brother . . . but you see your old sister Aunt Fuss has also faults & you must pardon them.'

Ella had become as keen a reader as Victoria. Long gone were the days when books bored her: she was now reading four concurrently. She wrote: 'In German reading Schiller's 30 Years War & the Grimm lectures about Goethe & in English two books Uncle Bertie sent Irène and me at Xmas 'Sense & Sensibility' & 'Mansfield Park' by Miss Austen.' How the slower Irène got on with her books is not known.

Ella was soon matching Victoria in her absorption with current events, shocked by the assassination, that year, of Alexander II of Russia. The young Princess had met him at Heiligenberg. 'How I pitty [sic] poor Aunt Marie & the present Tsar, who can never feel sure of his life,' she wrote. 'I will be so glad when [Papa] is back again from this dreadful St Petersburg.'

Within a couple of years, Ella would be engaged to the murdered Tsar's son, Grand Duke Serge. She was to see first hand how unstable Russia was and just how 'dreadful' St Petersburg could be.

In the autumn of 1882, Irène, now aged 16, was thrilled to buck Orchie's joyless regime and accompany her two elder sisters on a trip to Italy.

The sisters had three companions accompanying them around several cities: Miss Jackson, a General von Herff and a widower from Darmstadt. Victoria recalled wrangles, as the companions argued about which galleries the girls should visit and which pictures they should see. Miss Jackson marched Irène off to see paintings half remembered from a previous trip, General von Herff hurried Ella around pictures marked with a star in his Baedeker guidebook, while Victoria's widower treated her to a random selection of personal favourites.

Ella loved Milan and Florence. Irène was full of Venice and Lord Byron: '. . . in a gondola to see various objects of interest including the Lido where Ld Byron used to ride and where we gathered shells,' she enthused to the Queen. She was no less effusive to Ernie: 'something new & beautiful every day'. Victoria recalled that General von Herff was not so enamoured with the canals. At one point he upset Miss Jackson and a gondolier with a leaden jibe: 'molto stanco ici'.

Mistrustful of Italians, the General kept his money with him at all times, stowed in an inner pocket. Victoria recalled his roundly rejecting Miss Jackson's suggestion that he leave some of the cash at a hotel reception. While never actually robbed, the party were repeatedly swindled. As Victoria reported dryly: 'We . . . were more dreadfully cheated than I would have believed possible.'

In Modena, there were ructions over soiled bedlinen. It was, needless to say, Miss Jackson who found blood stains on pillows, where guests had crushed mosquitos or bedbugs. Miss Jackson never managed to relax into the holiday spirit. When she wasn't remonstrating with General von Herff or examining sheets, she was protecting the girls from Italian admirers. In London, she had attempted to keep Prince Louis Battenberg at bay; now she found herself dealing with gangs of Italian cadets. 'Ella who was very pretty, especially attracted their attention,' wrote Victoria. 'Their loud remarks, which Miss Jackson, who spoke Italian, understood, made her highly indignant, so Ella was ordered to keep close to her side.'

The three sisters' trip to Venice would mark Ella's last holiday before she set out on the path to Russia, where her fate would be sealed.

3

*'Anything is better than making an
unhappy marriage.'*
Queen Victoria

In 1878, the year of Alice's death, the Queen had issued warnings to the Princesses 'not to be married for marrying's sake & to have a position' and to be 'prepared & on your guard while such things are brought before Papa'.

Returning from their exotic Italian trip, the Hesse Princesses found Darmstadt something of a let-down. 'Poor Darmstadt looks very bare and uninteresting after the picturesque Italian towns,' sighed Victoria. The Princesses were enlivened, then, when, soon after their return, Grand Duke Serge dropped by on his way back to St Petersburg. He had timed his visit well.

Whether Ella had ever agreed with Victoria on the flaws of the young Grand Dukes is not clear. But, four years on, she was finding the towering Serge anything but lazy or silent. The couple spent two rapturous days discussing the charms of Italy. She sent a buoyant note to the Queen, reporting that Serge had also visited Italy and stayed in the same towns as they had. Did the Queen already hear alarm bells?

Victoria had accused the Grand Dukes of believing themselves perfect: Serge was especially known for his lofty manner. His niece, Marie of Romania, left a chilling description: 'There was something intolerant, unbending, about him: instinctively one felt that his teeth were clenched.'

Grand Duke Serge in 1884.

His defenders maintained that his manner was misleading. Ernie wrote: 'He held himself very stiffly and his eyes appeared hard . . .[which] caused people to get a false impression and to consider him proud and cold – which in general he wasn't.' Alix's lady-in-waiting, Baroness Buxhoeveden, echoed Ernie: 'A certain shyness made him seem outwardly stiff and unresponsive.'

If Ella was aware of any teeth clenching or stiffness, she was prepared to overlook it. As the neatest of the four sisters, she admired Serge's impeccable appearance, enhanced by a figure-hugging corset. His claim that he wore the controversial device as a spinal aid was rejected by his boisterous brothers, who ragged him mercilessly.

The young Prince Felix Yusupov, later famous as the assassin of Rasputin, was equally fixated. 'When in his summer uniform, the bones [of the corset] could be clearly seen through the white linen tunic,' he wrote. 'As a child it always amused me to touch them and this, of course, annoyed him intensely.' Serge's appetite for culture would presumably have been especially noticeable in what Victoria had termed Darmstadt's 'second-rate' society. As for Ella, when he informed her that he had learnt Italian in order to read Dante in the original, her entrancement was complete.

While Ella was falling for her '*homme sérieux*', Victoria received a proposal from Prince Louis Battenberg. It was Prince Louis, now an officer in the British Royal Navy, who had upset Madgie when he took Victoria and Ella out boating in London in 1878.

The Queen, who prided herself on her matchmaking skills, was offended not to have been consulted. In a letter to Victoria in June 1883, she reprimanded her: 'Darling Victoria I cannot be silent . . .'

But Prince Louis appeared suitable, and the Queen soon gave the union her blessing, adding that Victoria had 'done well to choose a Husband who is quite of your way of thinking & who in many respects is as English as you are'. She seems to have nodded through his declaration, years before, that he had fathered a child with her son Bertie's mistress, Lillie Langtry. In fact, evidence subsequently emerged that he probably wasn't the father. The Queen may not have been aware that he had a dragon tattoo stretching from his chest to his legs.

The engagement was officially announced in July. The exuberant groom-to-be wrote to Bertie's son Georgie, the future George V: 'I am nearly off my chump altogether with feeling so jolly.' He admitted that he and Victoria had to be circumspect around the Queen: he could meet his fiancée only 'by stealth as she didn't approve of engaged couples "spooning"'. Irène, then 17, had high hopes for her prospective brother-in-law, writing eagerly to the Queen: 'He will be such a kind elder brother to us.'

There were some detractors. Victoria's uncle Arthur grumbled to his mother, the Queen: 'I only wish his rank were a little higher & that they had a little more money between them.'

That summer their beach holiday in France was once again fraught with domestic difficulties; but this time it was Miss Jackson, not Orchie, in the dock. Victoria reported that Miss Jackson received complaints from some fellow visitors, the Queen of Naples and her sister, the Duchess d'Alençon, 'rigidly upright figures, who pointed out to Miss Jackson that we did not hold ourselves as straight as we should'.

The suitors now flocking to Darmstadt clearly found no fault with the Princesses' deportment. Indeed, the beautiful Ella was spoilt for choice, dismissing, at various points, two Danish princes, Prince Charles of Sweden and an English lord. Henry Wilson had, of course, been among the admirers gathering for tennis parties at Darmstadt. He was probably unaware that her heart was already spoken for; he may even have felt he had some grounds for hope. A contemporary gave a jaunty portrait of him: 'A tall gaunt youth with very long bony arms and legs, a merry eye and a most delightful laugh.'

Ella's attachment to Grand Duke Serge could have been viewed positively, as the young Princess committing herself to a suitable match. The Hesse Princesses and Romanov Grand Dukes had come to know each other quite well over the years, and Serge's father, the late Tsar Alexander II, always made it clear he would welcome the Princesses as daughters-in-law.

The Queen, however, was not about to drop her violent objections. While she knew no details, her suspicions had been aroused. She planned to oust any lurking Russians and replace them with the German Grand Duke Friedrich, 'Fritz', of Baden; it was his clumsy younger sister who had injured Irène's nose with a spade.

She sent anxious inquiries to Darmstadt, but Victoria remained tight-lipped, writing on January 9th 1883: 'You ask me about Ella and Fritz of Baden – he was here the other day, but said nothing, according to Papa's wish. Ella & I never talk about those sorts of things, but she seems neither to like nor dislike Fritz in any way . . . Says he is good-natured and nice – but I do not think she cares for him at all yet.'

Victoria's claim that the sisters never discussed suitors rang hollow. More hollow still was her assurance that Ella was indifferent to the Grand Dukes: 'I do not think she cares for one of the Russian cousins.'

Ella's final rejection of the Queen's unfortunate candidate, Fritz, was followed by an awkward dinner in Berlin. His parents, expecting her to accept the proposal, had placed the couple at the same table. Fritz's grandmother, Empress Augusta, was grievously insulted by her refusal. 'Empress cut Ella and me dead,' reported a mortified Victoria. The Empress blamed the Princesses' father for being too weak with his daughters.

Grandmama was equally dismayed, particularly when she got wind of Grand Duke Serge's successful advances. 'Oh dear! How very unfortunate it is of Ella to refuse good Fritz of Baden, so good and steady, with such a safe happy position and FOR A RUSSIAN,' she raged to Victoria. 'You told me, only quite lately darling child that you thought Ella cared for no one? What does this all mean?' In her reply, Victoria admitted that Ella and her father, at least, discussed those sort of things: 'Ella told Papa she found Friedrich too good and solemn a person for her taste.' The Queen pronounced herself exasperated by 'Papa's failure to direct, or even protect, his daughter'.

As someone who prided himself on appearing good and solemn, Grand Duke Serge might have found Ella's objections to his rival rather puzzling.

Summoning the 18-year-old Ella to Britain, the Queen was in a fever of anxiety. She was convinced that, if the marriage to Grand Duke Serge went ahead, Ella would spend her life in mortal danger.

Ella, for her part, did her best to avoid talking to her grandmother on the subject, welcoming diversions, not least the recent death of the Queen's devoted companion, John Brown. Before her visit Ella wrote: 'I feel so much for you in your sorrow but I hope . . . to be able to be of some comfort to you & enliven you a little.'

On their first evening at Balmoral, Ella duly accompanied the Queen to John Brown's grave. The pair travelled to Windsor, then to Osborne. Towards the end of July, Ella's father joined them, with Victoria and Irène. Ella ended up spending several weeks in Britain.

But there was no avoiding the subject of marriage. When they were not discussing Victoria's prospects, the Queen was bombarding her granddaughter with reasons for not marrying Grand Duke Serge.

By the time Ella left, she was in turmoil. The Queen made a disingenuous note of her granddaughter's upset: 'Dear Ella . . . seemed quite distressed to leave . . . take-leaves at night always seem particularly sad and painful.'

Within a week of that particular take-leave, Ella had broken off her engagement with Serge. The Queen had won, writing triumphantly to her daughter Vicky: 'Anything is better than making an unhappy marriage.' Two days later, she was still trumpeting: 'I rejoice that she has acted as she has done about Serge.' To Victoria, the Queen fondly called Ella 'our sweet but undecided and inexperienced Ella'. She delightedly outlined her tactics, insisting she 'had not set Ella ag[ain]st Serge but I did tell her to reflect well before she accepted him & to remember the climate and state of the country'.

At this point, it looked as though Ella was not going to marry Grand Duke Serge. Everything hung in the balance. Had the fates decreed differently, she would never have gone to Russia and would not then have encouraged Alix to marry the Tsarevich. Had Alix not been Tsarina, the history of early 20th century Russian history might have been very different.

The Queen's delight was not destined to last. Within a further two weeks, the indomitable Serge had reappeared at Darmstadt and won Ella around again. It fell to Victoria to break the unwelcome news to the Queen. In October Ella herself wrote: 'I am afraid this letter will not give you as much pleasure as I would wish, but as it concerns my happiness & you have always been so kind to me I wish you to know what I think about Serge . . . Those few days I saw him last month have convinced me that I shall be happy with him . . . I am afraid you will think me very changeable but I think I know what I am doing . . . If I am unhappy, which I'm sure I'll never be, it will be all my doing'.

She was destined to be extremely unhappy. That it had been her own doing may or may not have provided consolation.

The Queen was dumbfounded, writing despairingly to Victoria: 'I have got Ella's letter but I really do not feel quite able to answer her yet . . . I know how dearest Mama was ag[ain]st the idea (tho' personally she liked Serge) & I also feel that Ella will be quite lost to me.'

Irène was caught up in the fall-out. Incarcerated with Grandmama at Balmoral, she received a battery of instructions from Ella: 'You might put in a few kind words for Serge when Grandmama speaks about him . . . try & prepare Grandmama as she is not very inclined to this match & tell [her] that I would never take a person I did not care for & that is the chief thing.'

It is not clear how many kind words Irène managed to put in. She did share one of her less helpful suggestions with Victoria: 'I hope that Grandmama will bring herself to be pleased to see them once together . . . if one took her by surprise – do you think that could be arranged?'

The surprise tactic would definitely have gone down badly. Luckily it was unnecessary, as the Queen soon buckled. 'The Verlobung [engagement] is now a fact & Sergei is nice and seems devoted to her,' she wrote grimly to Victoria . . . '[but] what I say to Ella abt. marriage in general I wld also wish to say to you; for it is very necessary to look on it in a serious light. So many girls think to marry is merely to be independent & amuse oneself – whereas it is the very reverse of independence – 2 wills have to be MADE to act together & it is only by mutual agreement & mutual yielding to one another that a happy marriage can be arrived at.'

The Queen put forward conditions that she may have suspected would not be met. She said Ella 'ought to be 20 before she marries' and that she and Serge should live 'out of Russia' for much of the time. As it turned out, Ella was 19 when she married, and she and Serge rarely left Russia.

Grand Duke Serge, meanwhile, was as 'off his chump' over Ella as Prince Louis had been over Victoria, writing from Darmstadt to his brother Pavel: 'Ella is, if possible, even more beautiful. We both sit together a lot. In the mornings she is in my room and I teach her some Russian which is very funny.'

Returning home from Balmoral, Irène was charmed by the Grand Duke, bowled over by 'the most beautiful jewels' with which he showered his fiancée. 'We are so pleased to have Serge here and that the engagement may at last be openly known,' she enthused to Victoria. 'I assure you the more one sees of him the nicer one thinks of him [sic]'.

Victoria echoed Irène: 'Dearest Ella looked so happy with Serge, may she be so!' she wrote to the Queen.

The sisters' father, Grand Duke Louis, joined the chorus of approval, with a letter to Grand Duke Serge's brother, Tsar Alexander III: 'I know Serge from childhood. I see his good and pleasant manners and I am sure he will make my daughter happy.'

Within a few months, the Queen herself had agreed to meet the recalcitrant Grand Duke. Ella was full of cautious optimism: 'I am so happy that you want to see Serge when he arrives next month and I hope he will make a pleasant impression on you. Everyone who knows him loves him & says he has such a true & noble character.'

The defeated Queen's note to her daughter Vicky was bleakly optimistic: 'I think we shall get on very well, though he is a Russian and carries off my grandchild.'

The wedding between Victoria and Prince Louis Battenberg took place in Darmstadt on April 30th 1884. Upon her arrival at the Hesse Court, the Queen noted that Victoria looked tired and unwell. This was hardly surprising. Victoria's nerves regarding her own wedding were compounded by worries about a second, altogether more controversial, ceremony.

Her father, it seemed, had fallen for a racy divorcee, Countess Alexandrine von Hutten-Czapska, and planned to marry her at the same time as Victoria married Louis. While Victoria herself had no objections to her father's mistress, she dreaded the Queen's disapproval: 'We others quite liked the lady, who was full of attentions towards us, and I hoped my father would feel less lonely when married to a woman he was much in love with.'

Such had been Victoria's anxiety about what her grandmother would think that she had asked Irène to mediate for her while she was staying at Balmoral. When not putting in kind words about Grand Duke Serge for Ella, Irène had somehow to prevent the Queen from attending Victoria's wedding, a quest that failed: 'Grandmama has been speaking to me about coming to Darmstadt for your wedding and I mentioned all I could to dissuade her – as you wished . . . You should have seen how happy she looked at the idea of coming and how she wished to be with us then to take dear Mama's place.'

Word of the second marriage ceremony soon 'oozed out', as the Queen's secretary, Frederick Ponsonby, put it. Duly outraged, the Queen proclaimed: 'F[or] all our sakes I entreat him to delay at any rate so serious & I must fear, fatal a step.' Grand Duke Louis's wedding to the sultry Alexandrine went ahead, only to be annulled ten weeks later, by order of the Queen.

Was there some attention-seeking motive behind Victoria's wedding day mishaps? It was not her fault that she suffered a stomach upset after eating lobster on an empty stomach, but she could have avoided jumping over a coal scuttle and spraining her ankle.

The Queen, oblivious to such hitches, was enraptured by the wedding outfits of all four Princesses – although Irène was, as usual, slightly short changed. She described Victoria first: 'She came down looking so pretty in her dear Mama's wedding dress over white satin . . . & a wreath of orange flowers & myrtle, which I had given her . . . Ella was in great beauty, wearing some of Serge's beautiful presents, including an enormous cabochon sapphire drop, set in diamonds. Irène looked also very nice and Alicky lovely in a short white dress'.

Almost as eye-catching was the specially devised Battenberg cake, then comprising a full nine-chequered panel of sponge.

In normal circumstances, Ella might have supported Victoria through both weddings. But she herself was on tenterhooks, anxious about what the Queen would make of her beloved Grand Duke Serge. Fortunately, the Queen, with her weakness for a manly figure, was immediately taken, pronouncing him 'tall and gentlemanlike but very thin, pale and delicate looking'. Ella was relieved as Grandmama gave the couple her blessing. 'Serge IS nice and seems so devoted to her,' she declared.

If Grandmama had finally accepted Ella's Grand Duke Serge, she was well and truly enamoured with Victoria's Prince Louis. He had spent the previous Christmas with her. 'I have learnt to esteem your dear Louis,' she rhapsodised to Victoria. 'What a motherly feeling I have for him and what an exceptionally tender, kind & excellent husband you have in him!' Victoria re-assured the Queen she would not forget what she said about her duty to Louis: 'Indeed it will be easy to fulfill it, for I love him with all my heart.'

Ella visited the fond newly-weds at their home, Sennicotts, near Chichester: 'A perfect little house but seems so curious that it should belong to Louis and Victoria, one hardly understands it,' she mused to the Queen. It's not clear whether Ella was confounded more by the smallness of the house or her sister's ownership of it.

Victoria saw no shortcomings in her new life, enthusing to her brother Ernie: 'We take long drives in my poney [sic] cart or in the dog cart about the country, which is very pretty'.

The domestic idyll endured, despite the couple's contrasting characters. While Prince Louis was a stickler for uniforms and medals, Victoria retained her childhood indifference to her appearance, occasionally even being called a ragbag. Though they were both German in origin, Victoria was considered more English in temperament. As Louis said of her: 'She is really more English than German and we invariably speak English together.' Prince Louis's own efforts to assimilate were hampered by his German accent.

Married life did little to stem Victoria's chattering. Her husband became one of only two people able to silence her, the other being the Queen. Years later, her younger son, Louis Mountbatten, became a third. In her memoir, *Without Prejudice*, Victoria's friend, Gloria Vanderbilt, complained: 'Rarely can one get a word in edgeways'. The diarist Chips Channon pronounced Victoria 'garrulous to the point of madness'.

As Victoria established herself at Sennicotts and Ella focused on her imminent Russian wedding, it fell to Irène to tend their disgraced papa. 'The hatred here against the woman [Alexandrine], to [sic] the lowest classes, is very great – but I shall write no more about it so as not to distress you. But the feeling is fearfully strong,' she fretted to Victoria.

Irène accompanied her father to see the Queen, who was pleased to find her 'slow' granddaughter emerging from her elder sisters' shadows. 'Dear Papa is on the whole in better spirits, seems to be comfortable and happy here,' the Queen informed Victoria. 'Irène is in such good looks & very dear & nice & trying to do what she can for dear Papa.' Perhaps it helped that Irène was no longer trying to raise awkward subjects on behalf of Ella and Victoria.

The Queen's meeting with Grand Duke Serge, in Darmstadt, had put her mind at rest, but only up to a point. It did not stop her acting upon gossip circulating that he might be homosexual. It was rumoured that the Grand

Duke had been having affairs with subordinate officers and soldiers of the Preobrazhensky Regiment. He was constantly surrounded by members of the regiment, frequently spending nights away with them.

She launched enquiries with the British Ambassador to Russia, Sir Edward Thornton, on 'a very delicate matter'. Sir Edward then duly consulted the correspondent for the British newspaper, *The Standard*, John Baddeley, and it seemed the Queen's fears were borne out. As Baddeley put it, the Grand Duke's reputation had long been assailed 'by rumours of such a nature as, if true, would make his marriage to any woman, but above all with one so young, innocent and beautiful, hardly tolerable. I told him [the Ambassador] – as indeed he knew already – that the accusations were openly made in all classes of Russian society and commonly believed. On the other hand, proof in such cases was seldom possible'.

In fact, at least one of the accusations – that Grand Duke Serge was enjoying a relationship with his handsome, young domestic chaplain – could be traced back to Ella's jealous cousin, the future Kaiser. Cousin Willie had, of course, once wanted the Princess for himself. Ella's brother, Ernie, confirmed: 'Every bit of tittle-tattle which his agents reported to him he made use of, repeating it with exaggeration.'

Their descendant, the historian Prince Rainer von Hessen, now readily asserts that Serge was an established homosexual and that Ella later sublimated her sexuality into religion.

The haughty-looking Serge was also said to be a heavy drinker, devising a game in which officers dived naked into the snow, drank champagne from a bowl, then howled like wolves. He was rumoured to have opened a club for 'Oriental lusts' in St Petersburg.

Looking at photographs of him from the time, it is hard to imagine. Or is it? In one, taken during the year of young Henry Wilson's stay at Darmstadt, in 1883, he is posing with Ella, Victoria, the latter's then fiancé, Prince Louis, and the Princesses' father. Serge sits, back ramrod-straight, on the floor, astride a cushion. Stylishly arranged across his legs is an elaborately decorated cane.

The Queen dropped her investigations, simply writing rather wistfully to Victoria: 'I DO pray that (at any time) she [Ella] will come to see me once before she marries.'

Sadly, Ella did not manage to visit her grandmother, but she wrote a grateful letter saying it was 'such a happiness to know that you care for us like your children . . . If dear Mama was living how happy it would make her to see all your kindness to us'. She paid tribute to her father and siblings: 'All the family are most kind to me & my own parting will be a wee bit less hard in consequence, although there are moments when I feel very sad . . . Your dear letter touched me deeply.'

In June 1884, two months after Victoria's marriage, the Hesses travelled together to Russia for Ella's wedding. Grand Duke Serge met the party, including little Alix and Miss Jackson, at Peterhof station. The visitors were whisked off to the palace in St Petersburg in a gilded carriage drawn by plumed horses. Miss Jackson may have disapproved of the flummery. But she must have preferred Russia to Italy, with its pesky cadets and soiled bedlinen.

Victoria was impressed by the Russian landscape, reassuring the Queen that it resembled Scotland: 'I never saw any [country] so rich in water before. From the frontier on, it is full of fine rivers & the most beautiful little lakes. The vegetation is much the same as in Scotland especially the trees. Great forests of fir & the grassland [are] studded with birches.'

According to Meriel Buchanan, the Hesse Princesses were stunned by the 'baroque immensity' of the Winter Palace, while being put out by what she obliquely referred to as the 'inadequate sanitary arrangements'. However, they enjoyed shopping trips on the grand Nevsky Prospect and were relieved by the relaxed atmosphere of the Russian Court. For all the trappings, the Russian Court at St Petersburg was less stiff than its Berlin counterpart. In a letter to the Queen, Victoria spoke of jokes, parties and informalities.

Ella's grand wedding ceremony, however, was suitably daunting. On June 15th, she was driven to the Winter Palace in the coach of Catherine the Great, which was crammed with white flowers and drawn by six white horses. Dressing for the ceremony had taken a full three hours.

Victoria gave Grandmama a slightly disapproving description of her sister's new wardrobe, reporting that Ella had been provided, by the Russian Empress, with a complete trousseau: 'As Ella had nothing to do with the choice of the dresses, they were not half as becoming as the outfit Ella brought from home.' She was no less critical of the exacting ceremony: '[Ella] bore the fatigues remarkably well . . . in spite of the great weight of her dress and jewels, especially the tiara & crown which are horribly heavy.'

It was during that first trip to St Petersburg that Alix, then aged 12, struck up a fond friendship with the 16-year-old Russian Tsarevich, Nicky. The Tsarevich was Serge's best man, and he was immediately struck by the young Princess Alix of Hesse.

Processing with one of the tallest members of the Romanov family, Grand Duke Nicholas, Alix looked especially engaging. 'Alix was a pretty little girl of 12 at the time and with her loose hair and smart frock looked very well at the wedding,' reported Victoria. 'She was led into the ceremony by the immensely tall Nikolasha who had to stoop down to talk to her.'

Alix and the groom, Grand Duke Serge, had already developed a special relationship, centred on his impish joke that he had once seen her, as a baby, naked in the bath. 'He took a great liking to little Princess Alix, whom he very much admired,' recalled Alix's lady-in-waiting, Baroness Buxhoeveden. 'He used to tease her unmercifully, and often reduced her to a state of blushing confusion, which she really rather enjoyed.'

The banquet after the ceremony had its controversial elements. With all his plaudits for singing songs in Russian, Ernie complained that it went on far too long. Victoria was put out because her husband Prince Louis was placed 'below the salt'. Tsar Alexander later apologised, blaming the Hesses' snobbish Prussian cousins.

But romance was in the air. The Queen's heart must have sunk when she received an ecstatic letter from the blooming 17-year-old Irène: 'It was all like a beautiful dream.' More anguish followed as Irène appeared to have paired off with Serge's dashing cousin Michael Mikhailovich, known as Mishe Mishe.

Meanwhile, the teenage Tsarevich and Alix were getting on ever better, with Nicky referring to her, in his diary, as 'darling little Alix . . . whom I really like a lot'. The pair enjoyed japes: 'We jumped about together on the net . . . went completely wild on the maypole' and 'told each other secrets'. Nicky declared himself 'very very sad' when it was time for her to go, giving her a brooch memento, which she coyly returned. A week later, he was writing: 'We love each other.'

What the dour Miss Jackson thought of all the excitement is not known. She certainly noticed that Alix was getting behind with her letters to Grandmama. When Alix finally wrote, she referred to the Tsarevich's nine-year-old sister, Xenia, while delicately avoiding any mention of 'Nicky': 'I have been much with little Xenia and her brother and only come to our rooms at bedtime so Miss Jackson hopes that you will kindly excuse me not writing sooner . . . It is very pretty here and I enjoy myself very much.'

The Queen may have already started dreading that something was up between Alix and Nicky. She would certainly have noted Ella's enthusiastic allusions to Nicky, mentioning that he was as bright and clever as the Queen's lookalike grandson Georgie, the future King George V, 'only a little calmer'.

The down-to-earth Victoria soon moved on from the demands of her sister's wedding. During her party's return journey to England, she and Prince Louis stopped at Copenhagen and she reported gleefully that the sailors bought trinkets with wrapping bearing the shopman's name: WC Stinks.

Over the summer of 1884, the three elder Princesses kept in close touch, embarking on the intense correspondence that was to be so vital a part of their lives. Though the letters were mostly in English, there were lapses into German phrasing and word order. The sisters used Queen Victoria-style abbreviations and the more urgent or affectionate notes frequently lacked proper punctuation.

Irène wrote from Germany to Victoria in England, passing on news from Ella in Russia. Much of Ella's early married life was spent writing and sending minute reports to her 'cosy old home' in Darmstadt.

Following their wedding, Ella and Serge travelled to Serge's 2,000-acre country estate, Illinskoye, 40 miles from Moscow. Ella was struck by the picturesque approach, through wheat fields and pine forests. The estate boasted poultry houses, Holstein cattle and horses from the Ardennes. 'The other day we heard from dear Ella, who seems to like Ilinszkoe [sic] very much. She said the drive there was very hot & that they had to stop at different villages on their way to receive bread and salt,' wrote Irène excitedly to Victoria.

'Today I got again a letter from Ella . . . saying she was going to have a little dance – being about 6 to 8 pairs, & they were going to begin the dance with the cotillon figures, the quadrille then & so on . . . They intended also to hang up in a grotto 100 lampions wh. Ella, with her Russian teacher . . . had made themselves.'

What Victoria felt as she read Irène's garbled reports cannot be known exactly. She must have been struck by the contrast between Ella's exotic

Illinskoye and her more humdrum Sennicotts. Which of the homes Irène might prefer, meanwhile, was open to question. She certainly felt the absence of her sisters. 'Everything is as it was, the old clock playing as usual & yet the whole place so quiet. I always am expecting you or Ella to come into the room & miss something the whole day,' she groaned to Victoria from Wolfsgarten. '. . . The old times are gone & will never come back again! I dare not look forward & it makes me sad to look back. What will happen to us as the years go on! I hope I never will grow old – it must be the saddest thing in the world.'

She did not forget Papa and his trials. 'Miss Jackson of course told me I must be with Papa wh[en]ever he wishes & as much as I possibly can . . . Poor Papa, I do all in my might not to let him feel lonely . . . I like this place better than any other & there are so many pleasant remembrances.'

Irène's longing for her two elder sisters seems to have exacerbated her irritation with Alix: 'What you say of Alix is unluckily too true, she is getting awfully stuck up.' Alix's success with the young Tsarevich may have put her sisters out.

Grandmama would have been horrified to hear of her three elder Hesse granddaughters all, at this point, learning Russian. Victoria had begun lessons shortly after Ella's engagement, with Irène, as ever, on the back foot: 'Michael [Mishe Mishe] was very much struck how well you knew Russian already, please let us do a little together when we come to Darmstadt – it will be such fun!'

On her first Christmas away from the family, Ella lamented: 'How I miss you all today!' But then there were always Grand Duke Serge's gifts: '2 half moons in diamonds with a long ruby, uncut, in the middle & a fan in beaten gold with flowers in stones & a grey Tiphany [sic] looking glass.'

Irène sighed to Victoria from Darmstadt: 'We missed you & Ella sadly & I fear that she, poor girl, without a single relation must have felt very lonely & forlorn.'

Alix, aged about 12.

A month before her wedding, Ella had written an emotional note to Grandmama: 'I hope that when you see me again you won't find any change in my character for the worse, as I long to be simple in manners & as good as Mama would have wished me to be.' When the Queen finally saw Ella and Grand Duke Serge, she was favourably impressed. She found Serge nothing like the philandering, drinking, howling wolf of legend, insisting he was 'just the same sweet gentle creature as ever'. Ella's 'pale and thin' appearance she readily put down to the heat.

But, for all his apparent sweetness and gentleness, was Serge 'unbending' – as his niece Marie of Romania had put it – towards his wife? By the autumn of 1885, Ella was writing to her brother Ernie: 'I do not know if I can trip over this year because you see there is always duty over pleasure . . . Of course I never would go without Serge as I would have no pleasure then, being away for ever so short a time makes me long for him, he is so dear and good and all to me – yet that never makes you all at home less dear, only my first consideration must be my husband.'

Ella certainly claimed she was happy, writing in November 1886 to her brother-in-law Prince Louis: 'It makes me always so heartily glad when I hear how happy you both are, it is so pleasant that we four enjoy the same perfect contentment.'

Victoria's and Ella's weddings were followed, in 1885, by the marriage of the Queen's youngest daughter, Beatrice. Cousin Willie's brother, Prince Henry, accompanied the two unmarried Hesse Princesses to Osborne for the ceremony. Irène, 19, and Alix,13, were to be bridesmaids. The Queen was again captivated by Alix, whom she described as 'lovelier than ever and immensely grown'. But while Alix caught the Queen's eye, it was Irène who captivated Henry. Irène could never be as sharp as Victoria or as ethereal as Ella, but she had evidently developed her own armoury.

This despite a certain ungainliness. Victoria painted a vivid picture of her sister at the time, enjoying an ad hoc game of cricket: ' . . . dress tucked up, puffing and panting up & down between the wickets. The latter being constructed out of a heep [sic] of waterproofs and jackets.'

The Queen registered Prince Henry's interest in Irène – and disapproved. She had plans for her third Hesse granddaughter. Once again abandoning her reservations about first cousins, she had set her sights on a match between Irène and one of her Wales grandsons.

She was infuriated when she heard that Ella had invited Irène back to St Petersburg. Haunted by the spectre of Mishe Mishe, she huffed to Victoria: 'I must tell you how annoyed & grieved I am at dear Papa & Irène's going to Petersburg . . . And then for poor Irène it is most awkward, for no end of reports have been spread & I know that Olga Cecile is bent upon Mishe's marrying her.'

Ella did not allow her Grandmama's objections to get in her way. She had progressed from hosting cotillions in grottos to grand balls, and Irène must attend these balls and be agreeable to fellow guests, even if one of them was Mishe Mishe.

Irène thoroughly enjoyed herself. 'Ella looks flourishing has quite rosy cheeks & is even grown a little fatter . . . Ella's ball went off admirably, everyone danced like mad and said it had been the nicest ball of the season,' she gushed to Victoria. 'The Empress was quite enchanted . . . Michael [Mishe Mishe] asked how you were. Everyone is kind to me . . . & so I am as happy as can be & only wish you all were here too!'

Although Irène and Mishe Mishe managed no more than a chat, Ella may well have hoped, at that point, that Irène would join her in Russia, as his wife.

But the Queen's problems did not end there. Her anxiety about Mishe Mishe was soon replaced by worries about Irène's more serious suitor, Prince Henry. He was not as pompous as his brother Willie, but the Queen thought him feckless. She had not forgiven him for the way he and Willie treated their mother. As keen young German patriots, the brothers had never got over their mother's Englishness.

Henry may have baulked at his English nanny once calling him her 'little Regent Street swell'. He may have been similarly upset to be known as Henry – or even Harry – rather than Heinrich. In fact, in years to come, he would become quite Anglophile, at one point even being accused by his brother Willie, by then Kaiser Wilhelm, of developing 'Anglomania'.

In the autumn of 1886, Irène was due to visit Balmoral, and Prince Henry wanted to visit at the same time. The Queen refused to allow him to come. At one point, she extracted a promise from Irène that she wouldn't discuss marriage with Henry before he set off on a particularly prolonged naval voyage. But Irène, once so obliging, had become as headstrong

Henry and Irène around the time of their engagement.

as her elder sisters. She and Henry were engaged in early 1887 and the Queen was, for the third time, taken unawares, coming upon the story in a newspaper report. Irène had gone for her 'surprise tactic', and the Queen was incandescent.

'It is impossible for me to tell you what a shock your letter gave me!' she fumed in response to an emollient missive from Victoria. 'Indeed I felt quite ill – for I am so deeply hurt at Irène's conduct towards me . . . She assured me again and again that she would never do that! How can I trust her again after such conduct?'

A month later, the Queen sniffed to Victoria: 'I feel very deeply that my opinion and my advice are never listened to and that it is almost useless to give any.'

Irène eventually weighed in herself with another of her muddled notes, assuring Grandmama that Henry was 'openhearted and true': 'Harry is really the good angel here and go-between in all the difficulties I have already seen & felt that I scarcely deserve him too.' Just as he had defended Grand Duke Serge, the Princesses' good-hearted brother Ernie entered the ring, supporting Prince Henry in a letter to Victoria: 'Darling Irène is so very happy with Henry and a more dear boy one really could never have seen.'

She was evidently forgiven by the Queen. Within months, the pair were back in correspondence. At the Queen's Golden Jubilee, in 1887, it was Irène who tended Victoria, then suffering from typhoid. 'In the evening they gave her a very good medicine called Anti febrin, which took the fever down to 38 degrees c . . . Naturally she felt ever so much better & cheerful,' Irène reported to the Queen. 'Dear Louis is so touchingly devoted to her & she feels quite unhappy when he is away from her for even so short a time.'

The following January, four months before her wedding, Irène was still building bridges: 'I shall always try to keep your kind advice in remembrance and be deserving of my name,' she assured the Queen. 'I am sure your wish to replace dear Mama has been fully fulfilled for I feel more and more that you are a second mother to us.'

The Queen recovered from her grievances, though she lamented to Victoria that Irène's behaviour had reminded her, chillingly, of Ella and Serge's betrothal, 'which I grieve over as much as ever'.

Around this time, Victoria and Louis moved to Malta, then a British colony, where he had been stationed. Prince Louis had by now inherited Heiligenberg, but the couple never considered basing themselves in Germany. They were increasingly embroiled in their British life, with Prince Louis rising steadfastly through the ranks of the Royal Navy.

In Malta, Victoria made the best of her myriad interests, including botany, cartography and archaeology. Her life in Malta was a far cry from the Queen's splendid Jubilee celebrations, but she had not lost her

The Queen, well over her grievances, sent Irène an affectionate postcard: 'To darling Irène from her devoted Grandmama VRI, Villa Palmieri, Easter 1888.'

weakness for a domestic idyll, 'leading a quiet pleasant life, making driving expeditions of an afternoon'.

Her new life did present social challenges, however. 'I was quite inexperienced in shopping and shy of calling upon people,' she confessed. And entertaining was restricted. 'We have been giving a few small dinner parties lately – our dining room is so small that we can never entertain more than 5 guests at a time,' she informed the Queen. She acquired a particular distaste for Maltese goats' milk, so 'goaty' that '[you] couldn't put cream on strawberries'.

She never lost her lackadaisical attitude to possessions, having little more luck with jewellery than she had had with her hair ribbons as a child. At one point, she lost one of her brother-in-law Serge's expensive gifts – a bracelet of linked pearls – at a Maltese nightclub. It was eventually returned, but only after a series of narrow squeaks. The finder, a workman, passed it on to his child, who hung it around the neck of a family pet dog.

While Victoria and Prince Louis continued to establish their British credentials, Irène and Prince Henry took up their position at the centre of the Prussian Court, marrying on May 24th 1888 at the Charlottenburg Palace in Berlin. Following Victoria's example, Irène wore her mother's wedding lace, along with orange blossom and sprigs of myrtle.

The Queen, well over her gripes, wrote effusively to Prince Henry's grandfather, Emperor Wilhelm I: 'I cannot think unmoved of the union of the children of my 2 dear daughters.' But she failed to attend. This despite Irène offering to change the wedding venue from Berlin to Potsdam, which she thought her grandmother would prefer. In the end, Bertie, the future Edward VII, attended as the Queen's representative, joining the happy foursome – Victoria and Prince Louis and Ella and Grand Duke Serge – and 15-year-old Alix who, according to Baroness Buxhoeveden, created 'quite a sensation'.

Unfortunately the atmosphere of the ceremony was dampened by the extreme poor health of several of Henry's relations. His father, Emperor Frederick, gasped loudly as he struggled to breathe through a tube. His grandmother, Augusta, who had once so sniffily 'cut' Victoria and Ella, now shook with palsy in a bath chair. Prince Henry's brother Willie, the future Kaiser, gave a desolate description of the service: 'The solemnization . . . was entirely dominated by the profound sorrow caused in all those present by the terribly emaciated appearance of my father.' Victoria called it a 'sad wedding'.

Henry's mother, Vicky, took a fond interest in the young couple. She had always compared Henry favourably with his older brother Willie: 'Tho'

Henry often provokes me, he has a good heart, and, alas, William has no heart at all.'

Vicky was very keen that Prince Henry and Irène live nearby, at the Villa Carlotta in Berlin, but she was overruled by Willie. Following several arguments, the couple finally settled far away from the Prussian Court, at Kiel. Victoria wrote of Irène's subsequent satisfaction in a note to the Marquess of Lorne: 'She seems pleased & contented with her new life.'

4

'All is in God's hands.'
Ella

Young Alix was by now creating a sensation wherever she went – her beauty enhanced by a beguiling melancholy.

Growing up, she had undoubtedly undergone more than her fair share of trials. Her perky nicknames, 'Princess Sunshine' and 'Sunny', belied a traumatic childhood. As a toddler she had had to contend with the death of her brother, the haemophiliac Frittie. At the age of six, she had been faced with the deaths, first, of her little sister May, then of her mother. She was stricken with recurrent pains in her back and legs from sciatica. Such pleasures as she enjoyed were muted. Though she loved playing piano, she hated performing, pronouncing music sessions for the Queen 'one of the worst ordeals of her life'. She would have infinitely preferred banjo-picking with Queen Victoria's lady-in-waiting, Miss Minnie Coltrane.

As a teenager, Alix became ever more introspective, betraying signs of the religious fervour that consumed her in later life. She was even developing a macabre interest in the occult. Was Miss Jackson the best person to help Alix through her complex difficulties? The Queen clearly thought not, and complained about the governess in a letter to Alix's father. Victoria stepped in on Papa's behalf: 'I am so sorry you are so very much vexed with Miss Jackson who in spite of her hastiness I sincerely like and respect but Papa has told me you have written to him about her & that he will settle all himself with you.'

Months before Irène's wedding, the Queen had begun fretting about Alix having Miss Jackson as her sole companion. She pulled no punches, warning Victoria that Alix 'must not be left to Miss Jackson alone, with her bad health, hard ways & crabbed bad temper. It w[ou]ld ruin Alicky. Someone must be found for her, younger, softer, brighter, else her life all alone will be utterly miserable'. Victoria replied that, although of course it would be nice for Alix to have 'someone fresher & younger', the time was not right; 'Papa also would prefer no change'.

But Miss Jackson's days were numbered. It was decided that she would leave at Alix's confirmation. In that way, she would be gone just before Irène's departure. Irène reassured the Queen: 'Papa intends Alix to be confirmed at Whitsuntide as in that way Miss Jackson's leaving would be more agreeable for all and a natural end to her remaining.' Victoria attempted to defend their Madgie: 'In spite of her various faults we all owe her a debt of gratitude, as she has really tried to do her best & has shown us real affection & devotion, in spite of her unfortunate outward manner.'

What the Queen made of the four sisters' lifelong devotion to Miss Jackson is not known.

Having dispatched the crabbed-tempered governess, the Queen set about finding a husband for Alix. Her first choice was her fey Wales grandson Eddie, Prince Albert. Eddie was known as 'collars and cuffs' because of the elaborate efforts he made to disguise his overlong arms and neck. It seems that Grandmama was prepared, once again, to overlook the fact that they were first cousins.

Unsurprisingly, Ella was opposed to the match: 'I find the idea of his marrying Alix quite dreadful – first cousin is best to avoid – the chief thing is he does not look over-strong & is too stupid . . . England with a husband – not at all a place for Alix.' The Queen was not to be put off, at one point choreographing a pageant in which Eddie and Alix acted out the letter 'U for Union' as bride and groom.

But she was outmanoeuvred. In the autumn of 1888, it was Ella who oversaw Alix's launch into society. Despite all her worries about leaving her husband in Russia, she was determined to attend Alix's coming-out in Darmstadt. Baroness Buxhoeveden wrote that Ella 'saw to every detail of her young sister's appearance'.

And the following spring, Ella invited Alix back to Russia. That six-week visit to St Petersburg would seal her 16-year-old sister's fate. The Tsarevich, Nicky, stood alongside several Grand Dukes as they welcomed the Hesse party at the railway station in St Petersburg. The Tsarevich was immediately enchanted by Alix: 'She has grown up a lot and become much prettier.'

At the time of Ella's wedding, the Princesses had struggled with aspects of court life in St Petersburg. Five years on, Ella was very much at home. Her Russian teacher, Mademoiselle Schneider, had worked tirelessly, keeping Grand Duke Serge up to date with his wife's new words, so that he could direct meal-time conversations. Ella boasted gleefully to the family at Darmstadt: 'I get on beautifully and can scold to perfection.'

More importantly, she had established herself as a particularly adept hostess. The young Grand Duchess devoted herself to unending social events, preparing herself by bathing in rosebud water, before spending hours dressing. As Baroness Buxhoeveden put it, Ella 'loved dancing and organised all kinds of entertainment so that her house was very attractive to her young relations'.

She designed her own dresses, scrutinising French fashion magazines before drawing intricate sketches. She and her husband both took pleasure in selecting jewels to match her outfits. Ella's biographer, Christopher Warwick, makes much of Serge's 'feminine side' and his 'interest in Ella's jewels & dress'. The French Ambassador, Maurice Paléologue, for one, was always deeply impressed by her, confessing that she inspired 'profane passions'.

It was under Ella's practised eye that Alix attended her first large ball. But Alix was not as socially skilled as her sister and was immediately labelled, by one racy Russian Countess, as 'devoid of charm, wooden, cold eyes, holds herself as if she'd swallowed a yardstick'.

Was Alix's lack of charisma the result of the dampening hand of Miss Jackson, or a stiff English approach to manners? Alix's lady-in-waiting, Baroness Buxhoeveden, later insisted that the Tsarina combined her awkward manner with a rich sense of humour, laughing until the tears ran down her face. It was just that she didn't crack jokes: 'It wasn't in her to set the laughter going.'

With her recurring sciatica, Alix coped no better with the badminton and skating parties. She preferred the less elaborate social events; at one point, the Tsarevich thoughtfully persuaded his parents to hold a modest tea dance for her, with blinis and caviar. There were expeditions to the theatre, to see a production of *Eugene Onegin*, which the Tsarevich and Alix both loved, and the more controversial and bloody *L'Assommoir*, which they did not.

The Tsarevich was not in the least put off by Alix's various difficulties: 'My dream is some day to marry Alix H'; 'I have loved her a long while and still deeper and stronger since 1889 when she spent six weeks in St P.'

Ella was as assiduous as the Queen in driving her intentions home. After Alix had left, she created an affecting memento of the visit for the Tsarevich. Around a photograph of Alix, their brother Ernie and herself, she painted scenes of the merry times they had shared. The Tsarevich described the momento to Alix: 'There is the ice hill, the big hall, the skates, a clown'. Another photograph, of Alix and Ella in ball dresses, he now kept constantly before him.

Ella's chief worry was the Queen's opposition. 'Through all the idiotic trash in the newspapers she [the Queen] gets impossible untrue views and founds all her arguments on facts which probably never existed,' she complained to Ernie. 'God grant this marriage may come true.' She added: 'I had a letter from Pelly [her name for the Tsarevich] always longing for news & feeling very lovesick & lost & having nobody except Serge & me with whom to talk.'

The Tsarevich's dominating father, Tsar Alexander III, was also, at this point, opposed to the marriage. One of his concerns was that the gauche Alix was temperamentally unsuited for the role of Tsarina. He would be proven right. The more immediate problem was Alix's refusal to convert to Russian Orthodoxy. The conversion was essential for any Tsarina of Russia. This hurdle was, however, frequently overlooked, dismissed by Alix's elders as caprice.

The Queen was jubilant when Alix returned to Darmstadt still resolutely unattached. Her triumphant note to Victoria contained a dig at Ella: 'I was right in telling Uncle Bertie that I KNEW there was no question of a marriage for her in Russia & that you have brought her back safe and free. Uncle Bertie says he knows Ella will move Heaven & Earth to get her to marry a Gd Duke!'

She eagerly resumed her efforts to unite Alix and her grandson, Prince Albert, Eddie. Her failures with all three elder Princesses had not dimmed her passion for matchmaking. During the summer of 1889, Alix endured uncomfortable stays at Osborne and Balmoral. The Queen tutted to Victoria: 'She [Alix] shld be made to reflect seriously on the folly of throwing away the chance of a very good husband, kind affectionate & steady . . . & a very good position wh is second to none in the world.' Alix may have been relieved to visit a Welsh coalmine with her aunt Beatrice at Ruabon; even braving a grim visit underground to see the shafts.

Irène then muddied the waters further, brightly supporting Eddie's cause while throwing one of his brothers into the mix. She wrote to the Queen: 'Alicky is always so reserved that it is difficult to speak of such things with her but I really think it only wants time – for she is so young – & then these fancies against E[ddie] may come right . . . I believe, however, that ever since a small child Alicky cared for Georgie of Wales – but do not know now.'

Alix finally managed to turn down 'Drawing Room Eddie', as he was known. Though he was feckless and disengaged and probably homosexual, he declared himself heartbroken by the rejection.

A visit to Malta gave Alix a welcome break from the furore. She and Irène both stayed with Victoria, despite the island being besieged by outbreaks of influenza. All four sisters were exercised by the epidemic, which had started in Russia. 'Ella wrote me that half St Petersburg was down with it and that it attacked people so suddenly that their legs would give way under them and they would have to sit down in the street,' reported Victoria.

But Alix's stay with Victoria gave her only a momentary reprieve. Back in Darmstadt, she found herself once again in fraught discussion with Grandmama. The Queen had dropped by on her return from a holiday in France. She would have made the most of regular, intimate drives with Alix and Papa. She issued strict instructions to Victoria: 'Take care and tell Ella that no marriage for Alicky in Russia would be allowed, then there will be an end of it.'

Did Victoria pass Grandmama's instructions on to Ella? If so, they had no effect. Within weeks, Ella had brazenly issued another invitation to Alix.

During this visit, curiously, Alix saw nothing of the young Tsarevich. She and Victoria stayed at Illinskoye, Ella's country estate, where Alix enjoyed a rustic idyll, far from the glitz of St Petersburg. At Illinskoye, Ella and Grand Duke Serge tended to embrace the simple life. The couple went for walks and Serge would read to Ella while she painted or, less probably, cooked eggs on a portable stove.

When not caught up in domestic pleasures, the Grand Duke liked to devote himself to building projects: a new school or an extension to the greenhouses. At one point, he set up a horse milk farm, the milk being considered a good folk remedy. Whether Victoria found the Russian horse milk any more to her taste than the 'goaty' Maltese milk is not known.

The various houses and grounds of Illinskoye could not compare with the palaces of St Petersburg. But the contrast with Victoria's humble quarters in Malta were starker still.

As she described Ella's elaborate arrangements for dinner, Victoria may have cast her mind back to the five guests obliged to squeeze around her own dining table. Her tone, however, remained breezy enough: '[There were] villa-like houses where a great number of guests were lodged. Some of these were sufficiently far away to make it necessary, when it rained, for a carriage to go round and pick up the guests for dinner.'

Ella's guests were treated to drives in an Irish jaunting car, holding four people on each side, seated back to back. One popular destination was Archangelskoye, the neighbouring estate belonging to Felix Yusupov's family. The Yusupovs, then the richest family in Russia, were known for their 18th-century theatre and a grand piggery.

The British Ambassador's daughter, Merial Buchanan, wrote that the magnificence of Archangelskoye put Illinskoye in the shade. Felix Yusupov clearly agreed, giving a slightly condescending description of the interior: 'Their house was tastefully arranged in the style of an English country house: chintz-covered armchairs and a profusion of flowers.'

It is hard to imagine Alix managing any of the sporting activities at Illinskoye, but Victoria threw herself into games of lawn tennis, boating and bathing. Ella, unable to swim, entered the water fully dressed, floating on a rubber ring. Victoria was taken with a second, more elaborate swimming aid: 'Another amusing thing to go about on the river in, was a round inflatable rubber punt with two rubber leggings let into the bottom. This Serge had bought in England where it is used by duck shooters.'

Victoria was particularly grateful to the Grand Duke for organising archaeological digs at a site nearby, Nikolskoye. Following the digs, she would take her collections of bracelets, armlets and horse trappings back to a museum at Darmstadt.

The two sisters were not the only guests at Illinskoye. Victoria noted, without comment, Serge's strapping male entourage, 'half a dozen young Preobrazhensky officers'.

Among the female guests, meanwhile, for whom Ella made bouquets and wreaths, was the 'overpoweringly stout' Princess Masha Wassiltchikov, whom Victoria described as 'the life and soul of the party'. Felix Yusupov's description of the Princess was less tactful: 'As tall as a drum major, weighed over 400 pounds and in her stentorian voice used the language of the guardroom . . . anyone passing within her reach risked being snatched up like a newborn babe.'

Those at risk would have included a diminutive fellow guest, Count Olsonfieff, whom Yusupov described as a 'bald chubby little man' armed with 'a sword almost as large as himself which made an infernal clatter as it dragged and scraped along the ground'. While in church the insensitive Count 'would go the round of the icons' while speaking very loudly. Yusupov remembered Ella smarting: 'The grand duchess was most uncomfortable.'

The two sisters had little trouble dealing with their fellow guests. More disquieting for them were Illinskoye's peasants. Ella's stepdaughter, Maria Pavlovna, described journeys from the station, during which kerchief-wearing women, gathering mushrooms, 'would run away at our approach'. In the village, she added, 'dirty children played in the dust'.

Ella was shocked by the peasants' servility, as well as their suffering. But

Grand Duke Serge remained untroubled; he took the servility as his due, while holding them to blame them for their woes. 'His life is hard indeed, but drink is his ruin. If I were to close the Kabaks [taverns] both here and at Usovo, there would be mutiny.'

Nonetheless, all the sisters enjoyed the peasants' celebration of Ella's Russian name day. Victoria described a lottery, with presents comprising more kerchiefs, white china teapots, cotton dress-lengths and bags of boiled sweets. In a special tribute to Ella, the peasants sang and danced on the grass. And Alix, in particular, enjoyed sharing a nod '*de haut en bas*' with the peasants. As Baroness Buxhoeveden recalled, 'Alix loved playing Lady Bountiful, treating the peasants as children.' Years later, as Tsarina, Alix would be convinced that 'the peasants love us', developing a close relationship with the peasant 'holy man' Rasputin.

Ella judged the Illinskoye visit a success. But Alix's future life in Russia was still far from assured. Alix had allowed herself to be swept into a romantic dalliance with the Tsarevich, but her objection to converting to Russian Orthodoxy remained an insurmountable obstacle. Years later, the Queen supported Ella's decision to follow Serge into the Orthodox Church. While her thoughts on Alix's reluctance to convert are unclear, she would obviously have welcomed any obstacle to her granddaughter marrying the Tsarevich. All three elder sisters were aware of the growing stakes. By now Alix had dismissed several eligible bachelors in addition to the unfortunate Eddie. Admiring officers had become a feature of Alix's visits both to Victoria in Malta and Irène in Kiel.

With Eddie dispatched, the indefatigable Queen set her heart on Prince Maximilian of Baden. Max was a cousin of Ella's ill-fated suitor, Fritz, and, like Eddie, probably homosexual. The Queen was insistent: 'Dear Papa will lose no time in inviting him.' Alix later recalled: 'I did not know him at all and I shall never forget what I suffered when I met him for the first time.' She may have been put off by his appearance. Like King Leopold II of Belgium, Max of Baden had a prominent nose.

Meanwhile, Eddie, Prince Albert, died of influenza in January 1892. Irène was upset that Willie, now Kaiser, forbade her husband, Prince Henry, from going to the funeral – refusing to give any reason why. As a row brewed, Irène found herself in the invidious position of having to apologise to the irate Queen on behalf of her bossy brother-in-law, begging her 'not to think too harshly of his Brother [Willie] for he was really sorry afterwards not to have sent Harry.'

Thoughts of Alix's prospects were cast aside in March 1892, when the Princesses' father, Grand Duke Louis, became mortally ill following a stroke. The four sisters gathered in Darmstadt for a rare reunion. Each made an effort to keep Grandmama abreast. The Queen had experienced issues with the lackadaisical Papa over the years, but she fully understood his daughters' anguish.

In one letter, Victoria related how the Grand Duke had been cheered by Ella's arrival from Russia: 'Ella bent over the bed and took Papa's hand. I said "Papa, papa, Ella ist da" & Ella also called him, then he suddenly opened his eyes in a dazed sort of way, looked puzzled from her to Serge & then a pleased look came over his face. He murmured, "jeh, jeh, jeh", raised his whole head off the pillow, put out his hand and stroked Ella's knee.'

Irène was much taken with Serge's sensitivity. 'We were so intensely thankful & overjoyed this morning when dear Serge said good morning in French and we heard him [Papa] say "oui"!! Imagine! Poor dear Ella looks so pulled still, is so wonderfully brave, dear and good. It is such a pleasure having dear Serge too, who feels so deeply.'

Following Ella's appearance, Papa's condition seemed to improve. As Irène wrote: 'We all feel quite different now that there is a little hope & a turn for the better. To be all together again after such a long time, although under such dreadful circumstances, is such a comfort and even pleasure.'

Victoria remained, as usual, at the helm and Alix, equally characteristically, under the weather. 'Alicky has borne up wonderfully in spite of the dreadful shock but suffers still from rheumatism . . . Poor Victoria . . . is the one we go to for everything . . . and the most practical for everything,' reported Irène. 'I cannot imagine what it would have been without her . . . Oh! darling Grandmama, many, many kisses, doubly so in this dreadfully anxious time.'

The small improvement in Papa's health proved fleeting. The Grand Duke Louis of Hesse died, aged 54, on March 13th 1892.

The task of sending locks of Papa's hair to the Queen fell to Victoria: 'And now I must say goodbye for today. I will send the hair & the flowers in a day or two'. The sisters hid none of their grief from the Queen. 'The sad sad bells are ringing as they do every day from 11 to 12 ...' wrote Irène. 'We all cling together more than ever ... And you darling Grandmama, we all feel and know ARE our one help & stay in this fearful sorrow – our second Mother whom we can always feel such love and reverence for.'

Wrangles about suitors had not soured relations between Alix and her Grandmama. Alix sent a confiding note: 'It is such a comfort having dear sisters here. I am, beloved Grandmama, your ever very loving, truly devoted, dutiful, deeply sorrowing child.

'How happy he will be now, united with sweet Mama . . . I am sure they are now looking down on us, Alicky.'

For all her emotional notes to the Queen, however, Alix was causing concern. She was not, it was felt, showing her deepest feelings about the loss of her father. This was considered repressive, even in 1892, and Orchie was worried. As the Queen reported: 'Dear Alicky's grief, Orchard said, was terrible, for it was a silent grief, which she locked up within her'.

Irène (left) and Alix mourned the death of their father in 1892.

Mindful that her sisters would soon all be gone, Alix tortured herself with the thought that she was not as wise as Victoria and would therefore be unable to help Ernie with his new responsibilities as Grand Duke. According to her lady-in-waiting, Alix was forever in thrall to Victoria's 'active and clear' mind.

With the death of her father, Alix's position in Darmstadt must have seemed more precarious. The Queen wrote anxiously to Victoria: 'It adds to my quite overwhelming grief to think of your distress & dear Ernie and Alicky alone – Orphans!! It is awful.' In fact, the orphans would muddle along happily enough. Alix was Ernie's favourite sister. In years to come, Alix would shower her brother with Fabergé cigarette cases from Russia. The cases, stored at Wolfsgarten, were fondly signed, 'With love from Sunny'.

Months after the death of Grand Duke Louis, in the autumn of 1892, Georgie, the future George V, provided distractions at the Hessian Court. The Prince was visiting Germany in order to learn German. Victoria recalled: 'George was a good deal bored by his life in Heidelberg and felt himself too old to start working with a tutor again.' He amused himself by riling his tutor with noun genders: 'Der, die or das Sonne is really very hot today – choose which, Professor.'

The Queen would have been gratified to know that, at this point, Alix had resolved not to pursue her dalliance with the Tsarevich. Though the couple met again the following January, in Berlin, at the wedding of Alix's cousin Margaret, they had no intimate conversations and no opportunities to relive those happy weeks in St Petersburg. The Tsarevich's parents had finally given him permission to pursue Alix, but he found her tantalisingly remote, now pleading earache.

After Berlin, Alix made a trip to Italy, enthusing about Italian cities in a letter to Miss Jackson: 'It [Venice] is like a dream, so different to anything one has ever seen . . . The delightful sensation of being rowed in a gondola and the peace & quiet. What a dream of beauty Florence also.'

Back in Darmstadt, she wrote again: 'Darling Madgie . . . thanks for your dear letter and the sweet little book. I ought not to have opened the packet till the 6th [her birthday] – but I could not resist the temptation.' Her grief for her father was still raw: 'Oh Madgie dear if you only knew how too terribly I miss my own darling. It is too hard to believe that we shall never meet again in this world.' Madgie was also in close contact with Victoria. Alix concluded: 'I am glad that you are going to Folkestone and so will be near Victoria.'

Madgie and Victoria had, in fact, met three months previously, the pair getting off to an awkward start: 'I lunched with Miss Jackson on Saturday . . . it was quite a nice little lunch,' reported Victoria to Ernie, 'at first MHJ was all of a flutter, but calmed down soon.'

Six months after their failed meeting in Berlin, Alix and the Tsarevich missed a further opportunity to meet in London. In July 1893, the Tsarevich was invited to Prince George's wedding. He met Victoria and Irène, but Alix sent her excuses to the Queen: 'The journey would be scarcely worth the while & there it is so expensive also . . .' Nicky's disappointment at not seeing Alix did not detract from his appreciation of the wedding presents: 'They [the bridal couple] were given everything conceivable,' he chortled to his brother. 'Somebody even managed to present them with a cow.'

That autumn, Ella and Grand Duke Serge travelled to Balmoral, with Serge's brother, Pavel. The visit was a success, with the Queen regretting the trio's departure: 'Had to take leave of Sergei and Paul . . . whom we liked very much.' The party seems to have avoided discussing Alix and the Tsarevich. But if the Queen assumed that Ella had abandoned her matchmaking plans, she was wrong.

Ella's next ploy was to get the Tsarevich to travel to Coburg to meet Alix. At this point, confusingly, it was the Tsarevich who seemed to lose his nerve, sending a note excusing himself. Serge was infuriated, ranting: 'My wife was . . . outraged by your letter . . . If you have no strong character, no will or your feelings have changed it's deplorable you haven't told me or my wife.'

Whatever the reasons behind Nicky and Alix's failure to meet, the question of whether Alix would convert was clearly still a sticking point. She remained intransigent, and finally wrote to the Tsarevich in November 1893: 'It grieves me terribly and makes me very unhappy . . . I cannot do it against my conscience . . . Goodbye my darling Nicky.' When Nicky then appealed again to Ella, he received a further stern letter from Grand Duke Serge: 'Everything is over and my wife asked you not to mention this again.'

But everything was not over. For all her requests to the Tsarevich not to mention Alix, Ella had not given up. She described her hopes in a letter to Ernie at Darmstadt; her brother was evidently supporting her: 'It all looks vague & sad & yet I cannot help hoping for the best, I so perfectly understand all Alicky must be going through . . . If you find my presence necessary . . . do send for me & if only possible I should arrive directly, if it should be for a few days.'

The Queen would have been discomforted by the insinuating tone of Ella's letter to her: 'The best is to leave her [Alix] alone as of course it is a very very sore heart one touches . . . All is in God's hands & dearest Grandmama if she ever accepts – your motherly love will be what she longs for most – alas, the world is so spiteful & not knowing how long & how deep this affection on both sides has been – the spiteful tongues will call it ambition – what fools, as if this throne was enviable . . .' With regard to political instability, Ella's view was chillingly stoical: 'Are not our lives always in His hands? And may we not all die suddenly?'

While still more or less convinced that Alix would refuse the Tsarevich, Grandmama probed Victoria: 'I wonder if poor dear Alicky has talked to you about the end of Nicky's hopes.' She was still smarting over Ella's championing of the match: 'Our dear Ella always encouraged him instead of doing the reverse.' By March 1894, even Alix was bridling at the 'encouragement', complaining to the Tsar's sister, Xenia, that Ella would soon 'begin again' with accusations that she was 'ruining' the Tsarevich's life, driving him, like a Dostoyevskyan anti-hero, to drink and the gipsies.

Alix's feelings at this point are hard to gauge. She may have resigned herself to refusing the Tsarevich once and for all, relishing a sort of martyrdom. She may, equally, have secretly hoped to be talked out of her refusal.

Ella's motivations are equally unfathomable. She was obviously keen to have her sister in Russia; she was satisfied that Alix and Nicky were in love. But had she properly thought about having her little sister as Tsarina?

It was at Ernie's wedding, in Coburg, that Ella 'began again' in earnest. In April 1894, the young Tsarevich travelled from Russia to attend the ceremony. Ella felt it was now or never. The Tsarevich must propose and her sister be prevailed upon to accept, even if she was not in best shape. She had recently complained to the Queen: 'I have to keep as quiet as possible on account of my legs.'

And it was not just her legs. Alix felt generally uncomfortable about Ernie's marriage, anxious that her place within the Hesse household would be compromised by the arrival of her brother's new wife, Ducky. She might have been less stressed had she known that the marriage would last only seven years, with questions arising about Ernie's sexuality. Years later, Felix Yusupov described Ernie's domestic life: 'Having taken it into his head one day that his white pigeons were not in keeping with the old stones of the palace, he had their feathers dyed sky blue. His marriage was not a happy one.'

No sooner had the visiting Romanovs arrived at Coburg than Ella marched the Tsarevich into Alix's room. He described this first harrowing meeting in his diary: 'After coffee, about ten, I went with Aunt Ella to Alix. She looked particularly pretty, but extremely sad. They left us alone and then began between us the talk which I had long ago strongly wanted and at the same time very much feared . . . We talked until 12.00 but without success, she is still against changing religion.'

Ella had never been a fan of her former admirer, Willie, Kaiser Wilhelm II. But this did not stop her recruiting him to break the impasse. Willie very much fancied the idea of having a German cousin on the Russian throne. He had already bossily instructed the timorous

Tsarevich to press his suit with flowers and a ceremonial sword. In fact, so keen was he that he was prepared to sacrifice his religious principles for diplomacy. When Ella had converted to Russian Orthodoxy, Willie had accused her of desertion – *Fahnenflucht*. He had no compunction about instructing Alix to 'desert'. Indeed, he insisted that, if she refused the Tsarevich, she would be guilty of putting the future peace of Europe in jeopardy.

It is impossible to know whether it was Ella, Grand Duke Serge or the Kaiser who finally prevailed. For five years, Alix had wanted to marry the Tsarevich, but felt she could not disobey her conscience. She was now persuaded that the marriage was not just desirable but right.

The Kaiser accompanied Alix to the house where the Tsarevich was staying, stationing himself, with Ella and Grand Duke Serge, in the room next to the one in which the couple would have their momentous discussion. Alix accepted the Tsarevich immediately. His report to his mother was ecstatic: 'With her first words she consented.' They both burst into tears; he confessed that he cried 'like a child'.

For the unsuspecting Queen, in Coburg for Ernie's wedding, the news of the engagement was mortifying: 'I knew that Nicky much wished it, I thought that Alicky was not sure of her mind.' She made no secret of the efforts she had made to prevent the marriage, lamenting to her daughter Vicky: 'I had laboured so hard to PREVENT it and I felt there was NO LONGER any danger and all in one night EVERYTHING was changed.'

Alix couldn't wait to pass on her news to Miss Jackson: 'I am more happy than words can express; at last after these five sad years!' Though Madgie is likely to have shared the Queen's reservations, she may have liked the idea that two of her Princesses would be united in Russia. She would certainly have been 'a-flutter'.

The *Morning Post* shared the Kaiser's buoyant view, declaring that the Alliance 'cannot fail to strengthen in the highest degree the guarantees of European peace'.

The Tsarevich travelled with the four sisters from Coburg to Darmstadt. He and his fiancée then had to part for six weeks as Alix visited England with Victoria.

Still reeling from her fourth blindsiding, the Queen bombarded Alix with questions. History had repeated itself, with Alix's change of heart echoing Ella's ten years before. Alix wrote to the Tsarevich: 'She [the Queen] began by asking me so many questions. When, how and where and what had made me change my decision and so on, til [sic] I no longer knew what to say.'

Less romantically, Alix was still suffering from sciatica. It was decided that she should have a rest cure at Harrogate, and that Victoria would accompany her. Alix registered herself, in lodgings, under the pseudonym Baroness Starckenburg. Any idea of secrecy, however, was soon undermined when she insisted her landlady name her newborn twins Nicholas and Alix. Duly appointed godmother, Alix would regularly send them Fabergé gifts from St Petersburg.

Victoria wrote a reassuring note to the Queen from Harrogate. Her words about Alix being supported by Ella in Russia would one day ring particularly false, as the two sisters suffered repeated fallings-out. Victoria talked of 'the great blessing that sincere love between husband & wife is to all . . . As to living in Russia, it is not as if she were going quite among strangers, for Ella is there too'.

When not having cures, Alix struggled to learn Russian with Ella's teacher, Catherine Schneider, groaning to Miss Jackson: 'It is amusing but certainly not easy!'

Alix was reunited with her fiancé at Walton-on-Thames, where Victoria was temporarily based. In his diary, the Tsarevich described the couple's ecstatic reunion at Victoria's 'cosy cottage' – the actually quite substantial Elm Grove.

His allusions to size had echoes of Ella's bemused comments about Victoria's Sennicotts. Over the years, the Battenbergs based themselves at a series of English houses of varying proportions: 'I arrived at "Walton" in 25 minutes and at 3.45 met dear Alix. Again, I experienced the happiness which I had when I left Coburg! It is a rare, warm and friendly life for four people in Victoria and Louis's little house.'

Victoria and Prince Louis and Ella and Grand Duke Serge had once been the happiest foursome; now it was Victoria and Prince Louis and Alix and the Tsarevich enjoying idyllic boating trips. This despite, on one occasion, their having an altercation with a neighbouring landowner. The party had been enjoying tea on an island, in defiance of a notice barring trespassers. It fell to Prince Louis to offer excuses. As Victoria reported crisply: 'On Louis's explaining that we would do no damage and leave no litter as we knew what it was to suffer from inconsiderate tourists on our own property, he allowed us to finish our tea.'

Several days later, there were further excitements for 'the Waltonians', as Victoria called her neighbours, when Alix and the Tsarevich left for Windsor Castle. Victoria wrote: 'We four [were] fetched by a Royal carriage with an outrider to go to Windsor, much to the surprise of the Waltonians, who never realized who the important people stopping with us had been.'

The betrothed couple spent five days at Osborne House, on the Isle of Wight, before the Tsarevich departed for Russia. After Nicky left, Alix went with Victoria to Heiligenberg, where the two sisters were briefly re-united with Irène.

After all her worries and warnings about Russia and the Romanovs, the Queen had been worsted. Her favourite granddaughter, Alix, was set to follow her sister to an unstable country where both their lives would be in danger. In fact, as Tsarina, Alix would face a greater peril than her sister.

Alix's wedding was dogged, from the outset, by misfortune. After saying goodbye to his fiancée on the Isle of Wight, the Tsarevich travelled with his family to the Crimea, where his father became seriously ill. Increasingly anguished, he persuaded Alix to travel from Germany to join him.

A gloomy correspondent for the local newspaper recorded her departure: 'It is only with feelings of deep grief and pity that the German people can follow the gracious and beloved Princess Alix during her journey to Russia. I cannot banish from my thoughts the secret foreboding that this Princess, who wept much bitter tears when she left Darmstadt, will have a life full of tears and bitterness on foreign soil.'

Victoria and Ella accompanied Alix on separate legs of her journey to Russia. The sisters fired off telegrams to the anxious Queen at Balmoral. Victoria wrote from Darmstadt: 'Start tomorrow with Alix via Berlin for Warsaw where Ella takes her on by special. Serge and Paul (Serge's brother Pavel) have gone on straight. I return here.'

Before meeting Alix in Livadia in the Crimea, Ella made elaborate preparations. It may have seemed odd for Ella to find herself playing second fiddle to Alix, but it was surely a taste of things to come. Victoria had already referred breezily to Nicky and Alix as 'the important people' stopping in Walton.

Within weeks of Alix's arrival, Alexander III's condition had deteriorated further; he died on November 1st 1894. The betrothed couple wrote to the Queen at Balmoral: 'Dearest beloved father has been taken from us. God help us and darling Mama. He gently went to sleep. Alix, Nicky.' The following day, Alix was received into the Orthodox Church. Now Alix wrote herself: 'Thanks touching telegram. The service for me Victoria wrote to you about takes place this morning at 10.00. Kisses Alix.' She did not mention that the treatments in Harrogate had failed and that her debilitating leg pains had returned.

Describing the service to the Queen, Ella also avoided any downsides: 'Her [Alix's] confirmation . . . was so beautiful and touching. She read all perfectly and was very calm. [She] thanks God she is well, doesn't feel her life too much and as much as possible rests in the day.'

Alix travelled with the Tsarevich from the Crimea to St Petersburg behind Alexander III's coffin. The trip went on for days, during which the dead Tsar's body gradually decomposed. For Alix, the dark symbolism would have been exacerbated by paranoia, as the couple were accosted by excited crowds at every station. Ella's insistence that Alix wasn't feeling her life too much rang false.

Following their arrival at St Petersburg, Alix and Ella returned to the station to meet Irène, who was to attend Tsar Alexander's funeral as well as Alix's wedding. Victoria was, by then, back in Malta and unable to attend either.

Irène, Ella and Alix sent continual updates from St Petersburg to Victoria and Grandmama. First, there were the disputes over a wedding date; when it was finally fixed, Irène immediately notified Victoria: 'It was after all decided that the wedding was to be a few days later – on Aunt Minnie's [the Tsarevich's mother's] birthday, the 26th, which day Aunt Minnie chose herself.'

Two of the sisters' fond companions from Darmstadt helped Alix dress for the wedding: Orchie and a maid, Madeleine Zanotti, who had worked with the Hesses for six years. Alix herself sent Grandmama a breathless telegram at 11.30 on the day: 'Very tenderest thanks for touching letter and lovely presents, am wearing the ring, fondest love, leave in an hour for Winter Palace. Alix.'

Irène filled Victoria in the following day: 'Aunt Minnie fetched Alicky yesterday with 3 escorts from Ella's house at 11.30. The whole family &

Nicky awaited them here. She took her straight into the room where her crown and cloak were put on . . . Alicky was quite wonderfully composed the whole day.'

Ella gave the Queen a minute description of Alix's appearance: 'The dress is an embroidered silver cloth Russian court dress & very pretty. As bride she wears two curls . . . it looks very pretty and a pretty frame for the face . . . Alix being tall will look perfectly lovely.' She enclosed two detailed drawings, including one of Alix's profile, with elaborate earrings.

She gave cheerful assurances following the ceremony: 'Wedding beautiful[ly] touching, Alix looked sweet, just took tea with young couple looking happy, cosily established.'

Ella was, of course, especially eager to give the Queen glowing pictures of Alix's first days as the Tsarevich's wife. Though not yet crowned, the young Princess was already effectively Tsarina. Ella described a visit by the newly-weds to the Tsarevich's father's tomb, during which members of the crowd tried to kiss Alix's hands, an experience the shy Princess would surely have hated: 'It was touching to see their joy kissing Alix's hands, nearly pulling off her cloak . . . Those who saw it say the crowd was like mad with joy.' She insisted, perhaps over keenly, that Alix's sciatica was under control: 'Alix looks well & hardly feels her leg.'

Irène painted Victoria a rosy picture of the couple's domestic life, making further mention of Orchie, who, aged 64, was arranging 'all' for Alix: 'They live below Aunt Minnie in his old rooms & 2 other rooms added, very cosily, light-wood furniture & chintz arranged in haste. Orchie was bustling about very happy to be able to arrange all for Alicky, who had already put up lots of her frames and nicknacks.

'They have their meals quite alone for themselves, Aunt Minnie having insisted they should & she said when we took leave she hoped we did not think she would be an exacting mother in law & I feel sure she will not.'

Ella gave the Queen an equally exuberant description of Alix's relationship with her mother-in-law: 'She [Minnie] has quite adopted Alix as her own child & is delightfully kind to her.' Alix finally put in her own tribute: 'She is an angel of kindness.'

The sisters' assessments of that special relationship would prove sadly awry. In years to come, Alix found her mother-in-law very exacting and far from an 'angel of kindness'. Indeed, by the time of the revolution, relations had deteriorated to the point where the Dowager felt it necessary to remove herself entirely from the Russian Court, settling 800 miles away, in Kiev.

Days later, the Queen heard from Alix herself. Well over her 'thunderstrike', Grandmama had organised a celebratory dinner at Windsor on the day of the wedding. Alix said she had been 'immensely touched' to hear of the dinner. She added: 'The pendant with your dear portrait is too beautiful & I shall prize it very much. The lovely ring I wore for the wedding & ever since and when I look at it I have to think of the beloved giver . . .'

She was as determined as Ella to spare Grandmama any bad news, alluding only fleetingly to the sad departure of the Hesse family: 'Darling Ernie, Irène and Henry left late last night.. I will send you some of the myrtle and orange blossom I wore & a bit of the dress as soon as I can.' With Victoria, she was more candid: 'It was horrid saying goodbye to dear ones when they left again for home . . .'

Alix felt the Hesses' departure keenly, but she did at least, at that point, have Ella.

Weeks after her marriage, Alix acknowledged the challenges as well as the joys of her new life. 'One day in deepest mourning, lamenting a beloved one, the next in smartest clothes being married. There cannot be a greater contrast but it drew us more together, if possible . . . If only I could find words to tell you of my happiness – daily it grows more and my love greater,' she confided to Victoria. 'Life is so different to what it was in the past – tho' there are many difficulties & all is not easy where one comes first into a new country & has to speak another language.'

In her Christmas letter, written amid the splendour of the Winter Palace, Alix referred to Victoria's 'little garden' at Number 5 Piazza Regina, in Malta: 'I wish I could slip over and peer into your rooms and little garden – how glad I am that I know the dear place, so can picture you to myself . . . Are there still so many snails on the bushes which you used to have to pick off with the little gardener boy?'

Alix entrusted her interior decoration to Ella, who clearly saw herself on a sort of rescue mission. 'I am busily arranging plans for [Nicky and Alicky's] rooms which would have been vile from all the designs sent,' Ella informed Ernie. 'I draw coloured sketches & then an architect will copy them correctly . . . All will be bought and ordered in Russia except the chintz. You can get everything here only there is such a want of taste so that I must draw every detail myself. All I want to be pretty, even the door handles.'

The Tsarevich's diary confirmed Ella's dedication. On November 21st he wrote: 'At 3pm went with Alix to the Winter Palace where Ella was waiting for us. We went around together and discussed everything pertaining to the construction of our rooms.' Eight days later, he added: 'I went off with Alix to Uncle Sergei's where Ella showed us the construction plans for our apartments at the Winter Palace.'

Alix had mentioned the 'difficulties' of her new life in Russia to Victoria; but she was all positivity in her communications with the Queen. She concluded one of her letters to her with an artfully constructed paean to both husband and grandmama: 'He is so awfully good and dear to me & my great love for him increases daily . . . Having him all to myself is such utter happiness. I never can thank God enough for giving me such a husband & his love for you touches me also so deeply, for have you not been as a Mother to me, since beloved Mama died . . .'

How much comfort the Queen derived from Alix's words is open to question. She was horribly aware that the death of Tsar Alexander had spelt yet more danger for 'Alicky' as she would soon be crowned Tsarina. It was barely 13 years since the Tsarevich's grandfather, Alexander II, had been blown up by terrorists. His father, the bombastic Alexander III, had adopted ever more repressive measures as plots gathered against him.

5

'Orchie watches me the whole time in a
tiresome way.'
Alix

By the time of Alix's wedding in 1894, Victoria had three children: Alice, then aged nine, Louise, five, and two-year-old George. As the first Hesse great-grandchild, Alice had been a source of particular interest to the Queen. At the time of Alice's birth, she was still recovering from her bruising over Ella's marriage; she had been more than ready to take charge of the pregnant Victoria, issuing instructions to Sennicotts: 'I hope you walk regularly every day? It is the one thing to be attended to.'

Baby Alice was born at Windsor, in the same bed in which Princess Alice had given birth to Victoria, 22 years previously. The Queen was present throughout the birth, holding Victoria's hand, as she had held Alice's. 'The relief was great, for poor Victoria had had such a long hard time which always makes one anxious,' she wrote in her diary. 'How strange and indeed affecting it was, to see her lying in the same room & in the same bed, in which she herself was born.' The little girl was named after the Queen: Victoria Alice Elizabeth, though she was always known as Alice.

Irène congratulated the Queen: 'Your first great grandchild born in England.' Ella, who was made godmother to the baby, enthused from Russia: 'You can imagine how happy I am to be an aunt & long for the moment when I can see the dear Baby.'

The Queen, Ella and Grand Duke Serge attended Alice's christening in Darmstadt. Long reconciled to the Grand Duke, the Queen seemed satisfied with her placement: 'I sat between Ernie and Serge.'

Young Alice would make frequent visits to Germany, staying with her Aunt Irène in Kiel and Aunt Alix, then still in Darmstadt. Baroness Buxhoeveden recalled that Alix, aged just 13 when her niece was born, had thought of baby Alice as 'a delightful toy'. As a toddler, Alice developed some less delightful tropes. In the spirit of her aunt Ella's childhood suspicion of old ladies, Alice flatly refused to kiss her elderly great-grandmother. When the Queen reprimanded her with a 'naughty child', she snapped back, 'naughty Grandmama.'

Four years after Alice's birth, the Queen provided a trusty midwife for Irène as she gave birth, in Germany, to her son, Waldemar, who would be known as Toddy. The Queen had mistrusted German midwives ever since her daughter Vicky's son, Willie, the future Kaiser, had been born with a twisted left arm.

Shortly before going into labour, Irène thanked the Queen for sending various gifts, as well as the midwife, Mrs Paterson, writing that she was: 'so deeply touched and cannot find words enough to thank you . . . It is too dear & kind of you darling Grandmama also the delightfully pretty bassinet, basket – charming gowns and things belonging to it. The little cap & cloak are my delight too . . . Mrs Paterson I find such a nice person, one in whom one had confidence directly – she has seen the Doctor & they seem to understand each other very well and agree in everything which is a great comfort.'

Waldemar was two years old when Irène made the shocking discovery that he was a haemophiliac. The Queen registered the boy's illness. It was at around the same time that she warned Ernie against a marriage with Princess Maud of Wales because 'of the symptoms in dear Irène's beautiful boy'. This was probably the first time the Queen alluded to the illness's devastating effect on her relations. The Hesse Princesses had not forgotten their unfortunate little brother Frittie.

During Waldemar's early years, however, Irène was not inclined to dwell on his disability. Towards the end of 1891, her letters to the Queen were full of light-hearted chat. The Queen had given Waldemar a pony to match the Hesse Princesses' 'Ironsides': 'Baby has rather a cold today but otherwise he is well and merry . . . the little pony you kindly gave Baby is a great pet in the stables and beautifully taken care of . . . We have on the whole nice weather.'

The Queen was disappointed not to have Victoria at Windsor for the birth of her second daughter, Louise. Perhaps Victoria had found Alice's birth too much, with its intense focus on Grandmama. For whatever reason, Louise was born in Germany. The Queen made special arrangements for Mrs Paterson to travel to Heiligenberg for the birth. Victoria was as impressed as Irène had been, proclaiming the stout nurse 'a trained midwife and a delightful character'. Irène was appointed godmother.

While her two sisters became mothers, Ella remained childless. One of Ella's god-daughters took a buoyant view: 'She loved children . . . I think she might have been happier if she had had children, but then she would have been more materially inclined. Her childlessness helped her to develop spiritually.' But Grand Duke Serge lamented to his brother and confidant Pavel: 'If only I could have children, I think my life would have been heaven on earth, but it's exactly what the Lord denies me. His are mysterious ways.'

Was that really the root of the Grand Duke's problems? Ella kept an anxious note of her husband's maladies: 'Serge is in pain. He's unwell again. We're desperate for some salts and hot baths.' He was diagnosed with osteoarticular TB and suffered pains in his joints as well as regular toothache. In a development perhaps more harrowing for Ella, he refused to stay in bed, preferring to mooch downstairs: 'He feels more miserable then [when in bed] but he looks very wretched, poor dear,' she wrote.

The couple were increasingly keen to present a happy front. Evening games at Illinskoye included patience cards denoting Seven Reasons for Marriage: Money, Character, Boredom at Home, Beauty, Position, Parents' Persuasion and Love. They were proud to report that, twice in one evening, Ella's card had indicated *'aus grosser Liebe'* (out of great love). Ella enthused to her cousin Georgie's wife, May: 'I do so hope we shall meet soon especially as I would like all my dear relations to know my husband with whom I am so intensely happy.'

The Queen was not convinced by Ella's proclamations, even less so when she heard from Vicky that rumours were circulating, in Berlin, that Ella and Grand Duke Serge were actually on the verge of divorce. 'Ella's constant speaking of happiness I don't quite like. When people are very happy they don't require to TELL others of it,' she fretted to Victoria.

After her visit to England for the Queen's Golden Jubilee in 1887, Ella had tried to put her grandmother's mind at ease: 'All I can repeat is that I am perfectly happy and yet in my new house and life will never forget my old home and those which are all so dear to me.'

Victoria was inclined to believe Ella, though she worried about the couple's childlessness, writing: 'It is pleasant to see what a happy couple Ella & Serge are & I am only sorry they have no children.'

It seemed it was the spiritual dimension of marriage that sustained Ella, and her thoughts on marriage would become ever more severe. Years later, in November 1904, she wrote an earnest letter to Ernie's second wife. 'I think marriage is the most serious and holy act in our earthly lives . . . I need not tell you what a pure, good, honest man he [Ernie] is as I am sure it is just these qualities which draw one towards our husband.'

Had she found the Grand Duke pure, good and honest? Ella was reluctant to confide in her sisters, choosing, instead, to express her marital worries to Ernie. She may have found him more discreet, or perhaps she felt he was more understanding of Grand Duke Serge. 'I am quite alone,' she wrote starkly, during one of her husband's spells away. 'He is more occupied than usual & often has other occupations in the evening with officers and soldiers.'

Ella began diverting herself with amateur theatricals. In 1889, the same year that Victoria's Louise and Irène's Waldemar were born, she performed several plays with 17-year-old Prince Nicholas of Greece. At the wedding of one of Ella's brothers-in-law, the pair performed a Shakespearean tableau vivant. Prince Nicholas, though seven years younger, played King Lear to Ella's Cordelia.

The following year, 1890, Ella and the Tsarevich secretly prepared an extract from *Eugene Onegin*, the play he had enjoyed with Alix during her six-week visit to St Petersburg the previous year. According to another of the Grand Dukes, Konstantin Konstantinovich, the project was kept secret even from Grand Duke Serge. Ella may have wanted to surprise her husband; she may also have feared his disapproval. Grand Duke Konstantin wrote in his diary: 'I already knew before about Ella that she quietly, away from her husband, was studying Tatiana's concluding monologue, and that the Tsarevich was taking the role of Onegin . . .

'Both were in costumes of the beginning of the nineteenth century and very well outfitted . . . Ella spoke her monologue with great feeling . . . it was not yet six years that she had been in Russia and already she was appearing on stage . . . Of course her pronunciation gave her away, but she was totally immersed in the play with a depth of feeling.'

The Tsarevich modestly wrote that 'Aunt Ella's little show . . . went off successfully', but whether Grand Duke Serge appreciated the performances is unclear. However, from then on Ella's theatrical ventures seem to have petered out.

Shortly afterwards, Ella made the decision to convert to Orthodoxy.

The news was important enough to merit a mention in *The Times*. On March 21ˢᵗ, 1891, a correspondent claimed that she had been forced into the decision by her husband: 'I repeat most positively my assertion that Princess Elizabeth of Hesse is not changing her religion willingly, but is only yielding to moral coercion of a very brutal kind.'

Ella appealed again to Ernie: 'Never did he [Serge] complain and only now [do] I know that there were moments he was in despair . . . Let the people scream about me – but only never may a word be spoken against my Serge, take his part above all – tell them that I adore him also my new country and so have learnt to love their religion.'

Irène, upset by the conversion, feared that Ella had been attracted to the Orthodox Church by its trappings. But Ella parried this attack as forcefully: 'Nothing in the outer signs attracted me, no, the service, the foundation of the belief, the outer signs are only to remind us of the inner things.'

Ella had been deeply moved by a trip she and Serge had made to the Holy Land, in the autumn of 1888, writing at the time: 'How I should like to be buried here.' This wish would, years later, be fulfilled by Victoria.

She had described her awe to the Queen: 'Very dear Grandmama . . . the country is not really beautiful – all grey rocks and houses the same colour – & yet as one gets into it, one is struck by the splendour . . . I fear my letter is most feebly written – but my brains get into such a muddle if one passes by so many new impressions.'

The Queen was unexpectedly supportive of her granddaughter's decision. Ella expressed her gratitude: 'You cannot think how intensely and deeply touched I was by all you say . . . I have told now all relations here so that there is no more necessity keeping it a secret . . . The Greek church reminds me so of the English church & that is why I understand it differently to those who have been brought up in the German protestant church . . . then also to have the same religion as one's husband is such a happiness – the only thing which made me wait so long was that I knew so many would be pained & not understand me, but God gave me courage.'

Victoria, who had none of Irène's misgivings, also thanked the Queen for her support: 'Ella wrote to me that you had sent her such a kind letter on the subject of her going over to the Greek Orthodox church – she was so touched at the way you took it, for of course many people will be less tolerant & just & she dreaded lest you might be displeased with her too. I think she does it from sincere motives & hope it will make her happy.'

Ella became vegetarian, boiled onions becoming an unlikely favourite dish. One of her god-daughters later recalled her air of saintliness: 'I became ill with measles and waking up in my little child's cot I saw an angelic face bent over me and decided that this was an angel. In the morning I told my nanny about seeing this angel – only without wings. She was so beautiful and I can remember even now that she was in a light lilac dress. I never noticed any sign of décolleté.'

The young Felix Yusupov may have disapproved of Ella's English decor, but he never forgot his childhood worship of her: 'Nothing would have induced me to close my eyes until the Grand Duchess had come to say goodnight to me. She blessed me and kissed me and I was filled with a wonderful peace and went quietly to sleep.'

In 1891, Grand Duke Serge was appointed Governor General of Moscow. Ella wrote to the Queen with the news, trumpeting, yet again, her domestic bliss: 'May God bless our stay in Moscow, as He did the seven years of perfect happiness we spent here together [in St Petersburg] . . . if we had wings we would have wished to fly over to see you; it looks so ungrateful that we have not been for such a long time in dear England but I cannot leave my darling Serge.'

The new appointment meant the Grand Duke would be parted from his precious Preobrazhensky guards. Ella registered the men's upset without appearing to attach any particular importance to it. She wrote to the Tsarevich: 'It is really touching to see how all the officers love Serge and in what despair they are that he is leaving them.'

Over the ensuing years, under the Grand Duke's control, Moscow would be described as a showcase of law and order. The cobblestone pavements were clean, policemen were posted within sight of each other and the utilities worked like clockwork. Ella would presumably have had no issue with such efficiency drives, but she was mortified by her husband's expulsion of 20,000 Jews. The expulsion resulted, not least, in 25,000 Russians, employed by Jewish firms, losing their jobs. Ella lamented: 'I cannot believe that we will not be judged in some way for this in the future. He [Serge] believes it is for our security. I see nothing in it but shame.'

Needless to say, she kept her misgivings from the Queen, writing equably: 'Serge . . . on the whole in good spirits although he has many worries poor boy.'

It wasn't only Serge who was inviting criticism; Grand Duchess Ella had begun to acquire detractors of her own. By 1891, a particularly damaging story was circulating that she had been having an affair with Grand Duke Serge's brother Pavel. Since her arrival in Russia, Ella had frequently spent time with the two brothers. When Pavel's wife died in childbirth, it was rumoured to be suicide.

Such stories would have been fuelled by ongoing questions regarding Ella's marriage. She and Grand Duke Serge might keep turning up the 'aus grosser Liebe' card, but they often failed to create a good impression. Pavel's daughter, Maria Pavlovna, who was later adopted by the couple, wrote: 'She and my uncle seemed never very intimate. They met for the most part at meals and by day avoided being alone together.'

Maria also noted that, while Grand Duke Serge might initially have approved of Ella's conversion, he soon started worrying about her excessive religiosity: 'Uncle Serge regarded with anxiety his wife's increasing absorption in things spiritual and ended by regarding it as immoderate.'

She remembered the Grand Duke treating Ella bossily: 'Uncle was often curt with her, just like he was with everybody else . . . He often treated her like a school teacher. I saw the most amazing colour flushing her face whenever he took her to task . . . The expression on her face reminded me of a schoolgirl caught out making a mistake.'

The French Ambassador, Maurice Paléologue, who had once linked Ella with profane passions, recalled her reaction to one of her husband's eruptions: 'After a violent outburst on the part of the Grand Duke, old Prince B . . . offered the young Grand Duchess his sympathy! She seemed surprised and answered in a frank tone: "I'm not to be pitied . . . People may say what they like, but I'm happy because I'm dearly loved".'

Several of their acquaintances noted Grand Duke Serge's harsh manner. The Duchess of Marlborough commented that Serge had 'a cruel and elegant air . . . I thought what a magnificent Mephistopheles he would make and the self-satisfied gleam in his eye made me realise that he sensed my thought'.

Serge's niece, Marie of Romania, wrote that 'his lips were thin and closed in a firm line that was almost cruel . . . There was a tyrant within him ready at any moment to burst forth . . .' She recalled a disconcerting nervous tic: 'As abrupt of movement as he was short of speech, he had a particular way of clasping his hands in front of him, the fingers of one hand clasping the wrist of the other, making a chain bracelet that he wore continually jingle against his cuff . . .'

But when the couple eventually returned to England in November 1892, they managed to convince the Queen that all was well. Their stay was such a success that Grand Duke Serge told the Queen he hoped to return the following year. She was utterly won round: 'It is a pleasure to see how he loves dear Ella and how happy they are together.'

At around the same time, in November 1892, Victoria gave birth to her first son, George. Born in Darmstadt, the new baby was also named Victor, after his great aunt, Vicky, and Serge, after his uncle.

The presence of the trusty Mrs Paterson may have gone some way to appeasing Grandmama during this, Victoria's second German confinement. By the following year, however, Mrs Paterson had taken to the bottle. The problem emerged while she was working for the Kaiser. His mother, Vicky, felt compelled to issue a stark warning. 'Henry and Irène swear by her, so does Victoria Battenberg, but Dona [the Kaiser's wife] says she drinks and I'm not able to discover whether it is true or not,' she wrote to one of her daughters. 'She was over worked at the Schloss and kept in such terribly small rooms . . . she may have taken more than was good for her.'

If servants at the exacting Prussian Court were inclined to buckle, those at the less challenging Hesse Court thrived, not least the irrepressible Orchie, who travelled to Kiel to help her 'delicate' Irène.

No sooner had Orchie finished tending Irène's children than she was hurrying to Russia to help her youngest Hesse charge, Alix. The young bride was doubtless delighted by her old nanny's efforts with wedding dresses and interior decor. She was less delighted by Orchie's preoccupation with her pregnancy.

From the moment she was married, Alix was sorely aware of the general interest in whether or not she was pregnant. She was infuriated by what she saw as an invasion of her privacy. In common with her sisters, she saved some of her most aggravating worries for Ernie. 'Orchie watches me the whole time in a tiresome way,' she grumbled, adding that Irène was making inquiries and Ella 'fidgeted in December about it'. Having orchestrated the wedding, Ella understood all too well that Alix must now produce an heir.

Everybody would have breathed a sigh of relief when, just two months after her marriage, Alix was, indeed, pregnant. But she was predictably coy, even to Irène and Ella. Though she confessed to Victoria that she was expecting a baby in autumn, she hesitated to tell her other two sisters. Ernie was under strict instructions not to tell anyone about the severity of her morning sickness.

Still, nothing kept Alix from her duties. 'Yesterday was a baise-main for all the ladies; it was rather amusing, especially seeing those I knew in 1889 . . .' she reported to Victoria.

'Schneiderlein [Ella and Alix's Russian teacher] . . . was 38 or 39 the other day. She comes every morning for a good [Russian] lesson and reads to me an hour before supper, whilst Nicky is occupied with papers . . . we are scarcely ever to ourselves . . . Do let me hear from you soon again, dear, as your dear letters are a great joy to me. I am sure fat little George must be a great joy to you and now that he can walk more . . . No more today, else I shall bore you with this long rigmarole.'

Did Alix miss being part of her three sisters' ongoing get-togethers? That year Victoria's younger daughter, Louise, accompanied Irène and her cousin Waldemar, also aged six, to the German island of Amrum for bathing. The party then travelled to Wolfsgarten, where they met Ella, who had taken a cure in the town.

Victoria worried, at this point that Ella was under the weather. 'She may not ride & has to keep very quiet, she can't go to the manoeuvres but wants to come here [Heiligenberg] instead. Of course I shall be very happy to have her – as we do not meet so frequently but naturally I am a little disappointed not to be able to go with you too . . . [but] what can't be cured must be endured,' she wrote to Ernie.

Ella's cure seems to have worked. Her 'fidgeting' about Alix's pregnancy had been rewarded and she was now ready to keep a close eye on her sister. The Queen was, of course, kept abreast as Ella painted a happy portrait of the pregnant Alix: 'Alice [sic] looking remarkably well, thank God, so much plumper in the face, such a healthy complexion, better than I had seen [her] for years . . . full of fun quite like as a child & that dreadful sad look which Papa's death had printed on her disappears in her constant smiles.'

Alix's first daughter, Olga, was born in November 1895. Ella was present for the birth, she and Grand Duke Serge stationing themselves at the nearby Catherine Palace. As the Tsarevich wrote in his diary: 'About 2pm Mama came from Gatchine and the three of us – Ella and I – were continually at her side. At exactly 9pm we heard a baby's cry and all took a deep breath.' Ella and the Dowager spent much of the confinement on their knees in prayer.

There was some concern, inevitably, regarding the new baby's sex, but Ella hastened to put the Queen's mind at rest: 'The joy of having their baby has never one moment let them regret little Olga being a girl.'

Alix was ecstatic. 'It is a radiantly happy mother who is writing to you. You can imagine our intense happiness now that we have such a precious little being of our own to look after,' she wrote to Victoria. She breastfed the baby: her mother would have approved; Grandmama would not. Nicky was enjoying it all, as he chuckled in his diary: 'Alix beginning to feed the wet nurse's son and the wet nurse giving milk to Olga – too funny!'

*

The coronation of the new Tsar and Tsarina took place in Moscow in May 1896. The splendid ceremony seemed to mark an ominous change in the dynamic between the two Hesse sisters in Russia.

Victoria travelled to Moscow for the ceremony. She noticed a visible alteration in Alix. 'Quite a different person & has developed into a big handsome woman, rosy-cheeked & broad-shouldered making Ella look small near her,' she wrote to the Queen.

Rumours abounded that there was some rivalry between the sisters. Resplendent in a dress of cream velvet embroidered with gold fuschias,

Ella was having none of it. Her first priority was to reassure Grandmama: 'The abominable lies told about us [Ella and Grand Duke Serge] to them [Alix and the Tsarevich] are not eddifying [sic] the intrigues were simply disgusting . . . What I cannot understand is jealousy between sisters or not liking the younger ones to be of higher rank . . . May God grant we husbands and wives may always love each other as we do . . . I know people watched at the coronation to see would I kiss her hand . . . Why it was a joy.'

Ella had been instrumental in her youngest sister's marriage; she had been involved in the decoration of Alix's rooms in St Petersburg, quibbling over doorhandles; she had prayed at the bedside during Alix's hours of labour. At the coronation, she was again at her sister's side as Alix turned on the electric illuminations, creating what one Romanov described as 'a sea of fire'. She was nervous, however, about being seen as the power behind the throne: 'I find it lucky we live in another town. It makes [Alix] quite independent . . . nobody can say whatever she does I have counselled.'

Ella acknowledged her younger sister's newly formidable presence – and was aware of its damaging effect. The general consensus, among the Russians, was that their new Tsarina was haughty and standoffish. She had frequently voiced her disapproval of the Romanovs' divorces and morganatic marriages. She was prim, insisting that toilets be covered with cloths during the day; no one must see her in the bath.

On one occasion, she sent her lady-in-waiting to reprimand a racy Russian aristocratic for her low décolletage. The lady-in-waiting's tone had been condescending: 'Madame, Her Majesty wants me to tell you that in Hesse-Darmstadt we don't wear our dresses that way.' The brazen woman was unfazed, pulling her front down lower, before responding crisply: 'Pray tell Her Majesty that in Russia we DO wear our dresses that way'.

Meriel Buchnanan, who had known her in Darmstadt, was struck by her hauteur: 'I wondered what had brought the look of cold aloofness into the face of the woman I had known as Princess Alix of Hesse.' And she had little conversation. One of Serge's brothers, Grand Duke Vladimir, claimed that the only way to persuade her to talk was to misquote the Almanach de Gotha. According to the historian Robert K Massie, Alix had an atrocious French accent and was badly dressed, clumsy and a poor dancer.

During the coronation, Grand Duke Serge's niece, Marie of Romania, watched with misgivings as Alix peered solemnly at the crowds from a coach. She 'does not smile and her expression is one of almost painful earnestness . . . There is no happiness in those large, steady eyes . . . all dignity but . . . no warmth'. Later, Marie would give a graphic description of Alix's forlorn attempts at friendliness: 'No fiery sword at the gates of the garden of Eden could have been more forbidding than her tight-lipped smile.'

Victoria had not wholly enjoyed Ella's wedding, smarting at the demeaning table placement allocated to her husband. She had been in Malta at the time of Alix's wedding. Her determination to attend the coronation was matched by a desire to enjoy it. Though she had commented on her sisters' changes in appearance, she made no mention of rivalry. Ella, she wrote, was 'overwhelmed with social duties, having to receive and entertain & as the Governor General's wife to receive in audience the hundreds of ladies come to Moscow from every part of Russia and Europe'.

She saw no sign of Alix's off-putting manner, describing her as 'blooming and radiant'. Indeed, so many ladies kissed the new Tsarina's hand, she enthused, that it became swollen and looked as red as if she had been stung by a wasp.

It was Irène, pregnant with her second son, Sigismund, who missed out this time. Not that this put off her husband Prince Henry, who arrived with what the Tsarevich referred to, disparagingly, as 'an enormous suite'. The Tsarevich recorded a large lunch on May 12th with 'Uncle Serge, Ella, Henry, Ernie, Ducky [Ernie's wife], Victoria and Ludwig [Louis]'. Victoria was billetted with Ella, ever grateful to Serge for rushing to rescue her dresses, when a fire broke out in his chapel.

No amount of sisterly jostlings could diminish the splendour of Nicholas II's coronation; but unfortunately the ceremony would be overshadowed by disastrous events just four days later.

A crowd of 500,000 had gathered at the Khodinka Field at dawn, to down hundreds of barrels of free beer and collect free commemorative enamelled cups. Rumours spread that the gifts were running out and, in the ensuing stampede, 1,389 people were crushed to death.

As Governor of Moscow, Grand Duke Serge was implicated in the fiasco, accused by his own brothers of mishandling the arrangements. From the windows of Ella's house, Victoria watched in horror as hundreds of bodies were transported from the site: 'All that morning we saw the dead and wounded carted past the Governor General's house . . . I think he [the Tsar] and everybody who accompanied him could not shake off a feeling of profound depression.' At a state luncheon afterwards, Alix was seen surreptitiously wiping her eye with a napkin.

The situation was made worse by Serge's unwise insistence that the young Tsar and Tsarina attend a ball that night at the French Embassy. The Grand Duke's niece, Marie of Romania, sensed that Ella disapproved of her husband's stance, writing: 'Beautiful Aunt Ella's despair [at Alix being forced to attend] was pitiful to see.'

At Balmoral, the Queen monitored the events with alarm. She doubtless viewed the hysteria and mismanagement as all too Russian, and immediately recognised her grandson-in-law's folly: 'Would it not have been better to stop the balls etc for it looks so unfeeling to go on just the same.' A few days later, she added: 'Alas I fear poor Serge, as Governor of Moscow, may be blamed.'

In fact, Grand Duke Serge blocked any inquiry into the tragedy. But Ella was swift to reassure the Queen that she and the Grand Duke had forfeited none of their popularity: 'We try to do our duty and I must say [though] it sounds vain – people here like us . . . some people will intrigue and lie as long as the world exists – and we are not the first who have been calumniated.'

For all Victoria's talk of profound depression, the Romanov party seem to have recovered themselves with remarkable speed. Within a couple of weeks, they had all transferred to Ella's country estate, Illinskoye, where they gaily threw themselves into nightly romps. The new Tsar's diary brimmed with 'yelling and running around games . . . accompanied, according to the rules, by screams and cries from the ladies'. There was further fun with mimes, ombres chinoises and tableaux vivants. One jape involved upsetting the timorous peasants – 'frightening the local simple folk with a fat round effigy of the devil'.

Victoria's account was more sedate but no less bullish: 'It was lovely being in the country after the strenuous days we had just gone through.'

While Victoria, a young 33, always retained a tomboyish streak, it is hard to imagine the haughty Alix or elegant Ella joining in the screams and romps. But, as hostess, Ella must have approved and the Tsar's diary gives every indication that his wife was enjoying herself. He alluded exuberantly to the idyll he and Alix had once shared with Victoria and Louis at Elm Grove. Within a fortnight, he had entirely forgotten about the travails of the coronation: 'It is exactly two years from that happy day when we met in England at Walton! What a carefree life it has been since then.'

Two of the brothers-in-law, Prince Louis and Tsar Nicholas, even managed an agreeable conversation concerning the actually rather prickly relations between their respective countries. As the Tsar wrote optimistically: 'We are best of friends with England and he [Prince Louis] saw the outlook in Europe as generally hopeful.'

After their spell at Illinskoye, Victoria and Louis travelled with Ella and Serge to Venice, where both couples invested in paintings. The two sisters may have been enjoying fond memories of their Venetian break with Colonel de Herff and Miss Jackson, but their trip was dominated by their large companion, Masha Wassiltchikov. 'Her immense size always attracted much notice. She had, besides, a loud voice . . . Ella used sometimes to go in the morning to sketch inside St Marks, accompanied by Masha,' wrote Victoria. 'When begged by Ella not to make loud remarks which might disturb the worshippers, her attempts at whispering echoed round the church.'

But Venice retained its glow. Later that year, during a visit to Darmstadt, the Tsar recorded an outlandish proposal: 'We [the Tsar, Tsarina, Grand Duke Serge and Ella] had lunch at Victoria's in the Alte Palais . . . we were beginning to conceive the strange idea of buying a ready built house in Venice!'

Ella and Alix's ready-built house in Venice came to nothing. But, by 1896, following several years based at the castle in Kiel, Irène and Henry were building a property outside the town. From now on, the family would divide their time between the Schloss in Kiel and their new estate, Hemmelmark, near Eckernförde. Among Irène's first priorities was the creation of a bedroom for her younger sister. Though she never stayed overnight, Alix insisted on a place to rest after meals. Just as Ella had installed English chintzes at Illinskoye and at Alix's Alexander Palace, Irène now began creating her own English-style country house at Hemmelmark. There followed years of intermittent correspondence with Coles wallpaper company, in north London. The doors, painstakingly ordered from England, retained their instructions: 'push' and 'pull'.

Irène's mother-in-law, Vicky, disliked Kiel, describing it as 'more dismal and melancholy than I can say . . .' But she thoroughly approved of the new house: 'Henry and Irène were so nice and the Schloss looks so clean and well-kept and comfortable . . . Henry and Irène are quite devoted to the place, and the thought of it being their own makes them love it, they enjoy perfect liberty there, and live à la Robinson Crusoe.'

What Vicky meant by 'à la Robinson Crusoe' is hard to say. Relieved to be liberated from the more exacting goings-on at the lofty Prussian Court, the couple certainly cut down on formalities, with Irène holding 'hen parties' to match Prince Henry's 'beer evenings'. While her three sisters romped at Illinskoye, following the coronation, the pregnant Irène would more likely have been enjoying a round of 'Up Jenkins'.

During their days in Berlin, Prince Henry had been dismissed as lightweight and careless, while Irène had been criticised for her lack of '*esprit*'. And, though Vicky approved of the couple's move, she seemed inclined to agree, professing herself disappointed with their conversation: 'I am so unaccustomed to think and talk only of the little trifling occurrences of everyday life that I feel it very suffocating.' She noted that neither of them ever read a newspaper.

Another bone of contention was Irène's relaxed attitude to pregnancy: 'It is to me utterly incomprehensible why & how the ladies of the present days like to go about . . . I think it quite embarrassing & would never have dreamt of doing so, especially before gentlemen & children & strangers.'

For all the games and light conversation, Irène faced significant domestic challenges, not least her husband's erratic moods. But the genial Ernie readily defended Prince Henry: 'Her married life was happy but often difficult, especially in the early days, because my brother-in-law Heinrich was unpredictable, this led to arguments which she had to settle. But things always turned out well, because his gentlemanly feelings and good heart would finally help him to see reason.'

Perhaps it was as well that Prince Henry was frequently away with the

Imperial German Navy. The Queen was unsettled by Henry's absences, suspecting that the ill-natured Kaiser sent his brother away simply to part him from his wife.

Queen Victoria and her grandson, the Kaiser, continued to come to blows over the years. She was furious with him for preventing Henry from attending the funeral of Alix's former suitor, Prince Albert, or Eddie. When Eddie's brother, the future George V, got married, in 1893, the Queen refused to invite the Kaiser. In his turn, the Kaiser tried to prevent Irène and Prince Henry from going to London.

In the autumn of 1896, Alix and Nicky embarked on a European tour, or as the Tsar put it to his brother George, 'a series of intolerable foreign visits'.

Alix would find the European visits, with baby Olga, as intolerable as her husband did. She had not seen Queen Victoria for two and a half years. Nonetheless, her summing up of a ten-day sojourn at Balmoral in a letter to Miss Jackson was as dour as the governess could have wished: 'Dearest Madgie . . . Here we have not had the finest weather. My husband has not shot one stag, only a brace of grouse.

'It has been such a very short stay and I leave dear kind Grandmama with a heavy heart. Who knows when we may meet again and where? . . . Next Saturday morning, God Grant, we shall be at dear Darmstadt.'

At Balmoral, the Queen initially judged Alix unspoilt, writing to Irène: 'Darling Alicky's & dear Nicky's visit was a very great pleasure – but too short – just as you say in your . . . letter of the 10 Sept. Darling Alicky is quite unchanged.'

But this did not prevent her issuing weighty instructions to her granddaughter. She was rightly worried about Alix's decreasing popularity with the Russians. Alix never lost her social awkwardness, and her excessive sensitivity had not endeared her to her new subjects. Meriel Buchanan reported that when Alix was obliged, for some reason, to leave the Maryinsyky Theatre in the middle of a production, a 'wave of resentment' rippled through the auditorium. On another occasion, the French Ambassador, Maurice Paléologue, remembered having to hastily hush a ship's band: 'The poor lady seemed worn out. Suddenly she put her hands to her ears. I signalled sharply to the conductor.'

The Queen urged Alix to make more effort: 'It is your duty to win their love and respect.' Alix's riposte was as terse as it was misguided: 'You are mistaken my dear grandmama . . . Here we do not need to earn the love of the people. The Russian people revere their Tsars as divine beings . . . the opinions of those who make up this society and their mocking have no significance whatsoever.'

The Tsar and Tsarina's visit to the 'dear old home' marked Alix's first return to Darmstadt since her harrowing departure for the Crimea two years before. They would be joined there by Ella and Victoria. The only fly in the ointment, as so often, was the overbearing Kaiser. 'Wilhelm is unbearable – he does not give us any peace here and wanted desperately to invite us for lunch in Wiesbaden next week,' complained the Tsar.

Upon her return to St Petersburg, Alix wrote ecstatically to Ernie: 'Those happy weeks at Darmstadt with you darlings seem like a dream to me, so long ago it all seems . . . What a joy it was being again in my old home, after two long years, which I had left so suddenly & with such sad and unsure feelings . . . It touched me deeper than I can say that the people had not forgotten their Aaaahhlix.'

But by December it was business as usual, with Ella and Alix both taking to their beds. 'Ella . . . has influenza,' reported the Tsar, 'Alix and Ella lay down in opposite sides of the house.'

That year, Victoria returned to Nice, lodging with her daughter, Alice, at a villa near Grandmama's Hotel Cimiez. One of Victoria's more random bugbears, at this point, was the nuisance of motor cars, covering pedestrians with dust as they sped along rough tracks. Later she complained of children refusing to get out of the way and trying to hang on at the back.

It was during visits to Nice, in 1896 and 1897, that Victoria and the Queen met the two Princesses of Montenegro. The Black Princesses, as they became known, were later to introduce the Tsar and Tsarina to Rasputin.

6

'Don't believe all the horrors the foreign
papers say.'
Alix

Irène's second son, Sigismund, was born in November 1896. His elder brother, Waldemar, was by then aged seven. It is not known why there were such long gaps between Irène's births; she either had trouble conceiving or maintaining pregnancies. Or perhaps Prince Henry was away at sea too frequently.

At Christmas 1896, Irène's mother-in-law, Vicky, visited the new mother at Kiel. 'I found Henry looking very well also dearest Irène. The baby is a fine child . . . They give him the pet name of Budge but he will be christened Sigismund,' she wrote to her daughter. In fact, Sigismund would usually be known as Bobby, and the comment most often made about him, initially, was that he was 'cross'.

Months after the birth of Sigismund, Irène was off again to see Alix, who was herself pregnant for the second time. During this trip, Alix attempted to teach Irène some Russian. In her diary, Irène paid sheepish homage to her sister's patience.

Irène may have struggled with the Russian lessons, but she was unfailing in her sisterly duties. She wrote frequently to the appreciative Alix and made 13 trips to Russia between 1886 and 1913. There's no reason to doubt that Alix looked forward to the visits. But a Count Bernstorff remembered spending a curiously enervating hour with the Tsarina, awaiting Irène's arrival. The pair were seated in the little station waiting room at Tsarskoe Selo, mostly in deadening silence: 'I cannot remember ever having had such trouble over a conversation in my life. Every subject and every language was tried without much success, until the arrival of the Princess at last brought us deliverance.'

Alix's second daughter, Grand Duchess Tatiana, was born in June 1897, seven months after Irène's Sigismund. Victoria, already blessed with her own son, George, was appointed Tatiana's godmother. The Queen chimed in, instructing Alix not to breastfeed: advice Alix again ignored.

Over the next few years, Alix seems to have enjoyed joining the Tsar in several surprisingly robust pursuits. She gave Victoria hearty descriptions of visits to Polish shooting lodges: 'Generally out for ten hours – bisons, roebucks, stags, elks, wild bear, capercaillies.' The shooting trips in Poland were followed by less challenging trips to Darmstadt. In 1897, according to George Buchanan, the Imperial couple stayed at Wolfsgarten, attending the Darmstadt Tennis Club, 'where the Emperor sometimes played while the Empress sat and looked on'.

Victoria's highlights of 1897 included lunch with Captain Scott of the Antarctic on the ship *Majestic*. But more important would have been her appointment of a new lady's maid, recommended by Miss Jackson. Over the years, Nona Kerr would become one of Victoria's closest confidantes.

The Queen's worries about Ella and Serge's marriage seem to have been put aside as she welcomed the couple back to Britain for her Diamond Jubilee. She wrote: 'They were both so dear and pleasant . . .' And of Ella herself: 'She is so lovely and so good and sensible.' The couple gave the Queen portraits of themselves – which now hang in Windsor Castle's Round Tower. They attended Royal Ascot and a party at Windsor Castle, judged by Ella's implacable sister-in-law, Maria Alexandrovna, as 'a very dull affair indeed'.

Ella in elaborate dress, 1897.

Maria Alexandrovna was equally scathing about Ella and Serge's home life in Illinskoye. 'It is rather depressing and I fear I never quite appreciate Illinskoye,' she wrote in 1898. 'I find it dull. Uncle Serge disappears always for hours, Ella potters about her little drawings and little works and seems quite happy over it, the rest of the company wanders about and it is not the kind of life I like . . .'

She thought that Ella had lost her taste for reading: 'Au fond Ella is never much interested in a book and only reads insipid English novels, would you believe she hardly ever touches a French novel as she is too much afraid of reading anything improper.' Was she bowing to pressure from her husband? Grand Duke Serge forbade Ella from reading *Anna Karenina*, in case it aroused an 'unhealthy curiosity and violent emotions'. And perhaps thoughts of her own Count Vronsky?

Ella may still have fretted about being seen as wielding too much influence on her younger sister Alix, but she was not quite ready to abandon her efforts. During the winter of 1898, she tried to persuade Alix to do more entertaining, feeling strongly that this would increase her popularity. But Alix, already into her third pregnancy, felt unable to oblige, spending seven weeks in bed before succumbing to sciatica and finally being reduced to a wheelchair.

Except for Olga, Alix's children were all born in the spring or summer. This meant she was repeatedly incapacitated during the social winter season, either through pregnancy or nursing. Alix herself had no problem with such limitations, insisting stoutly to Victoria that fetes and amusements meant nothing to her.

That winter, Irène and her two boys came to Britain to visit Victoria; she then travelled to China from Germany with Henry. But after the couple had left, their haemophiliac son Waldemar, then aged nine, became ill. Victoria rushed to Kiel, staying until he had recovered. Her description of Waldemar's operation makes it clear she was aware of the boy's vulnerability: 'An operation, which would have been a simple one for any other children, was a very grave one for him,' she wrote.

Years later, in a letter to Queen Mary, written in 1950, Irène shared an altogether pleasanter memory of that time: 'Fancy one Christmas I spent with Henry in Hong Kong & dear Grandmama managed to send each of us a Christmas card – arriving on the day itself with such kind words. It was 1898 & I treasure it still.'

Alix's daughter, Maria, was born in June 1899. Weeks later, the Queen wrote baldly to Irène: 'I saw disappointingly that Alicky also got a 3rd daughter.' The following year, Irène and Victoria would both give birth to further sons. There was an imbalance all round, as Irène's mother-in-law,

Vicky, wistfully noted: 'I think she and Henry would have preferred a little girl but one or two will I hope follow later to keep their brothers company.'

In fact, Irène's third son, Heinrich, born in January 1900, was to be her last child. Vicky's report was otherwise positive: 'Henry and the children are here all looking very well. Toddy [Waldemar] grown and much stouter; Budgie [Sigismund] not as cross as he used to be and the baby I cannot judge as he screams and shouts every time he sees me.'

In June 1900, Victoria had her second son, Louis. In characteristically robust spirit, Victoria ignored her aunt Vicky's warnings about Mrs Paterson's alcohol issues, welcoming the nurse back to deliver her fourth child.

Louis was the Queen's last great-grandson born in her lifetime, and her last godson. Though officially christened Louis, he was called Nicholas, to differentiate him from his father; his name then evolved from Nicky to Dickie-bird to Dickie. He was christened, in July 1900, at Frogmore, with his father standing in for a further godparent, Tsar Nicholas. The future Louis Mountbatten claimed he began a rich public life by knocking the Queen's spectacles clean off.

That autumn, Alix had recovered sufficiently to travel to Germany to witness the completion of the Russian Orthodox church, the Chapel of St Mary Magdalene, in Darmstadt. But Irène was still anxious about her, fussing to Ernie: 'Please take care of Alix and see that she does not stand or walk much & if one does not remind her she forgets to sit down.'

The to-ing and fro-ing continued. In October 1900, Irène visited the Queen at Balmoral, then moved on to Victoria at Frogmore, both sisters tending newborn sons. Victoria retained vivid memories of Frogmore, not least a menagerie featuring two kangaroos and a couple of large ostriches. One clearly traumatised ostrich beat its flanks violently with its head. 'After it had done so at least 20 times it would get up, a little dazed, but none the worse for the performance.'

Two months after Louis's birth, Victoria wrote her already treasured companion, Nona Kerr, an affectionate letter: 'I have never managed to say to you, though I've wanted to all along, that I thank you much for doing a great deal more than just jobs for me all the time.' She claimed that she suffered, improbably, from the 'incurable complaint of never being able to speak out decently even when I much want to'.

During the last months of 1900, Alix experienced a dramatic domestic upheaval, as she took on the unaccustomed role of carer. The Tsar, Tsarina and their three small daughters were in the Crimea when Nicky succumbed to typhoid. Alix seemed to find her calling, forming a tight team with the stalwart Orchie. 'The shock of his illness and feeling myself necessary gave me new strength, as I had been very wretched before,' she wrote to Victoria. 'I rebelled at a nurse being taken and we managed perfectly ourselves.'

There was a downside: 'Now I suffer from head and heartache, the latter from nerves and many sleepless nights.'

Six years after her arrival, Orchie was very much at home in Russia, maintaining a strict regime in the nursery. She would chastise another English nanny, Margaretta Eager, for allowing the little Grand Duchesses to play noisy games. Eager was finally driven to a sharp retort: 'Old Mrs O, who had brought up the Tsarina, came into the room. She began to rebuke me for letting them romp and declared that their mother had never made a noise in all her life. And I said: "We have all heard so often that the Tsarina was a perfect angel when she was a child, but she has only given me human children to look after".'

Miss Jackson, as devoted as Orchie, now gave English literature lessons to Victoria's 15-year-old daughter Alice in London. In the 1901 census, M H Jackson, 63, is listed as head of the house, and her sister Emily Jackson,

68, as visitor at 8 St Katherine's Precincts. Emily is listed as being born in York, while MHJ still lists her birthplace as Kensington.

*

Queen Victoria died at Osborne House, on January 22nd 1901. The four Hesse sisters were devastated by the loss of their dearest Grandmama.

Notwithstanding the various conflicts they had had with her before their marriages, the sisters appreciated the Queen's love for them. For decades, the letters had flowed between the royal residences of Britain, Germany and Russia. And, though they had occasionally jibbed at her interference, they all four acknowledged that she had, indeed, become their second mother.

Victoria later gave an emotional description of the sisters' relationship with the Queen: 'Grandmama's death was a great personal loss to me. On account of our having lost our mother when we were so young, Grandmama had taken a special interest in her beloved daughter's children . . . She herself, though very gracious to her grandchildren, expected perfect manners and immediate obedience from them and would look and speak severely . . . My mother's death broke through many of these outward barriers and the constant signs of affectionate pity and interest gave to our intercourse a more natural ease.'

Over the years, Victoria had developed a particularly deep bond: 'As the one of us who was most in England I was the one who was in closest touch with her.' In recent years, she had even helped the Queen with her writing: 'I had to put my finger on the last word written before she could continue.'

Irène hadn't seen Grandmama at the New Year because her mother-in-law, Vicky, had been ill: 'How dare one leave her at such a moment?' she wrote. But the Kaiser, also her grandchild, had no such qualms, leaving his mother in order to be with the Queen when she died. Victoria and Prince Louis were sent for, but arrived a quarter of an hour too late.

Ella's acerbic sister-in-law Maria scoffed at the response of the Queen's own daughters: 'Those foolish childish aunts . . . lost their heads and did not know what to do . . . Nobody had even ordered the coffin.'

Of the four grieving sisters, only Victoria and Irène attended the funeral. Victoria's husband Prince Louis was obliged to step in during the ceremony, ordering his sailors to pull the Queen's coffin after the horses got in a tangle. They had bolted after a long wait at Windsor station and broken their traces. Alix, then into her fourth pregnancy, expressed her envy of Victoria, who would 'see Grandmama being laid to rest'.

She and Ella attended a service for the Queen at the English church in St Petersburg. They were both visibly moved. There may have been some sympathy for Ella, but there was a general feeling of disapproval about what was deemed Alix's hypersensitivity. Barely five years after her coronation, the Tsarina could do no right.

The birth of Alix's fourth daughter, Anastasia, in June 1901, was generally viewed as a disaster. The longed-for male heir had failed, yet again, to materialise.

Alix, however, was not about to give up her relish of motherhood, describing her sadness that she would soon have to abandon nursing. 'It is very hard – she will be given over to the nurses, a moment that always makes me melancholy, as now she is always in my room or next door,' she lamented to Victoria. Alix was frequently considered over-protective towards her children, fearful of the interference of outsiders. Her own close attachment to Miss Jackson may, paradoxically, have made her reluctant to procure such a companion for her daughters.

The Imperial Family's domestic life was rigorously maintained. Ella's stepdaughter, Maria Pavlovna, was struck: 'We often went to the Winter Palace to play with the little Grand Duchesses. Then we were happiest, for there we sensed ourselves in a real family atmosphere, tender, simple and calm. The Emperor and his wife held for each other, and for their children, a deep and unswerving devotion, and their conjugal devotion was beautiful to see.'

Weeks after the birth of Anastasia, Victoria visited Russia with 16-year-old Alice and baby Louis, travelling to Moscow to see Ella before journeying on to Illinskoye, where she thoroughly enjoyed herself. But on August 6th the news came through that Irène's mother-in-law, the Queen's daughter Vicky, had died. Irène alluded to her mother-in-law's death in a letter to Infanta Eulalia of Spain: 'Henry's one comfort too was his having been able to say goodbye to her before he left with his vessel – both had the feeling that they would no more meet on this earth.'

The sisters' meetings never flagged. In September 1901, Alix took her four small daughters on a by now rare visit outside Russia, to Kiel, leaving the eldest three with Irène, while she and the Tsar went on a state visit to France. Waldemar would by then have been aged 12, Olga six, Sigismund five, Tatiana, four and Maria two.

That year, Irène attended her neice Alice's confirmation in Heiligenberg. After the confirmation, Victoria returned to Malta, where her quiet life was spiced up by the arrival of a new neighbour: the charismatic Admiral Fisher. Sadly, she took an immediate dislike to him: 'He seemed to glory in his partiality for or against individuals and once said to me: "I love hating".'

There were rumbling difficulties between the Admiral and her husband. Fisher didn't approve of Prince Louis's plans for reforming the Navy. The Prince had risen through the ranks from Commander to Captain to Admiral; he had been appointed Head of Naval Intelligence in June 1899. Fisher was still more worried about the Prince's German forebears, fretting each time Victoria and Louis travelled to Darmstadt for family events.

*Irène's castle in Kiel in 1902. Irène and Prince Henry are pictured in the top
left- and right-hand corners.*

All four sisters, at this point, enjoyed happy marriages. The Tsar was
famously besotted by Alix, while Prince Louis remained 'off his chump' with
Victoria. Grand Duke Serge never lost his entrancement with Ella, even if
he did spend too much time with his fellow officers. Prince Henry, with all
his absences at sea, appeared to be a model of fidelity.

However, during a tour of North America, orchestrated by the
Kaiser, Prince Henry was thought to have been overly captivated by Mrs
Cornelius Vanderbilt. The Vanderbilt family visited Kiel in 1903 and
Princess Daisy of Pless noted gleefully that the Prince 'disappeared below
deck with Mrs Cornelius Vanderbilt our hostess, a fascinating (though
snobbish) little American, but with much charm; I always imagined the
Prince stiff and shy, certainly without a soupçon of flirtation, but still
waters run deep'.

Meanwhile, their brother Ernie's marriage had come unstuck. His unmatched skills as his sisters' confidant had not helped him with his own domestic life. The couple dutifully waited until the Queen's death before divorcing. While Ducky had long complained that Ernie was homosexual, Prince Rainer von Hessen, a German historian and one of Ernie's relations, believes he was bisexual.

Alix never made any secret of her disapproval of divorce, but she was relieved to hear of Ernie's break-up: 'Divorce is a terrible thing but now I can only thank God that it happened as it did, otherwise my brother's spirit would have been utterly broken,' she wrote to a lady-in-waiting.

Three years later, Ernie was engaged for the second time. Ella issued a warm welcome to his new fiancée: 'You bring peace and sunshine into our dear old home . . . He must have told you about his sisters . . . In a family where all are so united it is easy to find a home and become a link.'

In fact, all were not destined to remain united. Tensions between Ella and Alix were mounting, and the two sisters would die unreconciled.

In 1902, Ella, Victoria and Irène attended Edward VII's coronation in London. The King's private secretary, Frederick Ponsonby, took charge of Irène and Prince Henry, who stayed at Wimborne House in London. 'I liked both Prince and Princess Henry very much,' he declared, 'and they were both charming.'

Ponsonby was grateful to Prince Henry for easing his path through a diplomatic upset. Delicate arrangements were made regarding the order of carriages travelling from Wimborne House to Buckingham Palace for the ceremony. The fiery Field Marshal Count von Waldersee refused to travel in a demeaning fourth place. 'A fierce discussion followed and soon the hall was filled with irate officers all talking at the same time,' recalled Ponsonby. The eventual solution was that the Count would go five minutes ahead of the rest of the party; Ponsonby was impressed by Prince Henry's equanimity.

In fact, the plans all changed because the coronation was postponed when Bertie became ill and had to have an operation. Originally scheduled for June, the ceremony finally took place in August.

That year Victoria spent Christmas in Kiel with Irène. It was to be her daughter Alice's last Christmas at home with her family. The following year she married Andrew of Greece.

For all Admiral Fisher's worries about Victoria's German relations, the new King Edward VII appointed Irène's husband, Prince Henry, Vice Admiral of the British Fleet and conferred on him the Royal Victorian Chain. The Kaiser was miffed. He found Henry's vacillating loyalties intolerable, now accusing him of 'Anglomania'.

The Kaiser had long been incensed by the idea that the British preferred his more personable brother. He would have been enraged by a *Times* obituary of Prince Henry, published years later, in which his brother was referred to as Prince Charming.

The four Princesses of Hesse themselves all had a touch of Anglomania. Victoria spent most of her life in England. Her three sisters were known for the English style of their houses and interior decoration. Ella maintained an English atmosphere in her home. As her stepdaughter, Maria Pavlovna reported: 'The immediate household and all of the family spoke English to us.' As a child, Maria read Dickens, *Alice in Wonderland* and *Uncle Tom's Cabin*. Alix spoke English to the Tsar and her children.

Irène, meanwhile, took on a Norland nanny to look after her three boys. Beatrice Todd, aged 30, was the daughter of a clerk in the Ecclesiastical Commissioner's office. She had worked as a housekeeper at Windsor and was also a Froebel-trained teacher. In spring 1903, she sent a note to the *Norland Quarterly* from the Neues Palais in Darmstadt: 'This is where we are staying for Easter but I have my Baby in bed with a bad cough & I am dreading wh [whooping] cough.'

The real problem with baby Heinrich, in fact, was that, like Waldemar, he was a haemophiliac. It is not clear when exactly Irène made the discovery, or how much Miss Todd was told. As in the case of Waldemar, little Heinrich's haemophilia was kept under wraps. The secrecy maintained around the disease would have dire consequences.

A year after the birth of Anastasia, Alix argued with Ella over spiritual matters. Alix was feeling increasing pressure to produce an heir. Such was her desperation that she had ventured into the paranormal, enlisting the services of a mystic called Monsieur Philippe. She and the Tsar referred to M Philippe as Our Friend, the sobriquet they later bestowed on Rasputin.

Ella disapproved of such mystics and Alix was irritated by her disapproval. In a letter to her husband, in July 1902, Alix described an uncomfortable carriage ride with her sister: 'We drove around the Alexander Park, and during that time Ella assailed me about Our Friend . . . She has heard many very unfavourable things about Him . . . I explained that all came from jealousy and inquisitiveness . . . I am sure my answers are most unsatisfactory to her, let's hope she won't begin again.'

One of the mystic's more curious gewgaws was a bell with magic powers; Alix claimed that the 'bell would ring if they [ministers] came with bad intentions'.

Ella would 'begin again' on the mystics, as she had begun again on her youngest sister's failure to try and engage more with the Russian people. But for now a truce was maintained as she and Alix went on a pilgrimage to Tambov. In August 1903, the two sisters attended the canonisation of St Seraphim, a 19th-century hermit. Ella wrote rapturously to Victoria: 'Many beautiful impressions . . . Thousands and thousands [of pilgrims] from the whole of Russia came for that day to pray and brought their sick from Siberia, from the Caucasus . . . It seemed as if we were living in Christ's time . . . How many were cured!'

Alix is believed to have prayed for a son during the pilgrimage and, by the end of the year, she was pregnant with the long-awaited heir.

In October 1903, the four sisters enjoyed one of their rare reunions in Darmstadt, gathering for the wedding of Victoria's daughter, Alice, and Andrew of Greece.

Alix had wished the betrothed couple well: 'May she be as happy as we are, more one cannot wish.' As it turned out, after producing five children, including the future Queen Elizabeth's consort, Prince Philip, Alice and Andrew were not happy. They were destined to live separate lives, with Alice becoming increasingly religious and Andrew ever more hopeless and lost. He disguised his depression with jocularity and probably drank too much.

At the time of the wedding, Victoria, Irène and Alix had 11 children between them. The previous year, Ella, now 38, had become stepmother to her 13-year-old niece Maria and 12-year-old nephew Dmitri. The children's father, Grand Duke Serge's brother Pavel, had been exiled from St Petersburg following his second morganatic marriage.

Unfortunately, Ella's relations with her stepchildren began badly. Maria never made any secret of her preference for home life with her aunt Alix. More damagingly, she claimed that Ella was put out by Grand Duke Serge's close attachment to her and her brother. She wrote that Ella 'appeared to resent our presence in the household and our uncle's evident affection for us. At times she said things to me that wounded me'.

Did Ella have grounds for such resentments? It is true that the ascetic Grand Duke Serge held his stepson in high esteem, on one occasion declaring him 'as elegant as a Fabergé statue'. Maria found her uncle's devotion unsettling: 'Towards Dmitri and me he displayed a tenderness almost feminine.' The Grand Duke was unequivocal: 'It is I who am now your father, and you are my children.'

Ella would have been upset by his inclination to side with them against her. Meriel Buchanan later wrote: '[The] children adored their uncle in spite of his strange cold eyes, his rigid bearing, finding he often took their part when they'd been naughty, rebuking his wife for being too severe with them.'

But Serge also imposed his own strictures. Maria Pavlovna complained that Uncle Serge was furious when she spilt her tea with boiled milk and that he was obsessive about punctuality at mealtimes: 'Delay of a minute would bring remarks down upon us and even punishments.' She also retained unpleasant memories of the Grand Duke's Russian name day: 'It was a very fatiguing day for everybody.'

Whatever Ella's feelings were towards her stepchildren, they were not central to her life. The links of motherhood that they could have provided between her and the three sisters would never be.

Alice's wedding was held at Darmstadt's Neues Palais. Liberated from his responsibilities in St Petersburg, the Tsar enjoyed his wife's 'dear old home' to the full, chasing after the wedding carriage and merrily tossing a bag of rice at the bride through a window, followed by a satin shoe, which Alice deftly caught before leaning back and hitting him on the head with it. The Tsar was shrieking with laughter while the bride called him a silly ass.

Contrastingly sober photographs from the time show all four sisters in elaborate white dresses. Alix, as Tsarina, is now at the centre; she looks languid, sitting in a chair with a large magazine open on her lap. In one, she is looking up, but slightly away from the camera. Irène is perched on a chair arm, while Victoria leans in from a sofa. Ella stands behind. They are all facing in Alix's direction while looking down, as if in her attendance.

Within months, happy memories of wedding japes were dispelled by tragedy. Weeks after the wedding, Ernie and Ducky's only child, eight-year-old Elisabeth, died of typhoid.

Victoria rushed back to Darmstadt to help with the funeral. Her letter to Nona Kerr is full of desperate hope for Ernie: 'He will continue missing his dear little child terribly but there is no reason to fear he will brood & mope over his loss . . .'. In a letter to Ernie himself, she recalled their mother's suffering following the death of little Frittie. Irène followed with her commiserations: 'Oh Ernie dear it makes one's heart ache to think how you must suffer.'

Little Elisabeth's playhouse still exists, at Wolfsgarten. Based on one of her dreams, it has a chimney shaped like the eye of a needle and a solicitous 'eye' watching from the roof.

Irène then faced her own shattering loss. Her youngest son, four-year-old Heinrich, was climbing between a chair and table when he missed his footing. Irène was with him, but had turned away for a second. Little Heinrich fell to the floor, injuring his head. Failing to recover, Irène's 'sunny bright angel' died on February 26th 1904.

Days after the death, Irène wrote gratefully to Victoria: 'God bless you for your love and help & all you did & suffered for us in those terrible days & kisses over and over again from your sorrowing old Irène.' A week later, she confided in Infanta Eulalia: 'Daily life seems so hard without that sunny bright angel near us – he was so full of life.'

Alix thought of Ernie: 'The painful news from Kiel must have vividly brought back the sad remembrances of last November,' she wrote to him. 'Irène says you were such a comfort to her.'

Victoria worried about the effect on Irène's middle son, Sigismund. Well over his 'cross' days, Sigismund had developed into a happy six-year-old, with a particular affection for Heinrich. Victoria wrote: 'He [Heinrich] was a bright merry fellow and his loss was a hard one for Irène and for her second boy Sigismund, 'Bobby', who had been devoted to his little brother.' The usually undemonstrative Alix was seen crying in church the day the news of Heinrich's death reached her.

Alix gave 3,000 roubles towards a mausoleum for the little boy. Built in a field near Celtic graves at Hemmelmark, the mausoleum still stands, though it has lost the flags and medieval ship that once hung from its ceiling. An elaborate gold dome is testament to Alix's generosity.

Victoria was chary of mentioning Heinrich's haemophilia, writing that her nephew 'injured his head by a fall and whether from being a bleeder or from having, as one professor declared, TB of the brain, he didn't recover'. The Queen had, at one point, alluded to Waldemar's illness. But, according to the historian Robert K Massie, nobody at the Prussian Court wanted it known that haemophilia had emerged in the German Imperial Family. In Russia, the disease was to become so associated with the Hesse family that it was referred to as '*bolezn Gessenskikh*', the Hesse disease.

Shortly before Heinrich's death, their nanny, Miss Todd, had sent a photograph of Irène's three sons to the Norland Institute. It was taken just a week before Heinrich's fall; she had captioned it poignantly: 'Prince Sigismund, Prince Waldemar & My Baby – Prince Heinrich [junior] January 1904'.

A subsequent visit to Victoria would have provided the grieving Irène with some comfort. She, Henry and their two sons stayed at the house where Victoria and her family were then based: Kendal Hall, in Hertfordshire. Despite his grief, Prince Henry found the energy to entertain the four young boys.

Victoria's husband, Prince Louis, was less help. He had begun that year badly, as Victoria reported, 'laid up with a feverish cold, culminating with an attack of hiccups lasting nine hours'. Months later, she was writing about his gout, which 'continued to be troublesome'.

*

Four months after the death of Heinrich, Alix gave birth to the Tsarevich Alexis. The Tsarina's fifth pregnancy was especially exhausting: 'I cannot get about and spend my days on the sofa,' she grumbled to Victoria, 'walking and standing causes me great pain.'

The jubilation over the birth was short-lived. Alexis was only two days old when he started bleeding from the stomach; blood was found on his swaddling clothes. Alix faced the awful truth that her son was suffering from the very same disease that had just killed her little nephew Heinrich.

Ella shared her sister's anguish. Though Alix, like Irène, attempted to keep the illness secret, Ella had found out early on. Her 14-year-old stepdaughter, Maria Pavlovna, recalled Alexis's first days: 'Even in our house a certain melancholy reigned. My uncle and aunt undoubtedly knew already that the child was born suffering and that from his birth he carried in him the seeds of an incurable illness, haemophilia . . . From that moment

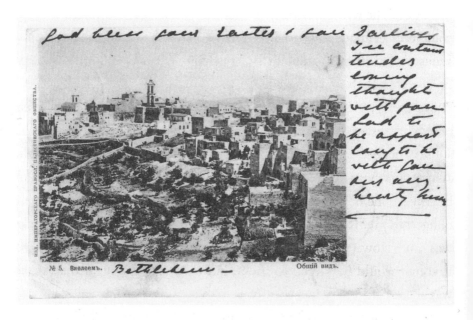

An affectionate, if muddled, postcard sent by Ella to Irène in 1904, weeks after the death of baby Heinrich. 'God bless your Easter and you Darlings, constant tender loving thoughts with you, hard to be appart (sic), long to be with you, our very hearty wishes.'

troubled and apprehensive, the Empress's character underwent a change, and her health, physical as well as moral, altered.'

Alix gave up the paltriest forms of exercise, becoming utterly absorbed in her role as a mother. Her devotion to domestic life had once attracted opprobrium. Baroness Buxhoeveden recalled that, following the arrival of the Tsarevich, an heir at last, there was no more public criticism of Alix the Hausfrau.

At the time of the Tsarevich Alexis's birth, the political situation in St Petersburg was dire. Six months previously, in February 1904, the Russians had declared war on Japan. Alix had been frustrated that pregnancy had prevented her from contributing more to the war effort. 'There is no end of work to be done, but it is a great comfort to be able to help one's poor sufferers a little . . . I like following all and not to be a mere doll,' she wrote wistfully to Victoria in June. She regretted that she could not get about and was forced to spend her days on the sofa: 'I know I must lie, it is the only remedy.' Ella swiftly threw herself into helping at hospitals and caring for the wounded.

By January 1905, the Russians were losing the war and the people were becoming restive. On what became known as Bloody Sunday, the Tsar's soldiers opened fire on a peaceful demonstration, killing 200 protesters. Alix furiously rattled off her own version of the events to Victoria: 'Don't believe all the horrors the foreign papers say. Yes, the troops, alas, were obliged to fire. Repeatedly the crowd was told to retreat and that Nicky was not in town (as we are living here [Tsarskoe Selo] this winter) and that one would be forced to shoot, but they would not heed so blood was shed.'

She seemed to modify the numbers: 'On the whole 92 killed and between 200 and 300 wounded. It is a ghastly thing, but had one not done it the crowd would have grown colossal and 1,000s would have been crushed . . .'

Retaining her buoyant conviction that the Russian people still loved the Tsar, her only regret, once again, was not being clever enough to help: 'Petersburg is a rotten town, not an atom Russian. The Russian people are deeply and truly devoted to their Sovereign . . . How I wish I were clever and could be of real use! I love my new country. It's so young, powerful and has so much good in it, only utterly unbalanced and childlike . . .'

She reserved criticism for the Tsar's late father, Alexander III, and his uncles, presumably including Grand Duke Serge. 'Had his [Nicky's] father seen more people, drawn them around him, we should have had lots to fill the necessary posts; now only old men or quite young ones, nobody to turn to. The uncles no good.'

Ella's husband, too, was under fire from his constituency in Moscow. It is hard to gauge what Ella's thoughts were about this. The net was closing in, and at one point Serge was even accused of embezzling money raised for the war effort. His response was to beg the Tsar to adopt ever harsher measures, insisting to Victoria: 'The people are not yet ripe for a more liberal government in Russia.'

Finally, however, the Grand Duke resigned, explaining sourly to Victoria: 'The important post of Moscow should be filled by a man more in sympathy with the new trend and more convinced of its success.'

Following his resignation, the British Ambassador, Charles Hardinge, wrote damningly of him, while paying tribute to Ella. The letter alluded to Bloody Sunday and was addressed to the King's private secretary, Francis Knollys: 'I hear from Moscow that on the outbreak of disorder in St Petersburg the Grand Duke Serge showed a lamentable want of nerve. He was living at a palace outside the town with the Grand Duchess and children, and immediately, on receipt of the news he simply fled to the Kremlin in the middle of the night with a large escort leaving the Grand

Duchess to follow next day. As a matter of fact she was perfectly safe, as she is as much loved as he is detested . . .'

'The placarding of Moscow with a telegram stating that the disorders in Russia were due to English gold was the doing of the Grand Duke Serge.' Though the Grand Duke had not written the incriminating telegram, he took it to the newspapers in Moscow.

No sooner had Victoria absorbed Alix's passionate defence of Bloody Sunday than she received an excited letter from Irène, blaming Russia's tribulations on the 'wavering' Tsar. Irène wondered if Alix might, after all, be able to help: 'Poor dears, what a time they are going through – if only Nicky remains firm . . . Ella wrote [that] Alicky seems to have woken up to the seriousness of the occasion, if only she helps Nicky in the right way.' Her sympathy, as ever, was for the sensitive Grand Duke: 'Poor Serge, it is so hard for him, but he seems to be very brave abt. it all.'

7

'I want to be worthy of a husband
like Serge.'
Ella

No amount of bravery would save Grand Duke Serge. On February 17th 1905, he was blown to pieces by a terrorist's bomb. It was 3 o'clock in the afternoon and Ella reported that he had just had lunch and been in an 'extremely happy' state of mind. Ella heard the explosion as the Grand Duke's carriage blew up; the bomb had gone off within the Kremlin walls. One of the police chiefs, Vladimir Dzhunkovsky, gave a statement: 'When the carriage reached the gate of the district court there was an explosion of [such] terrible force that a thick cloud of smoke [arose]. After a moment, horses were racing with a broken warped carriage without a coachman, who was thrown on the pavement at 20 paces from the blast, all wounded . . . it was only possible to see part of the uniform on the chest, a hand thrown up, one leg. The head and everything else were broken and scattered over the snow.'

One of Serge's booted feet, fingers and parts of his skull had been gathered up and put on a stretcher. His heart was found on a nearby roof. Ella set about frantically gathering up the remaining body parts and taking the rings from the severed fingers. In her deranged state, she worried about upsetting her dead husband: 'Hurry, hurry, Serge hates blood and mess.'

Victoria described how Ella courageously tried to find out for herself what had happened. Ella may sometimes have appeared remote towards

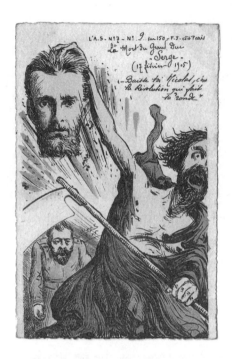

A savage French cartoon published on the day of Serge's assassination:
'The Death of Grand Duke Serge (February 17, 1905). "Take cover Nicholas,
it is the revolution that's patrolling"'.

her stepchildren, but she remembered them now. 'The governess of Maria Pavlovna, Mlle Djunkovsky, hurriedly threw a coat over Ella and wanted to go with her, but Ella would not have it, as she said that if anything had happened, the poor children must have somebody with them.' She reminded them of their stepfather's devotion: "He loved you so".'

When Ella returned to the palace, 14-year-old Maria was horrified by her appearance: 'On her right arm the sleeve of her blue dress was stained with blood. There was blood on her hand too, and under the nails of her fingers, in which she gripped tightly the medals that my uncle always wore on a chain at his neck.

'Dmitri and I succeeded in leading her back towards the rooms. She let herself fall weakly into an armchair. Her eyes dry and with that same peculiar fixity of gaze, she looked straight into space, and said nothing.'

With characteristic resolve, Ella soon pulled herself together, demanding paper and writing telegrams to all the family, beginning with the Tsar.

Alix's first impulse was to travel to her sister in Moscow. Her recurrent disagreements with Ella about holy men were momentarily cast aside. In the end, however, it was decided that Alix must not leave little Alexis, whom she was still breastfeeding. Ella, in any case, discouraged her, insisting she should avoid taking any risks, for her baby's sake. Alix admitted to Victoria that she was struggling with conflicting loyalties.

Maria Pavlovna remembered her mortification as they sat down to dinner with Ella on the night of the assassination: 'Facing her white, worn face, we were ashamed to eat.'

Victoria set off for Russia the day she heard of Grand Duke Serge's assassination. Finding her newly widowed sister so distraught, Victoria was convinced, once again, of Ella and Serge's mutual devotion: 'She could not sleep, neither could she touch a morsel of food . . . Contrary to the general belief, she and Serge had led a happy married life, though it was he who was completely head and master of the house. Ella was very willing that he should be it and he was full of affectionate attentions to her.'

She was impressed by the way her sister restored order, looking after 'everybody and everything in the house' and admired her determination to carry out her pre-arranged visit to a countess recovering from an operation. In an effort to spare the invalid, Ella had put aside her mourning dress. 'On the day after his assassination Ella went to pay her daily visit in her ordinary-coloured clothes,' Victoria wrote. 'It was difficult for her to keep from showing any emotion and talk in a natural manner and she took refuge in reading a book aloud to the patient.'

When Ella visited the Grand Duke's injured coachman, she assured him that his master had survived. Discarding her mourning clothes a second time, she was dressed in white as she delivered her comforting words: 'All is well with him. Why it is he who has sent me to see you.'

The coachman subsequently died. Victoria was coolly dismissive: 'The coachman's back was riddled with bits of bombs and stones but the man had no mortal injuries and would have recovered had he not been in the habit of drinking too much.'

More controversially, Ella also visited her husband's assassin, Ivan Kalyayev, in prison. Unbeknownst to her, Kalyayev had earlier spared her and the two stepchildren. He had been about to throw a bomb at Grand Duke Serge's carriage when he spotted the children, which meant that Maria and Dmitri had inadvertently saved their stepmother's life.

Victoria later remembered Ella's description of the visit: '[She] said to me herself, "I have nothing to do with earthly justice. It was his soul I was thinking of".' She apparently asked the killer: 'Did it not occur to you that with him you have also killed me?' She left a small holy picture in his cell.

Ella created a seven-metre 'Cross of Forgiveness' on the spot where Grand Duke Serge died. On the cross were inscribed the words: 'Forgive them for they know not what they do'.

In a letter to the Ambassador, Charles Hardinge, the British Consul Montgomery Grove described the ominous public indifference to Grand Duke Serge's death: 'Except in [the] actual neighbourhood of the Kremlin, very little difference was to be observed in the behaviour of the populace in general. Deep sympathy was to be observed for the Grand Duchess who by her indefatigable labours to assist the sick and wounded has rendered her universally loved.'

The day after the killing, Hardinge echoed Grove in a letter to Knollys: 'It is evident that the terrible news of the assassination of the Grand Duke

Serge reached London before it reached St Petersburg which is explained by the fact of the wires being in the hands of the Govt.

'A general feeling of horror and indignation was provoked in the highest classes in St Petersburg at such a ghastly crime, but the middle and lower classes show comparative indifference. I am told that last night the restaurants were crowded and bands playing notwithstanding the presence of numbers of officers in uniform who did not even suggest that the orchestras should stop. It is just like their nonchalant and fatalistic nature.

'For the last three or four weeks it has been an open secret that the Grand Duke Serge's name was on a list of five or six persons who have been condemned to death by the revolutionaries and it is stated that the Grand Duchess, who is loved by everybody, has been repeatedly warned not to drive with the Grand Duke.'

Ella's popularity received a further boost as she decided, on the day of Serge's funeral, to distribute food to the poor. Victoria, who attended the funeral, wrote: 'Ella had free meals served on the day of the funeral to all the poor people. These meals were served at the communal food centres called "The People's Palace", of which there were three, I believe.' She described how mourners dropped coins into Grand Duke Serge's coffin, 'the idea being that when a "True Believer" has been murdered, the whole Orthodox people should contribute to pay for masses for his soul.'

Victoria stayed a month with her grieving sister. She was convinced, wrongly as it turned out, that Ella would become more attached to her stepchildren: 'I think she will retain the charge of Marie and Dmitri & as they cling to her in such a touching fashion, she will have them to love & care for.'

In fact, within a year, Ella was more than happy for the siblings to live temporarily with Alix at Tsarskoe Selo. The arrangement would have suited Maria, who had always preferred the cosier life at the Alexander Palace. 'I want to leave Maria & Dmitri with Alix and Nicky who have kindly asked to keep them,' Ella wrote breezily to Ernie. 'They can go out freely & have their lessons. I shall live here & go from time to time to see them.'

Ella was intent on devoting more time to her reinvigorated spiritual life. She set about selling her luxury items and jewellery, including her wedding ring, and began wearing heavy black habits and square-toed boots. As she told her friend Zinaide Yusupov, mother of Felix: 'I want to be worthy of a husband like Serge.'

She rose daily, an hour after midnight, for Orthodox matins, before putting herself through unending rounds of hospital visits. In spite of past frictions with her stepmother, Maria was sufficiently worried about her to suggest she loosen her schedule. Ella refused, retorting that she needed to 'forget her grief at the sight of others' suffering'. Months later, she wrote to Ernie: 'I never remain a moment without an occupation . . . I talk, work, read along with my sick & assist at their dinner – they are my big babies who are so thankful to me for my care.' Ella had, at last, found an outlet for her maternal instincts.

Maria described Ella's room as resembling a nun's cell, painted white and hung with icons and pictures of saints. She added a macabre detail: 'In one of the corners she placed a large wooden cross in which were enclosed what remained of the clothes worn by my uncle on the day of his death.'

Irène, far away in Kiel, was beside herself with worry, fretting to Victoria in Russia: 'Poor Ella, do you not think she would come away a bit later on? Would she come abroad with me? & perhaps go to Ernie for a bit? . . . Only to have other impressions for a time. One must hope she will do it. One keeps on thinking what might be of some help to her – do tell me whatever you personally think would be happiest.'

As Victoria was preparing to leave Moscow, she arranged for Irène to meet Ella at Tsarskoe Selo, the following month. But Irène agonised about how Ella would manage after Victoria's departure: 'I have to thank you for the post-cards & 2 dear letters, the last received this morning about your & my journey. Harry & I would be very glad to join dear Ella at Tsarskoe on April 3rd – it makes me miserable to think that she will be alone till she goes there . . . they must let me know if she suffers too much alone – & I shall dash off in spite of it all.'

Days later, Victoria left Ella for Tsarskoe Selo. Staying with Alix, Victoria could admire the precious new baby Tsarevich, Alexis. During her journey back to England, she met Irène on a train in Germany; the sisters spent two hours exchanging news, before Irène proceeded on her journey to meet Ella, as planned, with Alix at the Alexander Palace.

Upon her final return to Hemmelmark, Irène was full of Ella's woes. These were primarily to do with Serge's murder. But there were also issues with Ella's stepchildren's father, Pavel, and his 'horrid' second wife. 'I returned back & dear Ella is remaining on at Tsarskoe. Today is their Easter. How she is altered – she often has that terrible look in her dear eyes, but remains as brave & loving as ever,' Irène wrote distractedly to Victoria. 'Only Paul [Pavel] is ungrateful & unkind to her . . . Ella hopes he will go to Moscow with her & children for a little, and help looking through the papers – but his horrid wife has egged him so nastily against her that she does not know what he will do.'

Despite her preference for 'trifling occurrences', Irène found herself unable to ignore the political upheavals in Russia. 'The chief heads of all these organisations seem now to have been caught at St Petersburg, so one must hope for better times, although the restlessness amongst the peasants is great,' she wrote, before adding one of her muddled conclusions. 'Ella only hopes the various seasons will have a calming effect, but one can never tell with cholera or bad harvest will not bring it all on more than ever.'

The sisters were right to be worried. By now all three of them were exasperated by the 'wavering' Tsar. Irène complained to Victoria: 'Poor Ella felt so hopeless about Nicky – just what you told me – the best intentions, excellent ideas, but not pushing himself, as so inexperienced . . . & through his wavering wearing out all who are doing their best to help him. Unfortunate man!'

Alix either had no inkling of her sisters' misgivings, or set no store by them. Her chatty note to Victoria, at the time, made no mention of her husband: 'The children are getting on nicely with their lessons, they have English and French masters too; they ride much also, which they greatly enjoy. Baby is getting on, thank God, splendidly. Do have Louise photographed, so that I can get a good idea of her now, as a big girl; Maria P [Ella's stepdaughter] also has her hair done up now.'

While the Tsar continued to waver, Prince Louis's position was ever more solid. Victoria was thrilled when the Prince of Wales, the future George V, appointed Louis godfather of his youngest son, John. In fact, the little Prince would turn out to be a rather sad figure: severely epileptic, he was to die aged just 13.

Later that year, Victoria would have been astonished to see early camera footage of Alix with the Queen at Balmoral during the Romanovs' visit of 1896. The film was shown in Darmstadt by the Tsar's court photographer. Victoria was chary of some technological advances, including radio and cinema, but with her passion for talking, she grew to love the telephone.

As she watched the party brought to life, Victoria must have thought of Grandmama and what she would have made of her two granddaughters in 1905, tangled up, all too predictably, in Russia's turmoil.

The end of the Russo-Japanese War brought little peace to the streets of Moscow. Alix's cheering news of her children at the Alexander Palace was at variance with Ella's grim picture from the Kremlin. Ella telegraphed Ernie, saying that she was well, 'though blockaded in the Kremlin and the town was without water or light'. For all her alleged popularity, Ella herself was in danger. Her entourage wanted her to leave Moscow, but she refused to relinquish her beloved hospital work.

Her sole concession to the emergency was to invest in two large motor cars: if the situation were to worsen, Maria and Dmitri could at least be transported to safety.

By December 1905, Alix's patter had resumed its habitual downbeat tone. 'Don't expect a long letter, one is not in the letter-writing mood,' she groaned to Victoria. 'Nicky slaves like a n———-, many a day passes without his getting out, or, if so, only in the dark. His poor head gets so tired, but he is brave and full of trust and hope in God's mercy.'

That Christmas, several Fabergé novelty gifts were successfully sent from St Petersburg to the British Royal Family at Sandringham. If Queen Alexandra had been anxious about the upheavals in Russia, she was less worried now. The arrival of the gifts reassured her that the establishment was still functioning and that 'things were much exaggerated in our English papers'.

Ella, however, remained pessimistic, writing grimly to Ernie of a 'bad time', during which the Kremlin had been threatened. The revolutionaries, she warned, could have got into the Kremlin: 'A month later they would go to Tsarskoe Selo & you can guess the end . . . there is still much of terror.' She begged the family not to visit: 'Please don't any of you come now, it really truly is a risk and would only cause me constant fears.'

Her small consolation was that her husband did not live to see the disorder: 'I know my darling Serge is at rest and thank God he does not live to see and hear all that is going on and I do not know how he could have borne it. How can I then feel sad?' She gave an obscure explanation of her beliefs: 'Shall I tell you why I feel calm alone, because the living and the dead are equally near me and I don't realise the entire earthly separation. I chat with you all in my heart.'

The following summer of 1906, Victoria managed to join Ella at Illinskoye. Eighteen months on, the Grand Duke's death still cast a shadow and the atmosphere remained ever more remote from those romps of 1896. The ambience was not improved by Ella's 'incurable invalids', her 'big babies', victims of the Russo-Japanese War, now installed at the estate.

Victoria noted the stepchildren's resentment of the 'invalids': 'The young people were very critical at the way she "spoiled" the patients, sending them out for trips in the carriages, the numbers of which were greatly reduced.'

She recognised Ella's continuing need to nurse; it was 'the only occupation which distracted her [Ella's] thoughts after the terrible time she had gone through'. But she worried about the impact on her sister's health: 'Ella was not at all well that summer. The shock of Serge's death had started an internal trouble which afterward turned out to be a malignant growth.'

Victoria later recalled her fraught departure from Illinskoye: 'When we left for Peterhof . . . [we] saw houses on fire not far from the station at Odinzovo and we were escorted to the station by a mounted guard'. She was unsettled by further events at Peterhof, where she lodged in the devoted Orchie's rooms: 'During my stay at Peterhof, General Min shot dead on platform of the Peterhof station, as he was sitting on [a] bench between his wife and his mother.'

Ella's malaise was exacerbated by her anxiety about Russia's political instability. She may have cast her mind back to Grandmama's warnings as she fretted to Ernie that revolution 'lurks in the background and the life for thinking people here has become very serious'.

*

In 1907, three of the Hesse sisters found themselves caught up in an unlikely matchmaking project. Despite her poor health and the growing political turmoil, Ella was determined to focus on a new venture: the creation of a

Martha and Maria convent and nuns' order. This was to be her life's work. And she was convinced, probably rightly, that she would have more time and energy for the project if her prickly stepdaughter, Maria Pavlovna, now 16, were married off.

It was Irène who suggested the suitable match; Victoria travelled to Moscow to supervise the engagement.

Irène had been approached by Victoria of Baden, the former playmate who had once hit her on the nose with a spade. The two women, now on the best of terms, agreed that Victoria of Baden's son, William of Sweden, would be a perfect husband for Maria Pavlovna. Ella had met and approved young William, then aged 24. Irène now sent Ella a telegram asking for photographs of the prospective bride.

Maria herself knew nothing of the plans until she discovered Irène's telegram. She later reported that she spent much of her time seeking out papers she believed were being concealed from her. She was intrigued by the telegram: 'It said that when the then Crown Prince of Sweden wished for my latest photographs they should be sent to Stockholm without delay.'

During that Easter period, Ella summoned Maria back from Tsarskoe Selo, where she had been enjoying another break with her preferred 'aunt', Alix. Maria returned to Moscow to find another aunt, Victoria, already in situ: Marie would refer, not always fondly, to all four Hesse sisters as aunts.

The plan was for William of Sweden, by then also in Moscow, to have tea with Maria and the two aunts. The tea was arranged with the specific purpose of bringing the couple together; at an agreed point, Ella and Victoria would leave the room and William would propose.

In the event, the normally robust Maria succumbed to measles and had to be wrested from her bed for the meeting. During the tea, the young couple showed little interest in getting to know each other; it was left to Ella to do most of the talking. Nonetheless, when the two aunts left the room, the proposal was uttered and duly accepted.

'That afternoon he proposed. There had been a tea table set up – two aunts there – they left – he proposed, he left,' wrote Maria bleakly. 'The aunts came back in and congratulated me. Then I was put back to bed.'

Ella was not going to let Maria's measles or a stilted tea party get in the way of her grand plan. She prevailed upon Maria to write an enthusiastic letter about her betrothal to her father, suggesting odd flourishes of her own. Maria was to write that love came upon her 'like a thunderclap'. Queen Victoria had used almost the same simile to describe her shock at hearing of Alix's engagement to the Tsarevich. Grand Duke Pavel was sceptical, receiving the surprise news badly.

A photograph of the young lovers was taken, with the two aunts: Maria Pavlovna smiles slightly, while her fiancé William looks quietly confident but a bit dopey. There is little sign, on either side, of a 'thunderclap'. Maria's brother Dmitri appears woebegone, doubtless dreading the departure of his much-loved companion. The two happiest parties are the aunts, Ella and Victoria, who are both smiling and looking full-square at the camera. They had pulled it off.

Victoria eventually returned to England, where she found Prince Louis laid up, once more. He 'had again been troubled by gout, this time in both feet'.

Maria and William's relationship may have begun inauspiciously, but the capricious bride-to-be was soon pouring out her heart to her fiancé. The scheming aunts would have been gratified by the odd flurry of passion, less pleased with the stream of complaints about 'Aunty' [Ella].

Maria had not got over her resentment of those invalids at Illinskoye. She sent her fiancé a sour description of Ella's response to her motor car breaking down: 'Aunty was excited only over the one question: that the motor should be ready to take the soldiers tomorrow to town!' She grumbled

Maria Pavlovna and William of Sweden as a mismatched married couple, circa 1910.

from the Crimea: 'She sent for two of her sick soldiers from Illinskoye . . . It makes you quite angry to see her run there and then come back and lie down directly and even not come to me.' Finally, she raged: 'She and only she has made my last years the unhappiest of my life'; 'She is like a rat . . . underneath the nails are sharp.'

While she looked forward to leaving Aunty, Maria was all too aware of her brother's dread. On Dmitri's 16th birthday, she commiserated: 'His life is not a gay one, not a happy one, without a mother or a real home . . . he who never cries, he went away to his room and cried all alone.'

Ella confused both siblings with a birthday telegram to Dmitri which read: 'Mama, children and sisters congratulate the dear young maitre of Illinskoye.' The pair got there in the end: 'Eventually we understood it was Aunty, she makes the soldiers call her Mama.'

Ella was Mama to her soldiers while remaining 'Aunty' to her motherless stepchildren.

Towards the end of 1907, Alix's health was creating more than usual anxiety among her sisters. Giving birth to the long-awaited Tsarevich had solved some issues; his illness had brought many more. Maria Pavlovna noted: 'Alix does not look well, she is very weak and lies [down] all the time.'

Setting aside her own travails, Ella travelled with her stepchildren to St Petersburg, to tend her younger sister. During Ella's frequent visits to Alix, Maria was relieved to have the house to herself: 'Aunty is in good humour but she is a bore and I am glad when she sets off to A. Alix and we stay alone . . .'

Maria occasionally accompanied Ella, on one occasion getting into an ugly tussle with her fiery cousins, the little Grand Duchesses: 'I had a dreadful fight with the children today, which ended badly; they took off my shoe and banged with the heel of it with all their might on my head. Anastasia pinched and bit me so long that I got really very angry.'

Months later, it was Ella who was at the centre of her sisters' worries. The growth that Victoria had attributed to grief and stress was having to be removed.

Irène hurried to Moscow to help. The fickle Maria was put out to hear of her impending arrival, insisting she had been looking forward to nursing Aunty herself. She groaned: 'Aunty operated on this morning. She had a tumour or growth in the stomach . . . Somebody got a telegram that A. Irène coming Sunday and I am in despair. The last real duty to Aunt and the only way of getting nearer to her.'

As it turned out, Maria herself would soon be ill again, and had to be kept away from Aunty: 'Aunt Irène arrived some days ago, when I was still in bed. I have not yet seen Aunty but A. Irène and Dmitri have and Irène will stay with her the whole time.'

Victoria, in England, was, of course, kept in the loop: 'On the 21st of January I received a telegram from Ella saying she had been satisfactorily operated on for a non-malignant growth at Moscow . . . She had not

The three elder sisters with their parents in 1866. Victoria and Ella returned from a visit to their Grandmama to find they had a new baby sister, Irène.

Irène (left) Victoria and Ella in 1875. The three sisters constructed intricate lamp-mats for Grandmama.

The four sisters with their parents, their brother Ernie and baby May in 1876. Victoria is on the left, Ella on the right and Irène at the front. Alix, at the centre, is being held close by her mother.

Above: In 1885, Alix sent Irène affectionate Christmas and New Year's cards.
Opposite: The sisters in mourning, 1879. Victoria (left), Irène, Alix and Ella.
Below: The sisters took pains to decorate envelopes for each other.

Above: Victoria and Louis at the time of their marriage, 1884.
Below: The menu of one Ella's wedding meals – and Ella in an elaborate dress.

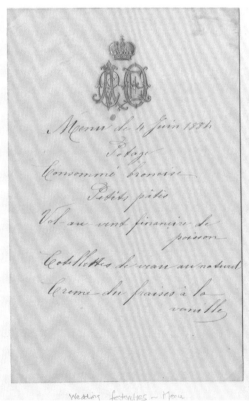

Above: Ella in court dress, 1885.
Below: Alix and the Tsarevich's official engagement photograph, 1894.

Above: Irène, Henry and her three sons: Waldemar (left), Heinrich and Sigismund, 1900.

Below: The Hesse Princesses with their spouses in 1903. Their brother and confidant, Ernie, is pictured alone, next to Alix, on the left.

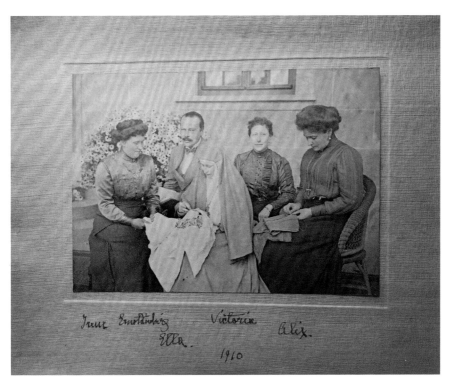

Above: The four sisters in Friedburg with Ernie, 1910.
Irène (left), Ella, Victoria and Alix.
Below: Ella in her nun's habit, 1913.

Above: Victoria in 1927. "In fond memory".

Below: The gold-domed family Mausoleum, orginally created for baby Heinrich, who died aged four in 1904.

warned us before that it was going to be a biggish operation so as not to alarm us . . .'

By the end of January, Maria had performed yet another volte face, paying tribute to Aunt Irène's efforts with Aunty and dreading her departure: 'A Irène is such a dear, she helps one in all [matters], it would have been dreadfully difficult for me alone. I am awaiting that time [Ella coming home from hospital] with horror. What will she do when A Irène goes away?'

Irène wrote to Alix's daughter Olga, in St Petersburg, from 'Aunty Ella's Hospital'. She asked after Alix, before alluding to her own struggles with Russian: 'Aunty is getting on steadily but slowly. I hope your Mama has had no more headaches. I know many more Russian words now but am too shy to say any sentences.' She described Ella's curious interaction with her 'babies'. 'In the evenings through the wall we hear sometimes the wounded soldiers singing songs, it is so pretty and Aunty can see them often of an afternoon from her bed walking into the garden, but they can only see her head or her hand when she waves to them.'

There is a photograph, taken that year, of Irène and Ella poring over a Russian fairy tale, 'Ivan the Tsar's Son and the Firebird'. The two sisters, both dressed in white, look absorbed and content as they gaze down: Ella reclines in an armchair, while Irène perches, less comfortably, on the arm.

Upon her arrival in Moscow, Irène had found herself facing an unexpected, additional problem. The match between Maria and William, so neatly engineered by Ella and Victoria, was fracturing. Maria, well over any flurries of passion, was now begging William to break off the engagement. He, in turn, was asking her to reconsider.

Aunt Irène was unsympathetic. Maria later recalled her reaction: '[She] told me my decision would kill my aunt [Ella]'. Irène deemed Maria's misgivings so unimportant that she didn't even mention them to Ella. Years later, Irène defended herself to Victoria: 'Poor Ella had only just got over her operation – otherwise I would have spoken up more then.'

When Ella herself subsequently found out about the ructions, she insisted her advice to Maria would have been very different from Irène's.

Grand Duchess Maria Pavlovna and Prince William of Sweden were married in St Petersburg on May 3rd 1908. Among the guests was the triumphant 'Aunty' Ella. Alix presented Maria with a ring on the day of the wedding: 'The Empress, always maternal, was very tender to me. That evening she put on my finger a beautiful sapphire ring, her parting gift,' gushed Maria. Alix and the Tsar would later visit Maria in Sweden. Maria wrote that the Imperial couple 'made me feel as though I were indeed – as they playfully used to call me – their "eldest daughter".'

The Hesse sisters' skills at matchmaking proved as chequered as their Grandmama's: William and Maria would be divorced after just six years.

*

Victoria might have played an important part in bringing Maria and William together, but she felt no obligation to attend their wedding. Instead, she travelled to Moscow weeks later, for what she and Ella clearly regarded as the more important event: the laying of the foundations of Ella's Martha and Mary Convent. On the outside of the church, a pair of angels in flight would be installed, their faces representing those of Ella and Grand Duke Serge.

The elaborate ceremonies were attended by Alix and the Tsar; Victoria was enraptured: 'We heard the wonderful choir of the Synod. It gave a beautiful concert in the drawing room.' Victoria brought her son, Louis, then aged eight, and daughter Louise, and her elder daughter, Alice, arrived with her husband and two daughters. Alice was profoundly impressed by Ella's enterprise, years later founding her own religious order.

Through selling her valuables, Ella had raised the modern-day equivalent of £2.5 million. She continued to have problems, however, grasping the concept of money. As the memoirist, Galina von Meck, later said: 'I remember my cousin [Ella's secretary] telling us that she wanted to spend another big sum of money on . . . a bigger hospital or something of that sort . . . My cousin said, "It is impossible to do it." Several months later another idea came into her head and she decided that she could do it. Why? Because she hadn't done the first one . . . So you see she had absolutely no idea about money – if she had it, in five minutes it went. Not on herself, of course, always on other people. But that was the charm of the woman.'

The Synod disapproved of the whole project, with one bishop referring to it as having 'a definitely Protestant leaven'. The Metropolitan of St Petersburg suggested Ella should offer herself to an existing convent. The Tsar joined the dissenters, insisting she 'could have done more good in [her] previous role'.

Ella was distraught, describing herself as 'taken aback when a whole battle broke out to prevent me, to frighten me about the difficulties . . .' She sent an impassioned note to the Tsar: 'I can't say if you are right or wrong but I will try, and He who is all love will forgive me my mistakes, as He sees the wish I have of serving Him and His.'

Victoria had accompanied Ella around various sites in Moscow the preceding year. She, at least, was unswerving in her support, believing that Ella was 'perfectly right to fill her life with useful work'. She even helped Ella create stipulations for the nursing order: women must be aged between 21 and 40 and be prepared to take practical roles, working as doctors and midwives. Ella had no truck with the Tolstoyan idea of charity, featuring gentlefolk masquerading as peasants. 'They need to be taught that neither lockjaw nor gangrene need be inevitable,' she said.

In a nod to her former self, Ella employed the Parisian couturier, Madame Paquin – dresser of the Queens of Belgium, Portugal and Spain – to design the nuns' grey wool habits and long veils. On feast days, the nuns dressed in white habits. The Russian Synod was again up in arms, maintaining that all habits should be black.

After the foundation ceremonies, Victoria and Ella went to Estonia for a course of restorative mudbaths. As Victoria explained, the mudbaths would help her sister 'to recover after her severe operation of the winter'.

The following year, in 1909, Victoria was back in Moscow, by which time the convent hospital had 34 doctors, two wards, 22 beds, an operating theatre, a room for bandaging and bathing and a library containing 200 books. Victoria gave a detailed description: 'The "obitel" consisted of a group of buildings, one of which was the hospital. There were buildings which contained a Dispensary and the rooms in which lighter cases were treated . . . There were orphan girls under the care of a chaplain, who had before been chaplain to one of Ella's regiments. [There was a] Little house at [the] end where incurable invalids were.'

The hospital had an emergency facility available in case of accidents. One day, when a cook was brought in with serious burns from an overturned oil stove, the nurses whispered to Ella that the patient was for the mortuary. Ella, however, was defiant: 'God willing she will not die here.' The cook survived, with Ella herself changing the patient's extensive, malodorous dressings twice a day.

Victoria was full of enthusiasm for the institution's 'nucleus of sisters' – never exceeding 60 – and their various charitable projects: 'Generous people donate material which is then sewn by poor people into dresses which they can sell for much needed income.'

The preceding February, Ella had moved on to the premises to live there full time. Victoria was less impressed by her sister's 'summer furniture', rudimentary wicker-and-cane chairs: 'Her reception room was furnished with basketware furniture, neatly covered with chintz, but emitting many squeaks as we moved.' Ella's sleeping arrangements were no less spartan.

She had no mattress, preferring to rest, for just two or three hours a night, on a hard wooden bed. Her one indulgence seems to have been chintz pelmets, decorated with her favourite flowers, lilies.

In July, Victoria spent time at Ella's Home for Incurable Women Consumptives, and reported a poignant exchange she had witnessed there: 'In one case, the husband, who was very devoted to his wife, was a communist, and he and Ella each held the hand of the dying woman. The husband said to one of the nurses that if all the members of the Imperial Family were like this one, the first he had ever met, his opinion of them would be very different.'

Later that year, Ella returned Victoria's visit and the two sisters inspected various English convents, including the house of Little Sisters of the Poor and the Convent of the Sisters of Bethany, in Islington. Nona Kerr, who accompanied them, was impressed by Ella's acuity: 'I was immensely struck at the quickness she showed in understanding their aims, though their methods were often so different from her own.'

*

That year, 1909, as the hostility towards the Tsar and his family was continuing to mount, and security was easier to manage on water than on land, the Hesse sisters arranged their get-togethers on yachts.

In Britain, there were rumbles of discontent as news spread of a prospective Romanov visit to the Isle of Wight. Protests were fuelled by angry speeches in Parliament against 'Nicholas the bloody'.

In August, the Tsar, Alix and their five children allowed themselves just three days in Britain, moored off Cowes. The family remained almost exclusively on board the Imperial yacht, *Standart*. According to Alix's lady-in-waiting, Baroness Buxhoeveden, that trip was the first time all five Romanov children had been abroad, except to Wolfsgarten.

Sailing on from the Isle of Wight, the *Standart* anchored at Kiel, where the Romanovs were visited by Irène and Victoria. The three sisters all had their children with them. In a taped interview from 1976, Irène's son, Sigismund, recalled the meeting. Then aged 12, he was impressed by the Russian yacht: '*Standart* was better than *Hohenzollern* [the German Imperial yacht]. Nicer, more elegant.' He was tickled by some comments from his nine-year-old cousin, Louis Battenberg (later Mountbatten), about the *Standart*'s Russian priest: 'Mountbatten said priest looked like 'Kycha' – a coachman. It was a priest with a beard!'

That Christmas, Ella kept Irène up to date with a book of photographs of her newly established convent. 'For my Darling Irène – Views of my Martha Mary Home of Charity – first photos made.' The collection featured a picture of '6 sisters in novice dress (we have no real sisters yet as they don't make their vows before a year & then get another white dress)'.

Ella also sent Ernie an unexpectedly glowing report of Alix's health: 'At last thank God Alix looks flourishing & lively & lovely, really a pleasant impression.'

In fact, at this point, it was more likely Ella who was finally – and briefly – flourishing.

8

'That crazy lunatic, my aunt
the Empress.'
Victoria's son, Louis

The Hesse sisters would all, to a greater or lesser extent, be entangled in the controversies at the Russian Court surrounding the so-called holy man, Rasputin. Years before, Alix and Ella had argued about Rasputin's outlandish predecessor, Monsieur Philippe, during their awkward carriage ride. But by 1909, Rasputin had become a much more serious problem, matching his soaring reputation for sexual exploits with increasingly frequent visits to the Alexander Palace.

He was summoned to heal the sickly Tsarevich Alexis; on several occasions he seemed to have been the only one able to stem the boy's bleeding. He may have been able to soothe Alix simply with his presence; as she relaxed so her son's blood pressure dropped. He also eschewed aspirin, which would have acted as an anti-coagulant. But none of this was generally known. Alix and the Tsar continued to keep Alexis's illness secret: the reasons for the 'holy man's' visits thus remained a source of unsavoury speculation.

Ella had no time for Rasputin's 'cures'. She disapproved of him as much as she had of Monsieur Philippe. But while she and Alix remained at odds over holy men, they shared a curious fascination with Rasputin's arch enemy and future murderer, Prince Felix Yusupov.

The wealthy Yusupov family were mainstays of the Russian Court, and over the years the fey, flamboyant Prince Felix and Alix had struck up an unlikely bond. He was entranced by Ella, whom he met regularly at Illinskoye. It was inevitable that he would hear intriguing tales of Rasputin; equally predictable that he would seek him out. At first curiously beguiled, he then performed a complete volte face, insisting, with horror, that Rasputin had tried to seduce him. He subsequently became increasingly hostile, put out by the power the 'holy man' wielded at Court.

Both of the Hesse sisters saw themselves as Yusupov's mentor. He would make theatrical confessions to Ella: '[I] broke down completely and threw myself at her feet. She gently stroked my hair until I had calmed down.' But while Ella stroked his hair, Alix preferred to cajole. 'Any self-respecting honest man should serve in the Army or take up a position at Court,' she snapped. 'I'm surprised that you do neither.'

Neither approved of Yusupov's decision to study at Oxford University. But he was disinclined to listen, duly enrolling himself at University College. Just before leaving for England, he met Alix, who instructed him to call on Victoria, in London, and pass on a letter. It is impossible to know, at that point, whether the pair discussed Rasputin, or whether Alix knew of the camp Prince's distaste for her grubby-looking 'Man of God'. Yusupov was certainly aware of Ella's view.

During Yusupov's lunch with Victoria, it became obvious that she shared his suspicions of Rasputin. Yusupov subsequently wrote of Victoria 'quizzing' him. He added: 'She was too intelligent not to see the catastrophe that threatened my country.'

For all her much-vaunted dislike of tittle-tattle, Victoria clearly found the subject of the outlandish 'holy man' irresistible. Yusupov may well have been the source of stories that Victoria then passed on to her friend, Gloria Vanderbilt.

Victoria told Vanderbilt that Rasputin had been spotted in Alexis's room, busily loosening screws holding up chandeliers and other heavy hanging objects. Following portentous prophecies, these would crash to the floor as if on cue. According to Victoria, these stunts had gone some way to convincing Alix of Rasputin's spiritual power. The story was that, when evidence of the screw-loosening emerged, Alix rejected it outright, refusing to see her meddling informant ever again.

That spring of 1910, Ella would have been put out to hear of the dismissal of one of Alix's maids, Sophia Tyutcheva. The maid, whose family were close friends of Ella, was fired after complaining to the Tsar about Rasputin visiting the young Grand Duchesses in their bedrooms. She'd first spotted him two years before, in the darkened corridors: 'A peasant in a tightfitting coat.'

With all their disputes about holy men, Alix and Ella remained ostensibly on good terms. Towards the end of 1909, Alix had written to Ella asking her to come to Tsarskoe Selo for a holiday.

More importantly, Alix stepped in to help Ella gain official recognition from the Synod for her nun's order. In March 1910, following several glitches, the order was established by Imperial decree. Ella wrote to the Tsar: 'Pray for me deary . . . my taking of vows is even more serious than if a young girl marries – I am espousing Christ and his cause.'

The Dedication of the Martha and Mary Convent took place on April 9th 1910. This time it was Irène who was present as Archbishop Trephonius gave the veil to Ella alongside 20 other women. Ella had readily gone from princess to peasant, pronouncing: 'I am about to leave the brilliant world in which it fell to me to occupy a brilliant position . . . I am about to enter a much greater world – that of the poor and afflicted.'

While willing to help Ella, Alix retained reservations about her sister's spiritual calling. Victoria, however, was full of admiration. 'There is something extraordinary about a person who has high ideals and tries to live in accordance with them, something shaming and refreshing for us ordinary people, that is what I find at Ella's home,' she wrote to Ernie's wife Onor. 'I am very sorry that Alix is so full of doubt, mistrust and envy about Ella and her undertakings; she doesn't really know Ella's art of living and I fear sometimes doesn't want to know. Ella and I are totally different in character and opinions and still I feel I understand her.'

Irène echoed Victoria in her support of Ella becoming a nun, though she had been the one who had struggled with Ella's original conversion to Russian Orthodoxy, admitting to 'crying terribly' when she heard.

Ella no longer set store by her lustrous hair. Before she took the veil, a friend had said: 'Shall we never see your beautiful hair again?' Ella had replied coolly: 'Have it as a gift', before removing and handing over some false curls, which she clearly wore in addition to her own hair. She shaved her head.

These steps were greeted with bemusement by various members of the Russian aristocracy. But Galina von Meck swore by the reverence in which Ella was generally held by ordinary Muscovites: 'Every morning she used to get up at 5.00 and go to the liturgy in one of the churches near the convent . . . she would stand quietly somewhere in the corner of the church . . . No-one ever molested her or touched her. They all knew her and loved her as a saint.'

*

After the dedication ceremony, Irène and Ella visited Alix in St Petersburg. Their stay at the Alexander Palace did not go well. At the heart of the sisters' upsets, once again, was Rasputin. Ella tackled Alix on Rasputin's misdoings. Alix then railed against Ella to Irène. From Irène's anguished account to Victoria, it was obvious that she was already solidly pitted, with her two sisters, against Alix.

The Tsar blithely referred to the two sisters' visit in his diary: 'Ella arrived in a great monastic outfit . . .' Later that same day, he treated Irène to a visit to an aerodrome. The outing sounds as if it would more likely have appealed to Prince Henry. 'At 5.15 I went with Irène and a few people from her suite to the city and in a big motorcar to the Kolomyazhskii aerodrome,' wrote the Tsar. 'I went round to the pilots, who showed us and explained each construction piece of their apparatus. The wind was blowing and we had to wait a long time until they decided to fly.'

But Irène, already anxious about Alix, was not inclined to be distracted by aerodromes: 'Poor Alicky lives in such grooves of thought one would like to shake her out of it, though gently I know it must be done,' she fretted to Victoria.

She then endured a painful supper alone with Alix, who clearly hoped for sympathy from her less strident sister. She had no idea that Irène was already partisan. Or that, when Irène claimed ignorance, she was simply obeying Ella.

Irène's report to Victoria was particularly incoherent, her German word order rendering her meaning additionally opaque. It seemed that Alix was accusing Ella of trying to get rid of Rasputin; and that she was still smarting after Ella had effectively dispatched his predecessor, Monsieur Philippe: 'Poor Ella when here the last time had to speak to Alicky about that horrid man and very hard words fell & has left a bitterness with Alicky who said she would never forget that Philip [Monsieur Philippe] had Ella wrenched from them.'

She added that Ella had tried to shock Alix with the 'terrible things' she had heard about Rasputin's sect. But Irène feared that Ella's warnings had had no effect; indeed she was convinced that Rasputin was about to strengthen his grip. Listening to Alix's ravings, Irène must have struggled to keep silent; 'Ella advised me to do as if I knew nothing at all.'

Irène was still with Alix when the sisters heard that their much-loved uncle Bertie, King Edward VII, had died. However upsetting, this news

Alix saw Rasputin as her son's saviour. But her three sisters were ranged against her: for Ella, he was a fiend and an imposter, for Victoria a skullduggerous fraud and for Irène 'that horrid man'.

may have provided a welcome distraction from Rasputin and those 'hard words'.

Certainly, Irène wasted no time in writing an altogether more composed letter from St Petersburg to her bereft cousin George: 'My dear Georgie, How deeply I feel for you in this great grief that has come so suddenly over you all, and can so well realize what a terrible shock it is. One cannot find the right words of sympathy in such a time, although one would so gladly say all one feels . . . Your dear father's memory will ever remain fresh and dear to me, with his great kind heart that never varied. How my dear Mama and Aunt Vicky loved him and how undeniably kind he was to us for their sakes, especially this last visit which will ever remain a very precious memory to me and Henry. I am here in Russia with Alicky and Nicky after having been with Ella in Moscow but my thoughts fly to you regretting I cannot be present for dear Uncle's last honours. I fear I would have been in the way too. Fondest love to dear May and yourself . . . cousin Irène.'

Victoria echoed her sister: 'Uncle Bertie was always so kind and good to us, his sister's children . . . that we mourn his loss as a personal one to ourselves.'

Belying the sisters' fond condolence letters, relations between Britain and Germany were, at that point, far from perfect. It was Irène's husband, Prince Henry, who broached this awkward issue with his admirer, Frederick Ponsonby. He began: 'Fritz why is it that we cannot get on?' Ponsonby attempted to fob him off with something about 'bad press', but Henry was persistent: 'No Fritz that won't do.' Cornered, Ponsonby crisply pointed out that Germany was building a fleet; if Germany didn't want to fight France, Russia or any other power, it must be aiming for war with Britain. Henry, exercised in his turn, took offence at the very suggestion. 'Prince Henry got very keen and excited and said that nothing was further from their thoughts than a war with England,' wrote Ponsonby. 'All they [the Germans] did want was to be strong enough to hold their own in the event of our attacking them.'

As Irène left Alix, she wrote one of her instructive notes to her niece, Grand Duchess Olga, from the train. There was no mention of the sisters' unsettling supper: 'My darling Olga, Many thanks for your nice little letter . . . Now you must be at the parade and I hope you are all enjoying yourselves. I am sorry I was not able to see it. I felt very sad leaving you all and hope Mama will not be feeling as bad as she was affraid [sic] of. Perhaps of an evening you can read to her again as you used to and think out some game to occupy the little ones, not to make too much noise.'

*

The final reunion of the four sisters, in autumn 1910, was, appropriately, in their beloved '*Heimat*', Hesse-Darmstadt.

They had all known that the visit would pose a massive security threat. It was just months since the Imperial Family's controversial visit to the Isle of Wight, which had been so unpopular in left-wing circles. The Tsar's reputation abroad had certainly not improved in that time.

Concerns about safety were duly raised before the Romanovs' arrival, with two of the sisters arguing about where the family should stay. Where would Alix be most content?

Needless to say, Victoria dominated the proceedings: 'The one to keep us all up and the most practical for everything,' as Irène once put it. But this had never stopped the other sisters weighing in.

'The happiest solution would be if she [Alix] lived in a small house alone . . . & only receive visits from her own family & us,' she wrote brightly to Victoria.

Victoria's rebuttal was so crushing that Irène immediately backtracked, replying in a fluster: 'Of course I am not going to make any suggestions to Alicky. I only wrote to YOU . . . what entered my head about a Liegekur [lying-down cure] . . . but it's not necessary. Of course [a] thousand times better she is with us all to cheer her up.'

Her next proposal was quashed by Ernie, who tutted to Victoria: 'Irène's idea of the hotel is quite out of the question. First the season is not over, so they would be mobbed the moment any one of them put their nose out of the house. Then as to guarding the house & all the surrounding streets, that also is not favourable. The quiet which Alix wants she would never get.'

After painstaking deliberations, it was decided that the Imperial Family and their 140-strong entourage should be installed at Castle Friedberg, around two miles from Bad Nauheim. The municipality of Friedberg did not take it lightly. So fearful were the administrators of an attack that they insisted the Tsar insure all their public monuments at his own expense.

The Schloss in Friedberg, in 1910. Pictured at the top are, on the left, Ernie and his wife Grand Duchess Eleonore (Onor), and on the right, Tsar Nicholas and Alix.

The ostensible purpose of the Princesses' visit was for Alix to take the waters at Bad Nauheim. Her devoted physician, Dr Eugene Botkin, had diagnosed 'progressive hysteria', before recommending a cure. 'At last Alicky tells [me] that the Dr has told her she must take the Nauheim waters . . . Thank goodness,' Irène had written to Victoria.

The 38-year-old Tsarina's medical difficulties showed no sign of abating. She suffered from what she perceived as a heart condition, daily registering herself Heart Number 1, 2 and 3 according to the severity of her condition. When her heart was not troubling her, it was the old leg and back pains. Her anxious husband wrote to his mother at the time: 'It is very important for her to get better for her own sake and the children's and mine. I am completely run down mentally by worrying over her health.'

A physician who saw the Tsarina at Bad Nauheim, Dr George Grote, found little sign of the fabled heart trouble. But he did confirm that she was below par: 'Had she not occupied such an exalted position she should have been sent to a sanatorium with two sisters of mercy to take care of her, not letting her see anyone. She takes too much on herself and hides her sufferings from everyone.'

In fact, she was not inclined to hide her suffering from her sisters. Months before the reunion she had given Victoria a distressing portrait of her diminished life: 'Don't think my ill-health depresses me personally, I don't care except to see my dear ones suffer on my account, and that I cannot do my duties . . . I give up my pleasures – they mean so little to me, and my family life is such an ideal one, that it is a recompense for anything I cannot take part in.'

Though the four Hesse Princesses all worried about each other, the most common pattern had always been the eldest three fretting about 'poor Alix'. The arrangement had suited everybody: Alix revelled in the attention, while her sisters felt they were keeping the Tsarina of all the Russias at a manageable level. Their mothering of her created the happy illusion that they retained some control.

The logistics surrounding the sisters' various journeys to Hesse-Darmstadt presented complications enough. Alix, Nicky and their five children travelled to meet Irène in Kiel. From there, the two families transferred to Bad Nauheim, where they met Victoria, newly arrived on the train from England. Victoria was happily at the helm. 'It will be awfully nice that we can all be together at Friedberg . . . [Prince] Louis can send a man to fetch the boy [Victoria's son, young Louis] & his luggage, bring him to London, take him to the dentist & look after him until you start on 28th,' she rambled to Ernie. Ella would join the party five weeks later, travelling from Moscow.

Upon her arrival at Castle Friedberg, Alix took to her bath-chair, as Victoria reported equably: 'Alix was not able to do much and spent the afternoons sitting quietly in the grounds where I generally kept her company.'

Barely five months had passed since Ella and Alix's furious argument about Rasputin. But all those 'hard words' seem to have been put behind them, as the four sisters enjoyed their reunion. It probably helped that the meeting took place hundreds of miles from St Petersburg.

At that point, in 1910, all four Princesses had reached relatively satisfactory stages in their lives. Three of them remained happily married: Victoria, 47, had four children with Louis, and Irène, 44, had two sons with Henry. Alix's five children now included the long-awaited Tsarevich, Alexis. Ella, then 45 was the only sister without husband or children. But, months after taking the veil as a nun, she took something of a pole position.

She arrived at Friedberg on October 8th. Her decision to notify Alix's daughter Olga – rather than Alix – of her plans may have had something to do with the sisters' recent spat. 'The sisters [nuns] are very busy at the moment,' wrote Ella to her niece. 'They are preparing for exams, in a few days we will resume our normal working life here after the summer: the hospital, the clinic, the pharmacy and the Sunday school. On 1 October, ten of them will take vows. So I hope to leave here on the 6th and be at my old home on the 8th.'

The Tsar mentioned Ella's arrival at the 'old home' in his diary, alluding to the nuns accompanying her, in their habits, as 'grey sisters'. Over the next few days, he would accompany Ella to several religious services, attending mass at Bad Nauheim and Darmstadt. On the 20th he reported that Alix and Ella made companionable confessions together; the following day, the two sisters returned to Darmstadt for mass.

As it turned out, the Romanovs' security problems were mostly limited to the inquisitive crowds. The eldest Grand Duchess, Olga, complained of being mobbed in Frankfurt. 'We have just returned from the city, where we went shopping and bought postcards. From every angle, all kinds of people were photographing us and we got terribly fed up with it,' she grumbled to her tutor.

The Tsar with Ella, in her nun's habit, at Friedberg, in 1910.

Guests at the genteel Bittongs hotel, in Bad Nauheim, were singled out for a reprimand. Years later in 1926, a British traveller, Violet Hunt, would recall: 'One evening a notice was posted up begging the guests not to pursue, persecute or mob the Tsar of Russia who was staying at Friedberg, three miles off, and who came in every day with the Tsarina and her children. Poor Alix of Hesse, mortally ill, had turned as a last resource to the healing waters of her native province and her husband had complained that the Nauheimers followed him and her about and stared. This would, if continued, prevent him from coming to that place.'

Violet Hunt could not, however, contain her own curiosity, ending with a heartless description of Alix: 'I often saw the Tsaritza, in black with pearls, going in and out of the baths, her face a tragic mask, stupid, incompetent, haughty, dejected – she looked a lovely fool; nay hardly lovely now – the morbid shadow of a queen.'

The nervy German authorities, meanwhile, were reduced to laying false trails regarding the Tsar's movements. As Violet Hunt added: 'When he was supposed to be going to the baths it was at the Kursaal you would find him; when it was the riding school, it was much more likely to be the lake.' He was still occasionally caught by the crowd, not least playing tennis with his brother-in-law Ernie in Bad Nauheim. Victoria recalled that the pair were 'gaped at through the wire enclosure like animals in a zoo'.

Entertaining the Tsar had been a worry: 'There must be somebody to help in occupying Nicky, although he is so touchingly kind, never expecting anything,' Ernie had written to Victoria. Subsequent efforts clearly paid off, with the Tsar reporting cheerily to his mother: 'Everything here is going well. There has been a whole kaleidoscope of relatives, as you might say, passing through.'

While he makes no further comment about the 'kaleidoscope', he evidently enjoyed the company of his in-laws. There were strolls in the park with Irène and Prince Henry. The couple took him for several drives, including to the Schwalheim curative springs, which boasted one of the largest water wheels in Europe. After dinner, the Tsar would join Victoria for games of trictrac, a French variation on backgammon.

The Tsar was feeling, as ever, liberated in Hesse-Darmstadt. One witness said: 'He seemed as happy as a schoolboy in holiday time.' The cheerless Violet Hunt would have begged to differ, swearing that she had spotted the Tsar looking as tragic as his wife: 'And once I saw him through the windows, like glass walls, of a shop full of Venetian glass, Japanese netsuke and plaques of green jade . . . the door of the shop had been left open and some sensible German passerby had shut it. Nicholas II looked up and out – he thought he was trapped!

'I saw his face through the beautiful clear glass; it did not exhibit mere terror, for he was a brave man, but all at once it seemed implicit with a summing up, a résumé of the composite agony of all this race of Kings consciously marked down for destruction. His grandfather [Alexander II] before him – his uncle [Grand Duke Serge] – and only the little son with his hand below the counter to carry on the monstrous imposthume of Russian Royalty.'

Alix, too, was bucked by the reunion. Her lady-in-waiting, Baroness Buxhoeveden, said that she enjoyed her sisters' company 'like a child'. Victoria's younger son, Louis, then aged ten, echoed the Baroness with his own bold summing-up: 'Even that crazy lunatic my aunt the Empress was absolutely sweet and charming'.

Louis's negative view of Alix's mental health probably came from his father. The boy had evidently registered his father's stark pleas to Victoria during the holiday: 'Alicky is absolutely mad – she's going to cause a revolution. Can't you DO anything'.

The previous year the sisters' children had shared happy meetings on the family's various yachts. That autumn, the young cousins played cheerily again, sharing relatively informal luncheons and dinners, marred only by visits from the exacting Kaiser. The Tsar referred to Willie bringing 'heaps of presents', which may or may not have made up for his strictures on dress.

Young Louis fell for the Tsarina's third and most attractive daughter, Maria, aged 11 (or so he later claimed): 'I was crackers about Maria, and was determined to marry her. She was absolutely lovely.' In a letter to her Russian tutor, Alix's second daughter, Tatiana, enthused about both aunts and cousins: 'I dreadfully like it here awfully much. It is not at all as I imagined it would be . . . There is a mass of aunties and cousins and it is so much fun here. We have been to Nauheim. Next week Mama and I will be taking baths and drinking the water at Nauheim.'

Victoria retained a poignant memory of Alix's six-year-old son, Alexis, falling for a toy engine while visiting a shop in Darmstadt. A kindly Russian student, unaware of the boy's identity, bought the engine for him. Victoria suggested wryly that this was the 'only time the Russian heir to the throne has been financially assisted by a subject'.

A number of photographs were taken of the four sisters during their 1910 reunion. In one, the Princesses are posing in the garden in Friedberg. Victoria stands to the right, in an elaborate black dress. Brandishing a walking stick, she looks magisterially away, into the distance. At first glance, it seems that she is the dominating presence. But finally it is Ella, in her light grey nun's outfit, who catches the eye. Her image is faint, almost luminous. She has retained her fine-boned beauty; she leans slightly forward, inclining her head to one side, eyes lowered, with the shadow of a benevolent smile. This photograph was always treasured by Irène at Hemmelmark, labelled lovingly: '1910 Garten Friedberg We 4 Sisters'.

A few days later, the sisters posed for more photographs, this time at the

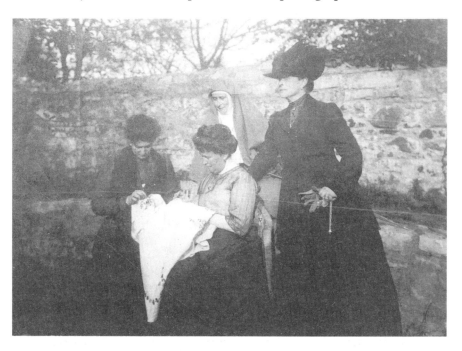

Irène's treasured photograph of 'we 4 sisters' – Alix (left), Irène, Ella and Victoria – at Schloss Friedberg in 1910.

beautiful estate of Wolfsgarten – to which they had moved after their stay in Friedberg. Again, they are pictured next to an outside wall, this time with a large bunch of flowers to their right. Ella is now at the centre. She and Alix are absorbed in their embroidery. They assume identical poses: turning their heads slightly to the right, away from the camera, eyes lowered on their work. But while Ella has an air of settled contentment, Alix appears put upon, with a certain stiffness about the mouth.

Victoria and Irène seem more engaged than their sisters. Victoria's faint smile is quietly confident. She is the only one looking square on into the camera: the pale-eyed gaze is bold and hints at her lively intellect and open nature. Irène is more diffident and ruffled-looking than the others. But she is also smiling, cheeks puffed, as she gazes admiringly at her sisters' handiwork.

On returning to their respective homes, the English, Russian and German cousins resumed their correspondences with renewed vigour. At Christmas 1910, Victoria's Louise wrote to Alix's Maria, with news from England: 'We spent a very nice Xmas and I got heaps of lovely presents. The whole family is here . . . We played the game in the dark like at Friedberg two nights ago. On New Year's Eve we are all going to dress up and after dinner we are going to Aunt Helen Albany who is living quite near Windsor at Frogmore.'

Young Louis, or Dickie, received an affectionate card from his purported new favourite cousin, Maria, and her sister Anastasia: 'We wish you darling Dickie a merry Xmas and a happy 1911 year. Much love to you all Maria, Anastasia.'

The Hesse Princesses themselves felt a little flat. Back in Kiel, Irène was plagued by existential worries. 'It is curious how all of us suffered each alone for himself, perhaps therefore the deeper & more lasting because we didn't speak of it,' she wrote to Victoria. Was she alluding to their mother's death.

Or May's? Or little Frittie's? Perhaps she was thinking of her unfortunate son, Heinrich.

Alix, meanwhile, moaned that the cures at Bad Nauheim had failed: 'I'm morally worried such tiring cures are no good,' she confided to Ernie. 'Personally I have felt no benefit from the cure & have been so bad again – am now slowly regaining strength, lie on the balcony when fine – was three days a little better then got overtired and again worse.'

She was, however, still enjoying the hiatus from hostilities with Ella. The sisters' elderly governess, Miss Jackson, would not have been surprised to hear that Alix languished while Ella flourished: 'We long for that rest [to go to sea], my husband has been working like a n—— for seven months and I have been ill nearly all the time . . . Ella spent a week at Tsarskoe Selo with us, looked well, pink and cheery.'

In June 1911, Victoria and her family stayed at Kensington Palace for the coronation of her cousin, King George V. Irène sent the new Queen congratulations from Hemmelmark, recalling 'bygone happy stays with dear Grandmama'. She wrote: 'My Dear May, To you and Georgie most heartfelt good wishes for your Coronation which I hope will not be too fatiguing for you and I am sure will be a most splendid sight . . . I remember the last Coronation when you had only just recovered from your last Baby – how the time flies – you were still living at St James's . . . God Bless from your loving cousin Irène.'

That July her ebullient husband launched his challenging 'Prince Henry Tour', for which motorists drove more than 1,000 miles, starting at Hamburg and finishing in London. The two-week tour involved sailing from Bremerhaven to Southampton, then driving to Scotland. Competitors motored through German and English countryside, contending with sheep, cattle and angry drovers. Upon their arrival in London, winners were selected and presented with trophies.

By the time the 'Prince Henry Tour' had run its course, three years later, the Prince had progressed to flying. *The Times* later described the Prince as a sailor, yachtsman, golfer, cyclist, aviator and motorist. Irène supported her husband in all his manly pursuits, but she rarely wanted to take part. Victoria was the only Hesse sister with derring-do, at one point taking an outrageously dangerous flight 'securely attached on a little stool hung on to the flyer's back'. It was Victoria, too, who, aged nearly 50, gamely attempted to roller-skate: 'After numorous [sic] tumbles I gave it up.'

*

The year 1912 proved momentous for all the sisters. Alix and Ella, who had never managed to entirely put aside their differences, now found themselves irresolvably divided over Rasputin.

The so-called holy man's visits to the palace were relentless. Two years before, Irène had complained to Victoria about the 'horrid man' and Ella and Alix had exchanged their harsh words. Now Ella felt compelled to 'begin again'.

She was furious to be thwarted by the Tsar, complaining to another ally, his sister, Grand Duchess Xenia: 'To HIM I only spoke as she [Alix] being so far from well . . . he did not like me doing so . . . Do you know how to explain this impossible obstinacy! It is a feeling of honour [that] they must save the innocent little peasant, a child of nature and of God's who is being falsely accused only because he dared overstep the threshold of their Palace!'

Upon her return to Moscow, Ella was visited by Victoria, who had just been to see Irène in Hemmelmark. The visit was not an unqualified success. Victoria lasted only one night in a house at the bottom of Ella's hospital garden. 'The house proved to be infested by bugs!' she exclaimed. 'We moved into Ella's house, I living in her room and she sleeping in her study.' Victoria evidently found Ella's squeaking furniture less challenging than the infestation.

There was a further upset when Victoria found herself caught up in one of Ella's medical missions. The Moscow Secret Police kept a record of Ella's movements for her own security: 'At 1.30pm, together with her sister, Victoria Battenberg, she left the house on Bolshaya Ordynka St and stopped in front of the Ossipov house where she saw on the pavement a man, aged 25 to 27, who was suffering from the effects of poison, probably a workman . . . Her Highness examined the stranger and immediately turned back to her own drugstore; she arranged for the sick man to be sent to the convent accompanied by two pharmacists by her own horses. The patient was brought 10 minutes later and received first aid in the presence of Her Highness . . . At 2.30pm Her Highness together with her sister went to the department of tuberculosis of the convent on Donskaya Street and at 4pm they came back.'

Then there were the monoglot abbesses. Victoria was just about able to manage the odd letter, in Russian, to her nieces, but she was in no way prepared for a chat. A keen talker, she found her situation especially frustrating: 'In spite of taking Russian lessons, both in London and with Mme Gordeev, my powers of conversation were extremely limited and as a number of the abbesses could only speak Russian, I was at a complete loss when Ella left the room.'

Back in Hemmelmark, Irène wrote a rambling note to Alix's daughter, Olga: 'I am so glad you are all enjoying your summer on the yacht, here we also have ideal weather, never too hot, masses of roses and flowers in bloom, also sweet peas that smell so good . . . In the morning before breakfast mostly some of us ride, at 11 we go to the beach for bathing, after luncheon rest etc, after tea, mow the grass, play golf . . . or tennis or make a staircase of stones, a row or motor to some place or other – in the evening guessing games etc etc.'

Victoria also wrote to Olga, reverting to the usual concerns about Alix: 'Dear Olga, how difficult and uncomfortable it is for me to write in Russian!

How could you do this! Don't blame me if my answer is very bad, still you can laugh at me. George [her first son] is here now, "Dick" [her second son] went off to school today . . . How is Mama? Better I hope.'

Meanwhile, Alix filled Miss Jackson in on her elaborate arrangements with her three sisters: 'Darling Madgie, I had Victoria's visit for a week, which was delightful, and Ella came also for three days, and I shall see her again in Moscow . . . Irène will come at the end of September to us in Poland, Spala . . . [I'm] painting flowers as, alas, have had to leave singing and playing as too tiring.'

Irène had visited the hunting lodge in Spala before, and would have looked forward, not least, to the extensive forest picnics, the food prepared in a kitchen wagon, then served at long tables with white tablecloths. But, as it turned, out, the holiday at Spala, in 1912, was clouded by disaster.

On September 19th, the Tsar made a fleeting reference to the arrival of Irène and her son Sigismund in his diary: 'Around noon we rode to Olen station and met Irène.' For the next few days, his entries dwelled exclusively on hunting and fishing: 'I killed a nice buck and wounded then killed a huge wild boar' . . . 'We fished for pike there at a new pond, but not very successfully.' Entertainments in the evening included what the Tsar called 'a common game of geography' and dominoes.

Those carefree days came to an abrupt end when the eight-year-old Tsarevich fell ill. Alexis had initially fallen over in a boat and injured his leg. He seemed to recover, but, in a bid to cheer him up, Alix unwisely took him out for a drive and the shaking of the carriage brought on a stomach haemorrhage.

Alexis's condition worsened and doctors were summoned. Alix stayed by her son's side, refusing to go to bed for a full 11 days. She was finally so shattered that Irène felt obliged to take charge of the Imperial suite. She appeared, white-faced, at the doorway of Alix's boudoir and told the suite to retire: 'As we were about to go upstairs after dinner, Princess Irène of Prussia suddenly stood in front of us,' Alix's companion Anna Vyrubova recalled in her memoir. 'She had come to bring comfort and succour to her sister. Pale and shaken to the core she asked us to [de]part as the condition of the heir to the throne was hopeless.'

Haemophilia had long constituted a terrible bond between the two sisters. Eight years before, Irène had lost her son, Heinrich, to the disease. Her eldest son, Waldemar, now aged 23, was frequently ill. As Alix's lady-in-waiting Baroness Buxhoeveden put it: 'They each had a child for whose life they trembled.'

Both sisters were haunted by the sad fate of their little brother, Frittie. Their suffering was exacerbated by their determination to keep the nature of the illness secret. Irène avoided mentioning Alexis's plight, even in her own diary, focusing instead on hunting, tennis and games of charades.

The news was not kept from Ella. She immediately wrote to Alix offering to come to Spala. Receiving no reply, she appealed to her niece Olga: 'I have proposed to Mama [that] if I can give her rest & Alexis a little variety, which always when one is sick one needs, I can come for a while to Spala. I long to be of help to you all as to know poor Baby is suffering & darling Mama so anxious & tired in spite of the strength God of course always . . . gives to [help us] bear up in such moments.'

It was also a testing time for 15-year-old Sigismund, who had been so attached to his younger brother, Heinrich. Years later, he spoke of the 1912 visit to Spala, where he had relished spending so much time with his Romanov cousins, and had been particularly entranced by Alix's youngest daughter, Anastasia: 'Spent one week with Alexis before ill . . . Ate together all the time. He got ill during time I was there . . . I saw Anastasia in Spala every day. She was impulsive and energetic all the time. She liked jokes. Her character was quite different from the others.'

For some days, the Tsar's diary entries echoed Irène's, continuing to focus on hunting. He made no mention of his son's condition until

One of Alix's elaborately decorated cards for Irène, with a photograph of Alexis,
in 1912, aged eight.

October 5th, when it appeared that Alexis was getting better: 'We spent an unhappy day today – poor Alexei has been suffering continually now for a few days from internal bleeding. This is the first time it has happened in Belovezh. Prof Fyodoroff arrived yesterday. Thank God today he found a certain improvement.' His account of the day concluded characteristically: 'During dinner the balalaikas played.'

Despite these respites, Alexis remained seriously ill. His predicament became so dire that priests were summoned to deliver the last rites. It was finally decided that Rasputin must be contacted. It is unclear who made the decision. Alix and her friend Anna Vyrubova must have reached an agreement before a telegram was dispatched to Rasputin in Siberia. The two replies from the 'Man of God' came immediately: 'The little one will not die' . . . 'Do not let the doctors bother him too much.' The boy started to improve the day the telegrams arrived. Alix was convinced that Rasputin had saved her son's life.

When the Tsar referred to his son's recovery, he made no reference to Rasputin: 'Today thank God an improvement appeared in the condition of dear Alexis's health . . . After this [communion] Alexis spent the day completely calm and cheerful. We all took heart. In the afternoon I took a good walk with Irène and all the daughters in the 'zelen' woods, while the Suite went shooting in the wild boar park.'

Alix's three sisters were horrified by her strengthened belief in Rasputin. Ella would have been additionally upset that her own offers to help had been ignored.

The Tsar was pleased to revert to more mundane activities, several involving Irène. On October 13th, he wrote that he went with Irène to the station to see Sigismund off.

Upon her return to Hemmelmark, Irène made it clear she would not forget the dramas at Spala. Her birthday greetings to Alix's daughter, Olga, contain yet more weighty, Queen Victoria-style instructions: 'Well you are getting on, Olga dear, in age and wisdom and hope you will be of real and great help to your dear Parents now that they are in such anxiety about dear Alexis – you will I am sure be able to help them in every possible way dear – in thinking for them, what they may like and how you can give them pleasure – even without their noticing that it is you who did it – and thinking for your dear sisters how you can help them if they feel lonely when Mama cannot see them much – you read to them, arrange games for them and see how you can make tiresome walks merry for them, through guessing games etc etc.'

Following the episode in Spala, stories spread swiftly about Alexis's haemophilia. On November 9th, a British medical journal broke the news and the following day the *New York Times* ran the headline: 'Czar's Heir Has Bleeding Disease'.

Irène was horrified to hear that gossip mongers in St Petersburg were talking of nothing else. In her flurry, her English grammar and word order went, once again, awry: 'Today in a Hamburg paper from a Russian source [it is written] that all St Petersburg speaks only about Alexis – it is openly said what he has got and also explained what 'Bluter' [bleeder] means, that it is hereditary & that amongst the relations an older boy has it – which could be easily ascertained,' she complained to Victoria. 'So there the "curse" of our family is known & poor Alicky and we must take the consequences.' The 'older boy' would have been Waldemar.

That Christmas, Irène and her family stayed with Victoria. Irène gave Alix a possibly unwelcome copy of *Treatise on Haemophilia* by J Wickham Legg, containing several strange theories about the disease.

*

Meanwhile, Victoria and Irène were full of their husbands' recent successes. Victoria's Prince Louis had been appointed First Sea Lord; Prince Henry's achievements were more obscure, but one involved conducting talks with the King on behalf of his brother, the Kaiser. At Sandringham, he had boldly presented a hypothesis to the King: if Germany and Austria were to declare war on France and Russia, would Britain help Russia? The King's response was equivocal: 'Undoubtedly yes, under certain circumstances.'

Unfortunately, in reporting this last exchange to his brother, the buoyant Prince Henry was inclined to overlook the 'yes' and focus on 'under certain circumstances'. In this way, Henry began convincing himself – and the Kaiser – that Britain would never wage war against Germany.

In February 1913, Alix and Ella were thrown together for the grand Romanov tercentennial celebrations. It was during these ceremonies that the unkempt Rasputin was particularly conspicuous, hogging places reserved for the smartest dignitaries. But the two sisters were still managing to put aside their differences, with the Tsar recording incessant meetings: 'Feb 16th Ella for lunch, 18th: Ella for dinner, 20th Ella . . . came for lunch.'

Nor were Irène and Victoria forgotten. Alix sent both sisters commemorative pendants decorated with eagles, 'in memory of the 300 years'.

Ever the dutiful aunt, Irène tried to cheer up her niece, Olga, now suffering from chickenpox, with a photograph of a game of tennis as a reminder of happy days in Hesse-Darmstadt: 'I am so sorry you have now alas got chickenpox. It itches so. I hope you will not scratch the places as it leaves marks. This is to remind you of the lawn tennis at Nauheim.'

The sisters' mutual support system remained sound. Ella may have failed in her attempt to help Alix in Spala, but in June 1913, she rushed to England to help Victoria through an operation for appendicitis.

The wires were abuzz as Irène fussed to Victoria from Kiel: 'Your telegram that you are feeling strong for the operation which is to take place on Monday has calmed me somewhat, above all that dear Ella is going to you & can stay with you . . . Really these appendixes are beastly inventions – but you may be sure I would have come to you if I did not know that dear Ella was able to . . . Ever your loving Sis Irène.'

Victoria was thrilled with Ella's visit, making special mention of her nun's habit: 'Kind Ella came all the way from Moscow to visit me, wearing her "Martha and Mary" dress and remained nearly three weeks.' Queen Mary was similarly impressed: 'Only think Ella of Russia had come over here to live with Victoria Battenberg who has just had an operation for appendicitis but is going on well. She looks lovely still but very thin.'

Though Irène was desperate to see both sisters, she restrained herself, insisting to Victoria: 'Keep her [Ella] as long as you can dear, never mind when she comes to me . . . then you must come & have a quiet time at Hemmelmark.'

She was jubilant when Ella eventually arrived, writing to Victoria: 'It is such a joy having dear Ella who looks so well & stood the journey . . . well, having had a good passage . . . Dear Ella was really very happy.'

A striking photograph exists of Ella at Hemmelmark in 1913, seated on a stool on the beach. Her brother Ernie is nearby, smiling, sitting on the sand in a suit, and Prince Henry is lying down on his front, his back to the camera, reading, with a cap on. Ella is looking down, with a subdued smile. She is in her nun's robes, wielding an umbrella.

From Hemmelmark, Ella travelled on to Sweden, where she visited her stepdaughter Maria Pavlovna. The pair had finally established a good relationship, which they were to maintain until Ella's death. Well over her beefs about Ella's 'babies', Maria was now rather in awe of her saintly 'aunty'.

However, within a year of Ella's visit, Maria Pavlovna's marriage was finished. Irène felt guilty for having suggested the match in the first place. Though it was Ella and Victoria who had orchestrated the lead up, she had also been the aunt in whom Maria confided her doubts. In a letter to Victoria, she blamed the break-up on the couple's inability to 'harmonise': 'But what will upset Ella dreadfully is about little Maria & William – she has left Sweden for good & is at Paris. We must all try & see what can be done – she is nervously and physically quite ill. [Maria has] nothing against W. except that they do not harmonise & she cannot bear Sweden. Must try & avoid a scandal & help her.'

She quoted Alix, who blamed William. In a foreshadowing of Irène's later criticism of the Tsar, Alix pronounced William insufficiently 'rough': 'Had William been a real man & not so weak & selfish he would have helped her . . . she lost all control over herself.' Both sisters took a brusque line, with Irène concluding: 'Poor girl with all her selfishness she is going through a hard school now.'

On August 31ˢᵗ 1913, Irène wrote to Queen Mary from Hemmelmark. Much of the letter refers to Mary's son David, the future Edward VIII, but Irène also mentions the ailing Alix: 'My Darling May, I must write and tell you what a pleasure it was for us to have dear David here – so charming and nice he was and I think liked the place. It was only very unfortunate we could not have him for longer as Henry left for Cowes and I am leaving tomorrow for Peterhof to see Alix, returning from there 19ᵗʰ as they start 20ᵗʰ for Livadia, Crimea. She is feeling very poorly again.'

Young David was impressed by Irène's unpretentious husband Prince Henry, writing later: 'He preferred working about his property or in his garage to the more pompous pastimes of those days . . . his great interest in the still comparatively primitive motor-car brought him often to Great Britain.'

While working in his garage, Henry had invented a type of windscreen wiper: it never caught on, perhaps because it had to be manually operated by the front-seat passenger. Victoria retained vivid memories of her brother-in-law's motor car: 'Coming back from Hemmelmark I was frozen up to the waist by the icy wind we faced, while the lower part of my body was being roasted like St Lawrence on the gridiron.'

The visits between the sisters continued through 1913. That summer, Irène made her last trip to Peterhof.

In May, the Tsar, Irène and Prince Henry had been in Germany for the Kaiser's daughter's wedding. But Alix, stricken with illness, had stayed behind.

Before she travelled to Peterhof, Irène was distraught to learn that

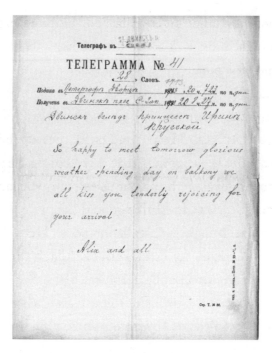

Telegram from Alix to Irène looking forward to seeing her at Peterhof in 1913, 'rejoicing for your arrival'.

Alexis had now suffered a leg injury. 'How is poor Alicky ever to get well with this perpetual wearing anxiety and the sort of character she is – poor girl,' she wrote to Victoria.

As the mother of a haemophiliac, Irène had always taken a special interest in Alexis's elaborate remedies, painstakingly passing them on to Victoria.: 'He . . . has all sorts of electric treatments in the bath too & warm cushions on the knee heated by electricity, [he] will have mudbaths later for the leg . . . as it has Radium in it. [He] Rows in the boat, has massage & lessons in between . . .' There were various props: 'He has ingenious apparatus[es] of every kind. He has a thing to wear that helps him to walk and he can go very fast then, but he hates to wear it before [in front of] people & prefers to hop on one leg . . .'

When Irène arrived in Peterhof, Ella was already in situ; the three sisters had 24 hours together, before Ella left to visit a monastery. It would be their last reunion.

By that time, Rasputin was visiting Alix and her family, at the Alexander Palace, on an almost daily basis. Two nights before Irène's arrival, Rasputin had, once again, apparently healed Alexis. The Tsar wrote in his diary: 'At 7pm Gregorii [Rasputin] arrived, he spent a short while with Alix and Alexis, spoke a little with me and the girls, and then left. Shortly after his leaving, the pain in Alexis's arm began to pass away, he himself calmed down and began to go to sleep.'

Upon her arrival, Irène was installed in what Alix's daughters then referred to as 'Aunt Irène's farm', La Ferme. Though she had witnessed the 'holy man's intervention in Spala, Irène remained as little persuaded by the 'cures' as Ella and Victoria. But the sisters would not have wanted to mar the atmosphere with their irreconcilable differences. It is safe to assume that all three avoided the thorny subject of Rasputin.

Ella left for the Solovetz Monastery the following day. She was accompanied on the trip by her wayward protegé, Felix Yusupov. He proved a predictably unreliable travel companion. 'I lost all sense of time as I strolled about the town [Archangel] and reached the quay to find the ship had left,' he recounted blithely. When he reached the monastery, he was dismayed by the privations of monastic life: 'The food was atrocious – we lived on holy bread and tea' . . . 'The monks were filthy and unkempt . . . as though it was necessary to smell bad to please God.'

At one point, the pair had to crawl through an underground passage to meet a hermit in a cave. Unusually, Ella seems to have enjoyed Yusupov's lampooning. 'Took snapshot of her [Ella] on all fours – to her great amusement,' he wrote.

During another unholy moment, Yusupov took it upon himself to buy a white bear in an auction. The bear was chained up in a cattle truck, coupled to Ella's train. He was amused to see that Ella was the only one to keep cool as the terrified bear emitted 'furious grunts' and 'blood-curdling snarls'. Ella was again 'convulsed with laughter', saying to Yusupov: 'You are quite mad.'

For all her laughter at comic snapshots and bears, Ella was not known for her levity, and the atmosphere at Peterhof may well have lightened following her departure. Certainly, the day after Ella left, Alix and Irène were enjoying meals 'on the sofa', as young Maria gleefully described them in her diary.

The placid Irène by all accounts favoured colouring books and eating meals on the sofa. But the Tsar was, as ever, intent on a packed schedule. Olga wrote that one day she and Irène accompanied him to Tsarskoe Selo in a motor car to inspect the regimental church and the grand palace. It was not until the afternoon that Irène was allowed to enjoy some scarf-dyeing: 'In the afternoon we 5 [all five Romanov children] dyed scarves downstairs on the balcony with Mama and the Aunt . . . There were so many flies, awful,' reported Olga.

Days later, Irène was whisked off again. 'At 9.30am rode to Krasnoye Selo for a public parade . . . Irène attended with Olga and Tatiana. They had lunch on the bluff,' wrote the Tsar. Six days later, he took Irène to review more regiments. Then she was off to an engraving factory.

On the day of her departure, Irène was accompanied to the station by the Tsar and several nieces. But first she enjoyed one final sofa breakfast with all the Imperial children.

Within 24 hours of her return to Hemmelmark, Irène wrote another of her anguished letters to Victoria. For all the young Grand Duchesses' cheery reports of scarf-dyeing and meals on the sofa, Irène was completely thrown by this last visit. She began with a dutiful reference to Victoria's dental troubles: 'I arrived back here yesterday & I hear you have safely got to Wolfsgarten. I hope your jaw where the wisdom tooth was removed hurts no longer . . .'

But then she did not hold back. 'It is with a terribly heavy heart that I left poor Alicky – I see little chance of her ever recovering as things stand now . . . she is slowly going downhill & I fear she will remain an invalid for life – unless Nicky and they all are vigorously shaken up & carried off some way or another. But that – alas – is hopeless.'

Irène had tried to persuade the Tsar to take Alix abroad for more cures; she had no idea that Alix no longer set store by such treatments. 'As I left I said once more to Nicky I had been trying to persuade Alicky to take some waters again . . . he answered with a sad voice and looking depressed: "You know she hates going abroad" . . . She has lost all energy & the perpetual worry and dread that her poor child should be seen as he is abroad is the cause!!!'

She deemed the 'wavering' Tsar to be part of the problem: 'Alas Nicky is no help to her & her dear family. A rough husband I believe is sometimes needful in such cases or at least one who takes her caring in hand . . . but he is not the man for it.'

Was Victoria also in favour of rough husbands? How did she treat Irène's dramatic conclusion that it was 'too late'? She knew that Irène was frequently a-flutter. But she knew that Irène might also be right.

As it happened, Alix enjoyed a burst of slightly better health before the curtain fell. By November, Irène was relaying more upbeat news to Victoria: 'Alicky has written to me [that] her heart is much better but [she] has such bad headaches so that she is unable to read or work for a time.'

A few months later, Irène passed on more good news from Russia: 'Ella wrote when she was there Alicky was SO much better & the little boy walking and running & scarcely dragging his leg.'

Immediately after her final trip to Russia, Irène visited Victoria at her London house on the Mall. Victoria had her own preoccupations at the time, not least an imminent move to Kent House on the Isle of Wight: 'We think that Kent House (a free gift as it would be) will suit us & our children,' she informed her companion, Nona Kerr. 'The Prince & I have lived in it in old times & though the garden was much smaller then, found one was neither overlooked [n]or disturbed by one's neighbours & that we were very comfortable, both summer & winter in the house.'

Irène was the conduit for news between her various nieces in England and Russia. Writing to Alix's daughter, Olga, in St Petersburg, Irène was particularly exercised by a dense fog: 'It was so nice the first night I was in England and I often went to the theatre, Louise too. Alice and children . . . were there still. We motored a great deal and I went shopping and to picture galleries . . .

'Once coming home fr Aunty Victoria in London, we had been to the theatre . . . and I got into a bad fogg so that the Chauffeur could really not see and we had to stop sometimes, once we got on to the trottoire [pavement] . . . There were autos, carriages with horses, omnibuses all round us and tooting away [so as] not to run into each other and one only saw the street lanterns when close under them . . .'

Still, she could not forget that it was only just over a year since those dark days in Spala. 'I am so glad to think that dear Alexis is better and able to walk without the machine sometimes . . . the worst time is always spring and autumn for those things and then it is always good to be in a dry and warm climate, plenty of sun.'

Victoria's daughter, Louise, wrote chattily to Olga's sister, Maria: 'Yesterday Papa, Dick [Louis] and I went to see a very pretty operetta called 'Gipsy Love' at Windsor. The day before Dick and I went to a very good cinematograph performance.'

But war was now imminent and the easy relations between the Hesse

Princesses' children in Russia, Germany and England were about to come to an end.

The beginning of 1914 saw Irène and Henry setting off on a seven-week tour of South America, visiting Argentina, Chile, Brazil and Uruguay. It was meant to be a holiday, but it is likely that Henry had been instructed by his brother, the Kaiser, to forge diplomatic links in the various countries. The German papers were assiduous in listing unending banquets, receptions and exchanges of greetings.

Before setting off, Irène responded to Victoria's thoughtful note about little Heinrich; she had apparently come to see the boy's demise as a release. This might have been as a result of witnessing the suffering of Alexis, or even of her own son, Waldemar. 'It is hard & difficult to think that it is now 10 years ago [that] sweet Baby lay so ill & was taken from us, & was so dear of you to remember it – sometimes I have a terrible longing – but it is better so – & I always see his sweet smile when he was well.'

There were other more humdrum concerns: 'I am still uncertain about keeping my maid – for me excellent but has a horrid temper & rather common nature.'

Writing from the steamer itself, Irène described her grapples with the fellow passengers: 'We are nearing Rio & hope to arrive tomorrow morning . . . many thanks for your dear letters & book that were handed to me at Southampton . . . In spite of the Southern Trade Wind which is most agreeable it is very hot . . . so that one is mostly moist from perspiration. Of course there is a very mixed set on board but [it] is amusing watching the different nationalities . . . Games . . . vary the life on board – the swimming bath too but I did not care to try it . . . In the evenings there is music – a piano, 2 violins & a cello – not too loud & really quite good.'

By the summer of 1914, Irène and Prince Henry were back in Britain and Henry found himself immersed, once again, in weighty discussions with King George V. Prince Henry was clearly a better diplomat than his brother, considered more level-headed and agreeable.

The King now reassured him: 'You can be sure that I and my government will do all we can to prevent a European War, we have no quarrel with anyone and hope we shall remain neutral.'

Upon arriving in Germany, Prince Henry blithely asserted, once again, that the King would not go to war. Later, when he was proven so wrong, he would ruefully admit that he had interpreted the King's 'anxious hope' as a 'definite assurance'.

For some British officials, Prince Henry would always be a puzzle. He and Irène may have been known fondly as '*les aimables*', but the Prince had his detractors, not least the British Prime Minister, Herbert Asquith. When Frederick Ponsonby asked Asquith whether he thought Prince Henry a fool or a knave, the Prime Minister went for a knave. He thought Prince Henry was simply pretending to have friendly intentions towards Britain. But Ponsonby disagreed: 'Personally I came to the conclusion that Prince Henry's visit had in no way been instigated by Tirpitz [Grand Admiral of the German Navy] and that, being a genuine friend of England, he had tried his best to smooth matters. He was a perfectly straightforward man and never gave one the impression of having any Machiavellian cunning.'

*

Victoria swiftly recovered from her appendix operation and the extraction of her wisdom tooth. By the summer of 1914, she was ready for what turned out to be her last trip to Russia. Her plan was to travel to Moscow with her daughter, Louise, then aged 24. The pair would then join Ella for a sort of pilgrimage through Russia and Siberia, before visiting Alix in St Petersburg. They would meet Victoria's husband, Prince Louis, in Russia, at the end of July.

She discussed plans, in faltering Russian, with Alix's 18-year-old daughter Olga; arrangements were now made entirely through Olga. 'What months will you stay in Peterhof this summer? I wish to visit Russia this year, and I hope to see you all again. Louise will be coming with me in July . . . Ask Mama please if it is convenient to receive so many of us and when?'

Alix replied that she could see her sisters only briefly. Had she realised she would be seeing her stalwart Victoria for the last time, her attitude might have been very different.

Ella, Victoria and Louise left Moscow for the Urals at the beginning of July 1914, Ella and her nun companion visiting several religious communities on the way. Louise's diary was bullish: 'She [Ella] can hardly pass a town with a church without thinking she should go to a service . . . the local populations always planned this as the high spot of her visit.' Victoria recalled more conventional attractions: 'Saw Imperial Factory where marbles and precious stones were cut.' Travelling on the Volga was conducted in style, as Louise enthused: 'Such very nice cabins, lots of bathrooms and excellently decorated.'

The trio visited Perm, where Ella took Victoria for a carriage drive around the town. As the sister of the Tsarina, Victoria said she was, mostly, 'hospitably welcomed'.

But in a macabre twist, the itinerary included trips to the two places where Ella and Alix would one day be held captive. As Victoria recalled some years later, of the many convents visited by Ella, 'one . . . was at Alapaevsk, the place in which she was interned in the schoolhouse during the Revolution and from where she was taken out to be murdered.' Both sisters drove past the Ipatiev House, in Ekaterinburg, where Alix would be held captive before being shot.

As chilling, in retrospect, would have been their drive near the Four Brothers mine, where Alix and her family's bodies were first stowed after they were assassinated in July 1918.

It was during a visit to the St Nicholas Monastery, in Belogorsky, that Ella met Father Seraphim, who was to play such an important part in her life and then, crucially, in her afterlife.

*

Victoria and Ella were still in Siberia when they heard that their cousin, the Kaiser, had declared war on Russia. Ella was, at this point, visiting the Verkhoturye Monastery, where the young Rasputin had begun his heady spiritual journey. Victoria received a frantic telegram from her husband, Prince Louis, begging her to return to Britain as soon as possible. There was no question of his joining them in St Petersburg.

Alix and her daughters were having dinner at the Alexander Palace when they heard the terrible news. They all wept.

Victoria and Ella travelled immediately to Peterhof, where they met Alix. In the panic of the moment, Victoria handed Alix the jewellery she had brought with her, for safe keeping. Alix had the jewellery packed in a special case and sent to the Imperial Office. It was never to be seen again. 'My mother and I left all our jewels we had brought with us for the official parties which we were expecting to attend later on in Moscow and St Petersburg, with Aunt Alix,' wrote Louise ruefully. 'All Mama's heirlooms – tiaras, big necklaces and bracelets – were left there in the great jewel box which we had brought with us and we had no idea that we should never see them again and presumably the Bolshevik government will one day sell them.'

After nearly three weeks of travelling in Russia, Victoria left for Britain. Alix and her two elder daughters came to see her off, as they had seen Irène off the previous year. 'Alix, Olga & Tatiana came to see Ella and me on the following forenoon and I spent the next day with her and her family at Peterhof,' recounted Victoria. '[Alix] came to see us before we left and, with loving forethought, equipped us with thick coats . . . for the sea journey.

'Left afternoon of August 7th. I little dreamt that it was the last time I should see my sisters again.'

9

'Don't laugh at silly old wify.'
Alix

Victoria arrived back in Britain ten days later. Her life was altered soon after, as her husband, Prince Louis, found himself obliged to resign from the Navy. He wrote starkly: 'My [German] birth and parentage have the effect of impairing in some respects my usefulness on the Board of the Admiralty.'

After 46 years of service in the Royal Navy, he was mortified by suggestions that he could be involved in any disloyalty. But he never lost his sense of humour. Years later, he had a droll exchange with Sir Henry Wilson, the diplomat who had so relished his tennis parties in Darmstadt. Sir Henry accosted him in Pall Mall: 'I'm uncommonly glad to see you,' he said. 'I heard you were in the tower.' 'Behind the times as usual Henry,' countered Prince Louis. 'I was shot last Thursday.'

Victoria was less forgiving, pronouncing darkly: 'The wise man . . . must . . . yield to the "man in the street" and the ignorance of the People.' She never trusted the First Lord of the Admiralty, Winston Churchill, after he had failed to return one of her books. Could she herself have been at fault? Though she condemned gossip, her reputation as a chatterbox never dimmed. There may have been fears that, with war pending, she had become a security risk.

Victoria and Prince Louis retired, with their son Louis, to the Isle of

Wight. It was there that Victoria was to envisage having Alix and her nieces to live with her in exile.

The war brought an end to the four Princesses' easy correspondence and regular meetings. On August 4th, three days after Germany's declaration of war against Russia, Britain had declared war on Germany. Irène's country was now ranged against the countries of all three of her sisters. In recognition of their changed circumstances, Victoria and Irène exchanged maids. Victoria sent Irène her German maid, Eugenie, while Irène sent Victoria her English maid, Knight. The English maid gave Victoria a bald description of her former employers: 'Irène has lots to do & is well though grown thin. Henry evidently lives on board his flagship but is fairly often at home.' It is to be hoped that Knight was not the maid Irène once complained to Victoria about, with the horrid temper and common nature.

While Victoria's husband was sidelined, Irène's husband rose ever higher, now appointed Grand Admiral of the Prussian Navy. Confusingly, he retained several of his British appointments too, remaining Vice Admiral of the Royal Navy and a member of the Order of the Garter. In 1915, he was expelled from the Order of the Garter; his Royal Victorian Chain was also revoked.

Victoria and Irène found themselves in the painful position of having sons in opposing navies. Irène's son Sigismund joined the German Navy, while Waldemar drove ambulances. Victoria's son George was already in the Royal Navy; Louis would join him two years later, in 1916.

After her initial horror at the declaration, Alix was oddly fired up, just as she had been during the Russo-Japanese War. She and the Tsar were briefly riding a wave of popularity and were cheered by patriotic crowds in Moscow.

In the tranquillity of the Isle of Wight, Victoria would have struggled to process Alix's giddy news, relieved to come across glancing references to

Ella: 'Awfully busy . . . Blessed two hundred sisters, going to the war . . . Fastening [religious] images on to strings whenever free. Returning over St Serge and there part from Ella . . .' she wrote, before adding, with less brio: 'Having bad health makes all more difficult and stops me from doing many things one would have wished to.'

Through the war years, letters exchanged between the Hesse siblings based in Germany and their three sisters abroad could take up to three months to arrive. One rather laborious process involved Daisy of Connaught taking notes from German relatives, copying them out and posting them within Allied territory. She was then married to the Crown Prince of Sweden and so was on neutral ground.

While troops built up on the Western front, Alix fretted about Ernie's birthday. 'Today is our Ernie's birthday, the first time in his life that three sisters can give him no news,' she complained to Victoria. 'How lonely he must be away from his dear ones . . . hating the war . . .'

There was no let-up in the sisters' jostles over who was helping whom. Alix was convinced that her Moscow visit had restored Ella: 'Glad for dear Ella's sake that we have been here to cheer her up . . . She has any amount to do, is energetic, here there and everywhere.'

Alix may have felt that she was the one cheering Ella, but she herself was the one who appeared careworn. She had not aged well and now looked older than Ella. The French Ambassador, Maurice Paléologue, Ella's long-time admirer, saw both sisters in Moscow during a service at the beginning of the war. He watched them kissing the figure of the Virgin of Vladimir and was particularly struck by Ella's grace. He described how Alix and her daughters made a 'clumsy attempt' at the kissing, while Ella managed it in 'one supple easy and queenly movement'.

The two sisters in Russia still managed their intermittently cordial relations, with Alix, at one point, suggesting Ella accompany the Tsar on a visit to Lvov (now Lviv). The Tsar's sister, Grand Duchess Olga, who also accompanied them, wrote movingly of their reception: 'The people gave us a tumultuous welcome and flowers were thrown from every window . . . it was for the very last time that I sensed that mysterious bond between my family and the people.'

Certainly, Ella would not experience such a tumultuous welcome ever again. Anti-German feelings were soon rife in Russia, with both Hesse sisters in the firing line.

A story circulated about a general who came across the little Tsarevich, Alexis, in tears. When the General asked: 'What's wrong?' Alexis replied: 'When the Russians are beaten, Papa cries. When the Germans are beaten Mama cries. When am I to cry?' The Tsar himself was succumbing to prejudice; when he caught Alexis throwing snowballs at his victims from behind, he snapped: 'Leave that sort of behaviour to the Germans.'

In the fever of nationalism, St Petersburg was renamed Petrograd. The British diplomat, Robert Bruce Lockhart, registered anti-German feeling extending even to pianos: 'Hooligans sacked the leading piano store of Moscow. Bechsteins, Blüthners, grand pianos, baby grands and uprights were hurled one by one from the various storeys to the ground.'

Letters with German stamps were regarded with suspicion. The Holy Synod considered banning Christmas trees because they were a German tradition. Alix was enraged, complaining to her husband: 'I am going to make a row.' The Romanovs' English nanny, Margaretta Eager, had remarked on the German flavour of Christmas, before the war, at the Alexander Palace, where Alix would decorate an elaborate children's tree 'fixed into a musical box which played the German Xmas hymn and turned round and round'. The hymn was probably 'O Tannenbaum', the same melody as the socialist 'Red Flag'.

Alix reported to Victoria, via a letter that got through, that she and Ella had spent a companionable Christmas together in Moscow. Those 'hard words' exchanged over Rasputin were, momentarily, a thing of the past.

Around the new year, Victoria managed a chatty note to Alix's daughter Maria, then 15, passing on news of her son Louis [Dickie], who apparently never lost his soft spot for the Grand Duchess. Victoria was convinced that the war would be over within months: 'I hope I shall see you all again in the New Year when the war is over for a little longer than in this year. Dick is beginning to drive our motor quite well, unluckily for us he goes to Dartmouth when these holidays are over, it would have been so nice if he could have remained on at Osborne a bit longer.'

Alix, meanwhile, boasted to Miss Jackson of tireless visits to 'heaps of hospitals'. Making several references to Ella, she presented the two sisters, once again, as firmly bonded: 'I cannot tell you how deeply touched I was that you sent Ella and me those books and we thank you heartily as also for your dear letter . . .

'I visited hospitals in 8 towns with my big girls . . . The result has been that my heart is SO bad again and such weakness – I utterly over tired myself. Nothing is more tiring than visiting heaps of hospitals and speaking by the hour to the poor wounded. So I have not been able to work in the hospital now, which is a great grief for me, as I love the work and find consolation in nursing the sick and binding up their wounds.'

Two months on, Alix sent further garbled updates: 'My darling Madgie, I hope this letter will reach you by Easter. There is so much to do, tho' I am lying [down] since a week again . . . overtired my heart and strength – so despairing when one wants to be useful, not only with the brain.'

Alix's war spirit was further compromised as she succumbed to facial neuralgia as well as sciatica. She continued to visit hospitals, but had to be carried upstairs. Her lady-in-waiting, Baroness Buxhoeveden, wrote that she disliked this procedure, averse to making a spectacle of herself.

Victoria was disturbed but perhaps not surprised by Alix's bulletins, as she'd always been brutally honest about her health. In March 1915, she was once again complaining about her heart, but insisting it was all worth it: 'The wounded's grateful smiles are a recompense for every fatigue.'

Alix's altruism echoed Ella's words about her 'invalids' at Illinskoye: 'One forgets everything in looking after those heroes and their appalling wounds,' she had written to Ernie.

In 1915, the Tsarina visited a hospital in Pskov, where Ella's stepdaughter, Maria Pavlovna, was working as a nurse. Maria's marriage to William of Sweden, so assiduously endorsed by all four Hesse sisters, had been formally dissolved the previous year.

Maria Pavlovna, once so keen on Aunt Alix, now compared her unfavourably to Ella: 'In contrast to her sister, the Empress, my aunt clearly understood that she had no right to bury herself entirely in her own affairs and preoccupations.' She viewed the Tsarina's hospital visits as a disaster. Alix's insistence on wearing her much loved nurse's uniform proved a particular bugbear, as the soldiers were dismayed by what they saw as a demotion. She recalled their disappointment: 'The Tsarina was just a nurse.' Then there were her poor communication skills: 'There was something in her, eluding definition, that prevented her communicating her own genuine feeling and from comforting the person she addressed. Although she spoke Russian quite correctly and almost without any foreign accent, the men did not appear to understand her.'

While Alix was carrying out as many hospital visits as her ailments would permit, Ella was running her own hospital and a convent as well as sending churches on wheels to the front. But their good works could not stem the growing anti-German prejudice. Although Maria Pavlovna had defended Alix's Russian, it was generally held that both sisters had strong foreign accents – sounding either too German or too English. And neither liked being corrected.

Throughout 1915, rumours abounded that both sisters were hiding their brother, Ernie, on their various properties. It was said that Ernie had spent a week with Alix in a secret room at the Alexander Palace. There were also stories that he had been concealed in Ella's convent. The Tsar's brother, Grand Duke Michael, received alarming reports from his wife in Moscow: 'They have broken all the windows of the Nikolaevski Palace, since a rumour was let out to the drunken crowd that Grand Duchess Elizaveta Feodorovna[Ella] was hiding her brother there.'

In fact, Ernie remained in Germany, receiving the occasional agonised outburst from 'Sunny', as he still called Alix: 'My hair is also changing colour fast – such misery as one daily sees & lives through . . . I think our prisoners are also at Friedberg – how strange all is in life. Thank God we do not know what lies before us & can only hope and trust in God's infinite mercy . . . Oh what pain!'

Alix was surprised to hear from her companion, Anna Vyrubova, that Ella's car had been stoned. Ella had never mentioned the incident. Both sisters shrank from admitting the extent of their unpopularity. Alix wrote a furious note to her husband: 'Could it be native population so wrong and wicked? Felix [Yusupov] told Anya that they threw stones at Ella's carriage and spat at her but she did not wish to speak to us about it'. Yusupov, who set such store by Ella's popularity, was dumbfounded.

Alix may have felt some sympathy for Ella but she was still sensitive about the way her elder sister wielded power. She was put out by Ella's continuing campaign for the promotion of a particular cleric, dismissing him to her husband as 'just one of Ella's not good, bigoted clique'. At the end of this particular rant, Alix acknowledged that she herself was being bossy, but could still not resist a further dig at Ella: 'Reading this letter you will say – one sees she is Ella's sister.'

Which of the two sisters the Tsar found more forceful is open to question. It was Ella, after all, who had orchestrated his betrothal; after the marriage, he had found himself contending with both. During the periods when Alix fell out with Ella, it was perhaps a relief for him to have just one Hesse sister on his case.

While still angry about the behaviour of the 'native population', Alix was even more exasperated by the Germans. In May 1915 she complained to Victoria: 'How too outrageous the sinking of the Lusitania. There are things one cannot understand.' She continued with news of her daughters' nursing trials: 'An officer died on the table. A very difficult operation succeeded, then the heart gave way. Hard such moments, but my girlies must know life, and we go through all together.'

She raged against the German '*Vorsprung*' [headstart] which had assured them superior equipment and tactics. This was the very subject Prince Henry and the King had once discussed. Which country was the more prepared for war? 'They [the Germans] are advancing at great speed. Our misery, the lack of rifles and heavy artillery like theirs . . . Will England and France never help us? . . . Must hope for an early, cold winter. We were not prepared for war and they were thoroughly and they are splendid at organising things, laying lines and so on, but God will help.'

In December 1915, the Tsar decided to base himself at the Russian front. This left Alix appearing to be in charge of the government in Petrograd. The decision would prove calamitous.

The idea of having the German-born Tsarina ruling Russia was abhorrent to the majority of Russians; the idea of Alix ruling alongside the ever-present Rasputin was even more intolerable. The pair would soon be held to account for all the country's misfortunes. Ella's young stepson, Dmitri, was among those who tried to dissuade the Tsar from leaving the capital.

As the news of the Tsar's departure filtered through, Alix's sisters looked on in horror. All three of them in their respective ways had warned

Alix about Rasputin's influence, and their hearts must have sunk as they saw their little sister stepping up now with that 'horrid man' at her side.

As for Alix herself, no longer plagued by the thought of not being clever enough, she felt she was more than ready. 'I long to put my nose into everything – to wake up people, put order into all & unite all forces,' she wrote to the Tsar, issuing him with firm instructions: 'Show your fist', 'Be the Master & Lord' . . . 'Don't laugh at silly old wify, but she has "trousers" on unseen.' She instructed the Tsar to use Rasputin's comb, insisting it would 'bring its little help'.

By December 27th of the following year, Alix's links to Rasputin were being mentioned in a dispatch from the Russian military HQ at Mogilev to the King's private secretary, Lord Stamfordham in Britain. One general warned that the hostility was 'getting worse every day . . . and even the cabmen talk about her. The mistake they make is in thinking that she herself is pro German – that is not so – but the mix up of influences through her special lady in waiting [Anna Vyrubova] who in turn is under the influence of that blackguard Rasputin is what causes the trouble and the idea that she is playing us in with the Germans'.

In December 1915, another family friend appeared to have got mixed up in war tactics: the larger-than-life Mlle Wassiltchikov, whom Victoria had met with Ella at Illinskoye, and then again in Venice, and described as 'the life and soul of the party'.

Now settled in Austria, Mlle Wassiltchikov turned up in Petrograd with open letters to the Tsar and Tsarina suggesting that Russia make a separate peace with Germany. She had apparently come at the behest of Ernie. '[She] went to Darmstadt at the invitation of the Grand Duke of Hesse, and had been sent by him to Petrograd, charged with the mission of inducing the Emperor to conclude peace,' recalled the Ambassador, George Buchanan.

'She was empowered to say that the Emperor William was prepared to grant Russia most advantageous terms; the English had already made overtures to Germany for a separate peace; and that a reconciliation between Russia and Germany was necessary for dynastic reasons. Mlle Wassiltchikov also carried two open letters to Nicky and Alix.'

The furious Tsar threatened to consign Mlle Wassiltchikov to a convent. According to Baroness Buxhoeveden, Alix was also horrified, refusing to have anything to do with Ella's one-time friend. As the Baroness reported: 'Wassiltchikoff [was] sent off to her estates and ordered to stay there until the end of the war.'

Victoria may have joined Alix in her heartfelt Christmas plea – 'Oh how one longs for 1916 to bring us Allies glorious victories and peace!' – but a glorious victory for the Allies would, of course, leave Irène and Ernie on the losing side. Had the two sisters forgotten Irène's son, Sigismund, in the German Navy?

Shortly after the beginning of the war, the sisters had begun arguing over the treatment of prisoners. Alix was enraged by claims in the press that German prisoners were being treated badly. Victoria was, as so often, on the receiving end: 'The amount of lies printed in the German papers . . . it is sickening,' Alix fumed. 'The fright of the German prisoners that they are going to be shot and noses and ears chopped off, and their surprise and contentment when they are well treated and fed, are great.'

A year later, Alix was back on the attack, this time regarding the state of Russian prisoners returning from Germany. She complained to Victoria that the prisoners were 'sad to look at. Clothes in an awful state, faces of those that had no arms, covered with crusts of dirt, thin and famished looking but intensely happy to be back'.

Ella was dragged in, now accused of cossetting German prisoners in her convent, which she strenuously denied. In May 1915, the Tsar's brother, Grand Duke Michael, received more disturbing news from his wife: 'They are saying there is a terrible bitterness against Elizaveta Feodorovna [Ella], everyone knows how she is connected to the German prisoners.'

At the beginning of 1916, Alix attempted to send food to Russian prisoners in Germany. This project had to be scuppered, she claimed, because 'they [the Germans] eat it all up'.

Irène, late to the fray, sent complaints to Alix, via the Swedish Red Cross, regarding the treatment of German prisoners. The Tsar made inquiries about German prisoners' working conditions, after which Alix sent an official, presumably frosty, riposte.

Alix then deluged Victoria with details of the lives of German prisoners working on a railway line: 'What one says about Murman railway is untrue. We have just seen people we sent to see all. The German prisoners won't eat cabbage, therefore fall ill more than ours of Zinga [scurvy]. They get 60 roubles a month for their work on the line, as they do it well. Out of that they eat for 40 roubles – have bed, huts and barracks. In summer they sleep well out of doors.'

Victoria was spared nothing as Irène and Alix carried on sparring. It is hard to believe that, barely three years previously, the two sisters had been companionably dyeing scarves and eating 'on the sofa' at Peterhof.

It was clear that Victoria was finding the war-time strictures oppressive. As she wrote: 'It is always a bit depressing getting news and letters in this way & knowing nothing will ever be the same again, except our personal affection for our relations. You know how wholly English we are & yet can understand these other feelings.'

The complications surrounding nationality could never quite be put aside. The three sisters who had left Germany – Victoria, Ella and Alix – had all tried, at various points, to downplay and even shake off their German roots.

They prized their strong British affiliations, not least as Queen Victoria's granddaughters.

But, by this time, Alix was failing to forge links even with the British community in Petrograd. That summer of 1916, Miss Dunnett, an English governess, went to a sewing party, organised by the Tsarina, at the Catherine Palace. Alix, she reported, was 'awfully stiff'.

Meanwhile, during dinners at the British Embassy in Petrograd, speculation had started about whether both the Emperor and Empress would be killed; 'or only the latter'.

The Ambassador, George Buchanan, once so friendly with the sisters in Darmstadt, was now regarded with suspicion at the Russian Court. In 1916, he was invited to the Alexander Palace to watch films highlighting the contribution of the British Army and Navy during the war: 'But though I sat between the Emperor and Empress during the representation, which lasted till past 8 o'clock, I was not invited to remain for dinner.'

In Britain, Victoria had some pressing domestic concerns of her own, having sought the King's permission for her elder son, George, to marry Nadejda Mikhailovna de Torby. The bride's father was Grand Duke Michael Mikhailovich, 'Mishe Mishe', the man who had so alarmed Queen Victoria when he was linked to Irène. Alix would probably have disapproved of Mishe Mishe too because, three years before she married Nicky, he had been banned from Russia on account of his morganatic marriage. The young couple married seven months later, at the Russian Embassy in London, the union marking a Russian-British alliance of sorts.

Over the years, the three elder sisters' worries about Alix had centred on her physical health. But as the hard year of 1916 wore on, they were increasingly concerned about her mental state. They were painfully aware of her growing isolation.

Victoria flinched as Alix alienated Irène with her rages about prisoners.

She and Irène would both have noted her chilling indifference to the fortunes of their sons. Alix had responded bleakly to the news of young George's forthcoming wedding: 'Seems quite improbable. He is all of 23 and has been at sea all the time.' In another letter, passing on news of Irène's sons to the Tsar, Alix's tone was throwaway: 'Bobby [Sigismund] will be promoted officer in the summer (he is Tatiana's age), Toddy [Waldemar] was yesterday 27. She [Irène] says the boy [Sigismund] has seen already many trying things – was he out on a ship, I do not know.'

She had made enemies of both the Tsar's sisters. Grand Duchess Xenia had long been openly critical of Rasputin; his other sister, Grand Duchess Olga, had upset Alix by getting involved with a lowly colonel. As Alix huffed to Nicky: 'I cannot tell you the bitter pain it causes me for you. She, an Emperor's daughter and sister! Before the country at such a time when the dynasty is going through heavy trials & many counter currants [sic] are at work.'

In her turn, Grand Duchess Olga was infuriated, writing to her sister from Kiev: 'I forgot to tell you in my last letter that I got one from Alix. She asks me where & when I intend getting married. Fancy?! She hopes it will be quietly somewhere in the country.'

Alix had occasional intimations of her jeopardy. In a note to Victoria, she wished again for peace: 'How one longs for this terrible war to end – two years' strain. Such awful losses all over the world.'

As for Alix and Ella's relationship, while the war raged around them, they managed to paper over some of their disagreements. But these would never be properly resolved. One central problem remained their different approach to spirituality: 'The two sisters did not get on at all well,' wrote Felix Yusupov. 'Both were converts to the Orthodox Church, both were fervent believers, but each understood our religion in a different way, the Tsarina was inclined to follow a complicated, dangerous road to perfection: she dipped into mysticism and was led astray. The Grand Duchess chose the true and narrow path, that of humility and love.'

The Tsar's nephew, Prince Dmitri, agreed, writing: 'The Empress favoured the more mystical approach while the Grand Duchess chose the path of humility and good works. The two sisters could not have been less alike . . . There was a pleasantness and warmth with Aunt Ella but uneasiness when with Aunt Alix.'

Ella's niece Maria Pavlovna noted their estrangement: 'The relationship between the two sisters . . . gradually cooled and the Empress soon began to feel oppressed in my Aunt's presence.'

Perhaps Ella could have borne Alix's 'mystical approach' had it not led so directly to Rasputin; perhaps she could have borne Rasputin had he not been so present.

Yusupov characterised Ella's attitude towards Rasputin as excoriating, reporting that she saw him as a 'a fiend and an imposter' and 'did not conceal her opinion from her sister'. Rasputin, meanwhile, had no time either for Ella or for Yusupov's mother, Zinaida, who was her close friend. Yusupov would never forget Rasputin's snarls: 'I don't like her, your mother . . . she's a friend of Lizbeth [Ella]. They're both digging pits for me . . . The Empress has told me time and again that they're my worst enemies.'

In fact, it was Yusupov who was digging the pit, conspiring with Ella's stepson, Dmitri, to murder Rasputin. Yusupov had convinced himself that Rasputin was lobbying for Alix to become regent and then sign a separate peace with Germany.

Any affection Yusupov had ever had for Alix was long gone; he now insisted that she didn't speak Russian properly and didn't know the Russian people. He had no truck with Rasputin's gushing prognosis: 'The Tsarina is a very wise woman, a second Catherine the Great.'

In December 1916, Ella went to the Alexander Palace to renew her warnings against Rasputin. She implored Alix to send Rasputin to Siberia: as long as he was at court, the public would believe that he was in charge. After receiving short shrift, Ella suggested to Alix: 'Perhaps it would have been better if I had not come?' 'Yes', replied Alix. 'She drove me away like a dog!' Ella cried afterwards. 'Poor Nicky, poor Russia!' The two sisters, once so close, never saw each other again.

*

The murder of Rasputin took place on December 30ᵗʰ 1916. Felix Yusupov lured him to his residence, Moika Palace, with the promise of meeting his beautiful wife, Princess Irina. Yusupov's fellow conspirator's were Grand Duke Dmitri and a highly eccentric minister called Vladmir Purishkevich. The story was that Rasputin ate cakes and drank wine laced with cyanide, and that, when the poison had no effect, Yusupov panicked, shooting his victim at point-blank range. This also failed and Rasputin allegedly ran outside into a snowy yard yelling: 'I'm telling the Tsarina everything.' He was shot again and appeared, finally, to die. The conspirators tied him up and loaded him into a car, before throwing him into the Neva River, where he disappeared under the ice. One of his boots emerged several days before his body was found. Water was detected in his lungs, indicating that he had, in the end, drowned.

The murder sealed the breach between the sisters. As Alix saw it, Ella's stepson, Dmitri, had teamed up with her former protegé, Yusupov, to assassinate the only man who could heal her son. She ordered that Dmitri and Yusupov be confined to their houses. She refused to see Yusupov.

Ambassador George Buchanan's daughter, Meriel, wrote that Alix had long harboured reservations regarding Dmitri, accusing him of 'scandalling about'. Now, added Meriel, Alix wanted Dmitri to 'suffer the extreme penalty'. Yusupov concurred, writing: 'The wrath of the Empress seemed directed chiefly upon Dmitri – she was enraged by what she called Dmitri's ingratitude in relation to her and to the Emperor.' Dmitri himself was full of muddled regrets, even toying with shooting himself.

When Alix heard that Ella had sent an effusive telegram to Rasputin's other avowed enemy, Yusupov's mother, she was furious. 'My prayers and thoughts are with you all,' Ella had written. 'God bless your dear son for his patriotic act.' She had also signed a petition asking for clemency for the two main plotters.

The death of Rasputin marked the final falling-out between Ella and Alix. In the days after the murder, Ella made several attempts to bridge the divide but these came to nothing. 'Grand Duchess Ella sent her sister several sacred icons from the shrine of Saratov,' reported Alix's companion Anya Vyrubova. 'The Empress, without even looking at them, ordered them sent back to the convent of the Grand Duchess in Moscow.'

Alix was inclined, however, to try and make peace with Ella's stepdaughter, Maria Pavlovna, for whom she retained a strong affection. But these attempts were equally doomed. Maria had been horrified by Alix's harsh attacks on her adored brother Dmitri. She was not won over by Alix's peace offering, a small wooden icon of the Virgin Mary. An accompanying note, with assurances of her 'unchanged feelings' towards the young woman she had once called her eldest daughter, was no more effective. Maria sent Alix a curt reply.

As for Victoria, she was initially relieved to hear of the murder. 'I do so hope that this time the news of Rasputin's death is true, though poor Alix will probably fall ill at it,' she wrote to her companion Nona. 'I fear that among the masses in Russia she is hated, chiefly due to that vile creature . . .'

But she soon began to have doubts about the details surrounding Rasputin's death. It was said that Yusupov had shot Rasputin in his side, while his victim was praying. Victoria found it hard to believe that the fey Yusupov was capable of such a murder. She felt the more likely culprit was Yusupov's rough-hewn father. As she wrote to Nona: 'If either Yusupov had a direct share in the killing of that brute, I feel sure it was the father, Felix is not made of stern or violent stuff.'

Ella was also amazed by Yusupov's involvement. Weeks afterwards, she wrote to the Tsar: 'I return and find out that Felix killed him, my little Felix, whom I had known as a child, who had been afraid to kill a living creature all his life and did not want to become a military man so as not to shed blood.' She closed with misplaced jubilation: 'Finally a black wall between us and our Sovereign disappeared, finally we will all hear, feel him for who he is.'

Rumours now spread that Rasputin's most likely murderer was a British Secret Service agent. George Buchanan assured the Tsar that there were no Englishmen involved. Was Buchanan himself suspected? Buchanan had in fact met Yusupov months before the murder, in April 1916, but this was probably just a coincidence. The meeting, in the Crimea, involved a bizarre ritual in which Tatar villagers presented the Buchanan family with bread and salt. The headman had expressed his admiration for England.

When Buchanan eventually returned to London, he received a kind and gracious telegram from the King and was invited to lunch at Buckingham Palace.

Ten days after the murder, it was already clear that the death of Rasputin had done nothing to improve Alix's popularity. The Tsar's sister, Grand Duchess Olga, wrote from Kiev to her sister Xenia: 'Vera Titova returned from Petersburg full of gossip about all the past and last events & [people] say awful things about sister-in-law [Alix] and the poor dear children.'

*

For Buchanan, Alix became the Mouse that Roared. During his days at Darmstadt, he had been so taken with the shy, young Princess Alix; but his view of her, after the Revolution, was damning: 'Her fatal misconception of the meaning of the crisis through which Russia was passing made her impose on the Emperor Ministers who had no other recommendation than that they were prepared to carry out her reactionary policy.'

Back in England, Victoria followed news of the growth of civil unrest in Petrograd with alarm. When the British Government first hit upon the idea of sending Sir Henry Wilson's mission to Russia, Victoria's husband Prince Louis was mooted as the ideal person to talk to the Tsar. But Louis was rejected by Lloyd George, not least because of his German origins.

When Sir Henry was in the end dispatched, he was tasked with establishing Russia's wartime needs, but also with drawing out the Imperial couple. 'The Emperor and Empress, though very pleasant, made it quite clear that they would not tolerate any discussion of Russian internal politics,' he reported being told by a fellow delegate. In the end, he found that Alix preferred to discuss the 'dear old home'.

How responsible was Alix for the growing unrest? She was still dominating her husband, wearing her 'trousers unseen' and instructing the Tsar to 'be the master'. His mild defences were certainly too little, too late. 'What you wrote about being firm – the master – is perfectly true,' he once replied meekly. 'I do not forget it, be sure of that, but I need not bellow at the people right and left every moment.'

Weeks before the revolution, the Tsarina was still denouncing the interfering Russian Parliament, the Duma, to 'Hubby'. Her strident views were interspersed with random news about a kitten climbing into the hearth.

It fell to Romanov relations to take her to task. The Tsar's brother-in-law, Grand Duke Alexander, 'Sandro', had once been one of Ella's husband's fiercest critics. He now pleaded with Alix for a full one and a half hours: 'Please Alix leave the cares of the State to your husband,' he implored. 'You have no right to drag your relatives with you down a precipice.'

Grand Duke Serge's niece, Marie of Romania, described a rum state of affairs: 'Tsarskoe Selo was looked upon as a sick man refusing every doctor and every help. And it was always Alix's name which was mentioned as the chief stumbling block.'

But it was not in the Tsar's nature to bellow, or to be the 'rough' sort of husband that Irène had favoured. Victoria's grandson, Prince Philip, later maintained that the Tsar's small stature had been a factor in the revolution: 'The trouble with Nicholas II was he wasn't a big man. He didn't fill the picture that people expected. Russian leaders always appear to be twice life size.' Nicky was about 5' 6" and Alix appeared taller than him, which may well have been one of the causes of her problems.

Whatever Alix's ultimate responsibility, the blame for Tsar Nicholas II's final abdication in March 1917 and the ensuing horrors was to be laid firmly at her door. In Britain, Queen Mary protested to Stamfordham: 'What mischief the Emp. A is making in Russia, she must be insane to act as she is doing, why do stupid women have such a bad influence on men?' King George echoed his wife in his diary: 'I fear Alicky is the cause of it all & Nicky has been weak.' Victoria's husband, Prince Louis, had always deemed Alix 'mad'. Now he wrote to their daughter, Louise: 'No news from Russia of our dear ones. It is terrible and really all A[aunt] Alix's fault.'

Banished to Persia, Ella's stepson, Dmitri, joined in the attacks. In a letter to his co-conspirator Yusupov, he wrote: 'The final catastrophe has been brought about by the wilful and short-sighted obstinacy of a woman. It has naturally swept away Tsarskoe Selo, and all of us at one stroke.'

In the Kremlin, the cross that Ella had erected in memory of Grand Duke Serge would be among the first statues pulled down by the revolutionaries.

10

*'Forgive them for they know not
what they do.'*
Ella

The Imperial Family was incarcerated at the Alexander Palace for several months. Their spirits could not have been improved by soldiers marching past the gates playing the 'Marseillaise' and Chopin's 'Funeral March'. The funeral march was what the four sisters' mother, Alice, had been playing before little Frittie fell from the window to his death.

The only communication that the captives received from outside Russia was a telegram from Queen Mary, inquiring after the Tsarina's health. The Provisional Government leader, Alexander Kerensky, delivered her message to Alix, adding pointedly that: 'Relatives abroad were taking a keen interest in their welfare.' This was a needling reference to her German relations. Alix responded crisply: 'There is nothing German about me. I am English by education and English is my language.' In happier days, she had kept her husband awake at night as she tucked into English biscuits.

She drove her point home with an instruction to her ladies-in-waiting: 'You Russian ladies don't know how to be useful. When I was a girl my grandmother, Queen Victoria, showed me how to make a bed – I'll teach you . . .'

Writing to her friend Nona, Victoria clutched at straws, hoping the Tsar's abdication might benefit Alix: 'I am very grateful that Nicky has abdicated for himself & the boy, for no-one can tell how far the revolution will go . . . Had Alix still been Empress they might have fallen on her . . . I hope the rumour that they will be sent to the Crimea is true & that later on they can leave Russia.'

Victoria would have been ecstatic if she'd heard of plans to rescue Alix and her family and bring them to England. King George had agreed that they should come, and Kerensky had arranged for the family to be taken to Murmansk, from where they would be picked up by a British cruiser. The Imperial couple briefly embraced the idea; the Tsar listed the things they'd need for an English exile while Alix constantly talked of Osborne. But the plan failed, partly because neither of them could acknowledge the extent of their jeopardy.

Fifteen days before her husband's abdication, Alix had been pre-occupied by her children, all five of whom had succumbed to measles. She had given her lady-in-waiting, Baroness Buxhoeveden, an update: 'Olga 39.9 (103F) Tatiana 39.3 (102F) Alexis 40 (104F) . . . It's normal when, rash coming out, very strong. Thank God none so far have complications.' Baroness Buxhoeveden thought the children's measles was the central obstacle to the family leaving Russia: 'Had they not been ill, the whole Imperial Family would probably have left the country at the outbreak of the Revolution.'

Within weeks, George V had, in any case, withdrawn his offer of a British exile. He had buckled, after his private secretary, Stamfordham, successfully played upon his fears of revolution in England. Stamfordham had earlier received complaints about Alix from both the Russian military HQ and Queen Mary herself. Years later, Victoria's grandson, Prince Philip, was philosophical and broadly supportive of Stamfordham's view. 'There was a very strong revolutionary movement throughout Europe at the time, I think the King effectively said: "Well let's not stir it up by bringing it here". Things deteriorated after that and the window of opportunity was gone.'

Unaware of the withdrawal of the invitation, Victoria at this point still clung to the hope that her sister might escape.

At one point Buchanan suggested the Imperial Family might go to France. But the British Ambassador in Paris roundly rejected the idea: 'The Empress is not only Boche by birth but in sentiment . . . she is regarded as a criminal or a criminal lunatic and the ex-Emperor as a criminal for his weakness and submission to her promptings.'

In a bid to rescue his cousins, the Kaiser too contacted Kerensky. Irène's Prince Henry, as Commander-in-Chief of the naval forces in the Baltic, was to have taken a central role, guiding a rescue ship through minefields and torpedo boats. But it came to nothing, not least because Germany and Russia were still at war.

Ella's response to the Russian upheavals was radically different from Alix's. Victoria found her stoical attitude reassuring, writing: 'Ella has acknowledged the new govt & asked to be allowed to continue at the head of her sisterhood.' Ella had accepted the Tsar's abdication as the will of God; she was now content to obey orders to stay in the convent.

But then Ella knew little of outside events. In March, she had received a visit from Father Seraphim, the monk she had befriended at the Belogorsky Monastery just before the outbreak of the war; he brought news from the battlefront. But no messages had reached her from Tsarskoe Selo and her own telegrams to Alix had been returned. It is hard to say how much of a privation this was: the two of them were still at loggerheads over Rasputin's murder.

It was Ella's stepdaughter, Maria Pavlovna, who finally brought news of the captive Imperial Family to Moscow, offering to take a message back to Alix. But Ella was not yet prepared to communicate beyond her stark telegrams. 'She could not send a letter, she had nothing to say, she and her sister, the Empress, had long ago ceased to understand each other,' reported Maria.

Ella intended to stay out of the political morass. As one visitor, a Mme Langen, who visited Ella just after the revolution recalled: 'Not a single word did she say against Kerensky or anyone at all or members of the Provisional Government . . . She told us all, "I am not going to leave for anywhere. My duty is to stay here. You must only pray and pray".'

When salacious newspaper cartoon sketches of Alix were left on the convent doorstep, Ella calmly ordered them burnt. On one occasion, a group of foul-smelling, drunken reprobates crowded into the convent. Their brazen leader demanded to know who she thought she was, now she was not Her Imperial Highness. She replied quietly that she was his servant, at which point the leader exposed a viscous ulcer in his groin, demanding she attend to it, which she duly did. The patient himself was thrown but his comrades were unrepentant, insisting that Ella was 'still a German'.

A few months later, two trucks full of rough-necked revolutionary soldiers and ex-convicts from the Lubyanka prison arrived at the convent. Accusing her again of being German, they claimed that she was storing arms and harbouring German prisoners. Ella faced them down, insisting they leave their arms by the door and attend a service.

The memoirist Galina von Meck's cousin acted at the time as Ella's secretary. She recounted his description of the incident: 'A group of revolutionaries all with arms and matching gun bullets draped around their shoulders, and so on, knocked at the door and just rushed into my sitting room . . . 30 people crammed into that small room, but they did as she told them, put down everything they had, their guns and everything, went across the courtyard and into the church . . . They all prayed and they all came back, took their weapons and disappeared.'

Ella was able to laugh off snarling bears and to confront revolutionaries but she never shook off her fear of mice. Von Meck continued: 'When my cousin was going to the front after the First World War had broken out, he came to say goodbye to her before he left and she was blessing him with an icon when a mouse ran between them and, forgetting all about the blessing, she picked up her skirts, jumped on a chair, grabbed a huge book and threw it at the mouse. She laughed after and said: "That's the only thing I'm afraid of – mice".'

In the early summer of 1917, the Provisional Government suggested Ella move to the Kremlin for her own safety but she refused. Ella explained some of her feelings towards the Russian rebels: 'Those that I love from all my heart, truly they are morally ill and blinded not to see where we are going and one's heart aches, but I have no bitterness.' Later she added to Victoria: 'Our whole country is shredded into small pieces. Everything that has been gathered for centuries has been destroyed – and by our own people . . . but I have no bitterness. How can you criticise or condemn a man in deliriums or a lunatic?'

But Father Seraphim noted that Ella was increasingly 'emaciated and exhausted'. By June, the strain was worsening, as Ella fell ill with typhoid. Her niece, Maria Pavlovna, recalled her dismay when she visited her: 'I was struck by her tired and ill appearance . . . She who had always been on the go, now spent most of her time upon a wicker chaise longue with a piece of embroidery or knitting.' Ella had once insisted that her duty was to stay in Moscow, but Maria had the impression that she now wanted to leave and live in a hermitage.

Ella was also visited by Yusupov, whom she had so praised for his murder of Rasputin: 'You could not act otherwise,' she reassured him. 'You made a supreme attempt to save your country and the dynasty.' Yusupov had the impression that, for all her annoyance with Alix, Ella was intensely worried about her. 'She had few illusions about the seriousness of the situation and was greatly alarmed over the fate of the Emperor and his family,' he wrote.

Soon after Ella had been asked to move to the Kremlin, the Kaiser made another attempt to rescue her, but this also came to nothing. Though Victoria and Irène might have wished she would accept help, they must have understood her reasons for refusing. There were the obvious war-time objections: namely that the two countries were still at war. But Ella would not have forgotten the Kaiser's unwelcome romantic pursuit of her, nor his subsequent deriding of the sainted Grand Duke Serge.

In the meantime, Victoria had her own worries, as in June 1917 King George withdrew British peerages and titles from all his German relations and changed his name, Saxe Coburg Gotha, to the robustly English Windsor. Victoria's family were no longer Princes, Princesses or Serene Highnesses. Their family name, Battenberg, had transformed into Mountbatten.

There were compensations. Four months later, Prince Louis and Victoria were ennobled as Marquess and Marchioness of Milford Haven. After another two years, Victoria began to use letter-heading with an elaborate 'Victoria' coronet. She readily justified her decision: 'As a grandchild of a British sovereign and being entitled to it I do not feel it is snobbish to use it.'

*

In August 1917, with the British plans for the Imperial Family's rescue from Russia having been abandoned, the Romanovs were forced by the Provisional Government to travel to Siberia, where they were held, for several months, in the Governor's house at Tobolsk. In November, Alix sent her last letter from there to Victoria, thanking her for birthday messages. The note would have been extremely tardy: Alix's birthday was in June.

That Christmas, in snowy Tobolsk, Alix rhapsodised about English gardens, drawing a picture of holly for Baroness Buxhoeveden's English governess and referring to her mother, Princess Alice, in the inscription: 'Allow a fellow countrywoman's daughter to send her the small gift she has made for her with warm wishes.' But the press remained unconvinced by the Tsarina's acquired Englishness. A waspish article appeared in the Washington Post: 'She has always manifested, nevertheless, a distrust and a disdain for all things English. Her training and traditions have been as intensely German as those of the Kaiser himself.'

In fact, Alix ascribed most of her important 'training and traditions' not just to Queen Victoria, but to her former governess, Miss Jackson. The pair maintained their keen correspondence after the revolution, Alix sending Madgie her last letter in late 1917. There is no record of Miss Jackson ever receiving it, but then she died in January 1918, and was ill during the months leading up to her death. Miss Jackson was buried surrounded by pictures of her Hesse charges.

Over 20 years before, another of Alix's faithful childhood retainers, her maid, Madeleine Zanotti, had come from Darmstadt to join her in St Petersburg. In 1917, Madeleine took the brave decision to follow Alix to Siberia. The pair were never properly reunited, but Alix had been thrilled to catch glimpses of the maid from a window; in one of several unpublished letters in German, she instructed Madeleine, chillingly, not to wave, for her own safety: 'It is such a joy to see you in the street, only don't give any indication that you have seen me.' In another note, she betrayed her deluded optimism: 'We must show that we are strong God's children, full of confidence in better, sunny days.'

In her final letter to Madeleine, written at the end of March 1918, Alix mentioned talk of moving the family to a 'bishop's building' for their security. She hoped Madeleine would join them there. Alix's last letter to Miss Jackson had included a map of the house in Tobolsk; it was suggested that the map was intended for use in a British rescue.

Rumours began to spread that some or all of the family might break free. Victoria and her husband Prince Louis were confused when, on December 16th 1917, they received a telegram: 'Tatiana has arrived.' For a second, they thought Alix's daughter, the young Grand Duchess Tatiana, had reached Britain. But it was actually from their son, George, telling them that he and his Russian wife had had a baby daughter, whom they had named Tatiana.

In the early days following the October Revolution, Ella seemed to have fared better than her sister's family. She successfully ingratiated herself with the various revolutionary regimes, and soon reached an agreement with the new Bolshevik Government.

When twenty Chekhists turned up at the convent, Ella even suggested that they might have a common purpose: 'You and I may be making for the same goal – by a different road.' For several months, a lorry delivered food twice a week: she and her nuns may have run short of meat, but they were amply supplied with bread, dried fish, cooking fat, root vegetables and potatoes.

Everything changed again, however, when the Treaty of Brest-Litovsk, signed by the Bolsheviks in March 1918, created a separate peace between Russia and Germany. On learning of the treaty, which ceded Russian land to the Germans, the captive Tsar and Tsarina were outraged. The Tsar ranted: 'I should never have thought the Emperor William & the German government could stoop to shake hands with those miserable traitors'.

With the two countries now at peace, Alix and Ella might have accepted help from Germans. But Alix was resolute: 'I would rather die in Russia than be saved by the Germans.' Ella turned down two further offers of help from the Kaiser's envoy.

By the Russian Easter of 1918, which fell on May 5th, Alix, Nicky and their 18-year-old daughter Maria had been transferred from Tobolsk to Ekaterinburg, where they were held in Ipatiev House, a former merchant's dwelling. This was the town Ella and Victoria had visited just before the outbreak of war: the town where Victoria had felt such hostility. The rest of Alix's children would join them a few weeks later.

The Bolsheviks now returned to Ella's convent. Knowing nothing of any rift between the sisters, their leader asked Ella if she would care to join Alix, and told her that the Imperial Family had been moved from Tobolsk for their own safety. He made no mention of Ekaterinburg. Would she like to join them? She replied that she was ready to go wherever God willed.

Around this time, she was able to send an obscure, final message, via an American well-wisher, to Victoria. Though the note was meant to be reassuring, Victoria found it unsettling: 'The last, written shortly before her removal from Moscow, was only to say all was all right with her & was written in a feigned style, as if from a girls' schools in New York, as the bringer was American.'

Days after the Bolsheviks' visit, an armoured car came to take Ella away. She asked for two hours to prepare, but was given just half an hour. While she maintained her calm, some of her nuns were more demonstrative, making the sign of cross, falling to their knees and beating their heads on the earth. She left with just one fellow nun, Varvara Yakovleva.

As she was leaving, she dropped an ordinary-looking white glove. It has remained at the convent to this day, conserved as a holy relic.

It is hard to know whether Ella grasped the true seriousness of her predicament or whether she half-expected to be reunited with Alix. Though she had shied away from sending Alix a letter, she never lost her desire for a reconciliation.

Ella was taken first to Perm, then to Ekaterinburg, where she was held captive with several Romanov relations, including Vladimir (Volodya) Paley, the 21-year-old half-brother of her two stepchildren. Ella had long ago fallen out with their father, Serge's brother Pavel. Irène had kept Victoria abreast of the froideur that had also developed between Ella and Pavel's 'horrid' new wife. But her attitude softened towards the family during these months of captivity and Volodya would write to his mother of Ella's 'great kindness' to him.

The British Government attempted to keep tabs on both Alix and Ella. Thomas Preston was a young British businessman working in Ekaterinburg when he was asked by the Foreign Office to take on the job of acting consul. Years later, in Feb 1921, Preston wrote a confidential report of what he remembered of events in Ekaterinburg. The report was addressed to Lord Curzon and specified that Ella had arrived at Ekaterinburg on May 1st.

At that point, Ella didn't know Alix's exact whereabouts, but she was keen to send her Easter gifts. In the same spirit of rapprochement in which she had sent icons to the Alexander Palace, Ella packed up eggs, coffee and chocolate. The parcels were delivered to the Imperial Family by nuns based at a convent nearby. The Tsarina wrote plainly in her diary: 'Received coffee and chocolate fr. Ella. She has been sent out from Moscow & is at Perm (we read in the papers).' Ella was, of course, not in Perm but much closer by, in Ekaterinburg itself.

Alix never wrote to thank her sister. She left it to her young daughter Maria, Ella's goddaughter, who concluded a warm letter with their bleak return 'address'. Maria wrote: 'He is risen indeed! We kiss you thrice dearest. Thank you very much for the eggs, chocolate and coffee. Mama drank her first cup of coffee with great pleasure . . . It's very good for her headaches and as it happened we had not taken any with us. We learnt from the newspapers that you had been sent away from your convent and were very sad for you. It is strange we should all end up in the same province under arrest. We hope that you will be able to spend the summer somewhere out of town in Verkhoturye or in some monastery. We have so missed having a church. My address is: Ekaterinburg, the Regional Executive Committee, to the chairman, for transmission to me. May God keep you, Your loving goddaughter.'

Maria also wrote to her siblings, then still in Tobolsk, with instructions to send a rosary to Ella. While Maria attended to the logistics, the idea would surely have come from her mother. Was this Alix's final response to Ella's efforts at reconciliation? Maria wrote: 'Ask Tatiana to look for the large ivory rosary, to have it blessed and sent to Aunt Ella in Perm . . . We received from Aunt Ella: three eggs, coffee and chocolate.' There is no record of Ella receiving the gift; it would have marked the last communication between the sisters.

Irène succeeded in posting various items to Tobolsk. Sent via the Swedish Legation and then Alix's friend, Anna Vyrubova, in Russia, the items included money, a German poetry book and underclothes. While the money and underclothes were welcome, the German poetry was less so. Irène had clearly not grasped the extent of Alix's struggle to shake off her Hessian roots.

Hostility to the German-born Tsarina was not restricted to the largest cities of Russia. Years later, Thomas Preston recalled the animosity in Ekaterinburg. Her detractors, he said, were 'selling obscene pamphlets of the Empress and the monk [Rasputin] and exhibiting a series of disgusting pictures at the local cinematograph, in which the daughters and Empress also figured with him.' The press were printing lurid tales of the Tsarina and Rasputin with depictions of Alix bathing in a tub full of blood.

According to her lady-in-waiting, Baroness Buxhoeveden, the disabled Tsarina was wheeled out of the Ipatiev House, where the family was being held captive, every day. Soldiers smoked in her face or exchanged crude jokes, swearing at her for refusing to walk. Her loyal sailor, Nagorny, who pushed the chair, was plagued with letters condemning him to death.

She enjoyed the odd triumph. The Baroness witnessed Alix's successful winning-over of a Soviet deputy. The pair discussed the shortcomings of the Germans, before the deputy finally admitted: 'I was mistaken about you.'

After several days, Ella's group was transferred to Alapaevsk, 90 miles north of Ekaterinburg. A British officer, Colonel Blair, later wrote to the War Office from Vladivostok: 'The Grand Duchess Elizabeta Feodorovna and her lady in waiting Yakovleva were taken on the 6th May from Ekaterinburg to the school house at Alapaevsk.' A Russian officer, Colonel Rodzyanko, added: 'They were lodged in a deserted school without any furniture and told to sleep on the school forms. After a day or two of remonstrance, beds were furnished to them by the population of Alapaevsk.'

Ella was good at adapting to the captives' pared-down life: cooking, mending and doing laundry. Still vegetarian, she refused horse meat, surviving primarily on turnips and milk. Under her auspices, the party cultivated and ate lettuces, radishes, peas and cabbage. Her fellow captive, the young Volodya, was full of admiration: 'Aunt Ella knows more about vegetables than any of us.'

News of the Imperial Family's predicament filtered back to Britain. From the age of 15, Victoria had felt responsible for her younger sisters. Queen Victoria had issued stern instructions to her as the eldest of four motherless sisters to look out for them. Forty years on, Grandmama's words lost none of their resonance.

In May 1918, she sent a desperate letter to the Foreign Secretary, Arthur Balfour, begging him to let Alix and her four nieces live with her on the Isle of Wight. Writing from Kent House, she pointed out that, though the Tsarevich, Alexis, might be a 'political asset', the women could be 'of no value or importance as hostages to the Russian Government'. Balfour replied that the Foreign Office couldn't trust the Bolsheviks to do any kind of deal. He added that any such plan might be construed as a Tsarist conspiracy. He promised to search for other opportunities.

In Germany, Irène's husband, Prince Henry, had taken on a semi-official role as representative of the Romanovs in Russia. In June 1918, he received an alarming dispatch from Petrograd: rumours were spreading that the Tsar was dead. Upset by the rumours, Prince Henry was additionally dismayed by the reaction of the Russian populace: 'The effect of this news on the masses was barely perceptible. . . . Although the rumour was not retracted for almost two weeks, a requiem mass did not take place anyway. This notoriously proved that the ex-Tsar has lost all sympathy from the people.'

*

On the night of 16th/17th July Alix, the Tsar and their five children were murdered in the cellar of the house at Ekaterinburg. The Ipatiev House had been disturbingly renamed the House of Special Purpose. Alix's diaries in Ekaterinburg were in English and characteristically out of touch. Her last entry read: 'Played bezique with Nicholas 10.30 to bed. 15 degrees.'

The Imperial Family, by then reunited, were told, once again, that they must be moved for their own safety. They assembled in the cellar, clutching an assortment of bags. They were then instructed to line up against the wall for a photograph. The 11 gunmen had each been given a human target: there were seven Romanovs and four retainers. But in the end, several of the gunmen, who were mostly drunk, rounded on the reviled Tsarina: Alix was one of the first to die.

Years later, one of the killers gave more detail: 'At his last word, he [the Bolshevik leader Yakov Yurovsky] instantly pulled a revolver out of his pocket and shot the Tsar. The Tsaritsa and her daughter Olga tried to make the sign of the cross, but did not have enough time . . . Nicholas was killed by the commandant, point blank. Then Alexandra died immediately.'

The cellar filled with smoke. Confusion mounted as the killers' bullets ricocheted off the bodies. It was later discovered that the women had sewn impregnable jewels into their corsets. The bodies were still warm as gunmen began pocketing the precious stones. Yurovsky was furious, declaring that anyone caught with an item of jewellery would be shot.

The assassinations were followed by botched burials, strung out over more than two days. The corpses were loaded on to a truck and driven into nearby forests. When the truck's wheels became stuck in the mud, it was decided to transfer the bodies to some horse-drawn carts. A second gang of drunken revolutionaries, who happened upon the scene, insisted on helping. Finding jewels in the clothes, they began manhandling the bodies: two groped under Alix's skirts. One said: 'I can die peacefully now I've felt the Royal——.'

Attempts were made to lower the bodies into a mine, but the shaft wasn't deep enough. The killers then tried to destroy the bodies with grenades and acid, but to no avail. As dawn broke, they gave up the struggle, leaving the mine with the victims' limbs still protruding above the earth.

The following morning, Yurovsky loaded the corpses back on to the truck, which promptly got stuck again. In a fit of exasperation, he buried nine of the bodies under nearby railway sleepers. Two of the children – Maria and Alexis – were buried separately to confuse anyone trying to identify the seven Romanovs. Yurovsky later said in a report that the body he had really wanted to destroy was the Tsarina's.

Colonel Blair wrote to the War Office from Vladivostok relating the events: 'The bodies were taken to a wood some distance from the town and were there burnt, it is believed.'

Eight days after the murders, the White Army arrived at Ekaterinburg and investigations began. On August 31st a Foreign Office telegram confirmed that some charred bones had been found in a mineshaft twenty miles from Ekaterinburg. Investigators uncovered Alix's spectacle case and one of her fingers.

A day after the murders at Ekaterinburg, on July 17th, Ella's group were told, as Alix's family had been, that they were to be moved for their own safety. They were instructed to have their supper an hour and a half early, at 6.00pm. Colonel Blair wrote: 'Their guard, which had been chiefly of Magyars, was changed on July 17th to one of Russian workmen.'

The party were ordered to climb on to carts. They were told not to bring luggage; they could fill their pockets with anything they particularly needed. The streets around the school at Alapaevsk were generally deserted, but a brewer later claimed to have seen the grim procession: 'They were taken that night 20 versts [about 13 miles] to a coal mine in Troikas,' reported Colonel Blair.

The Russian Colonel Rodzyanko was party to more vivid detail: 'When the carts were stopped, at a place near where there were coal mining shafts, the family . . . began to understand that something was going to happen to them, so as they all walked on together they sang religious hymns, while the Bolsheviks laughed at them.'

Ella and the other nun, Varvara Yakovleva, were pushed into the mine first. Rodzyanko reported that Ella made a curious request: 'She asked only one thing – that they should wrap her head in something.'

The two women managed to heave themselves on to a ledge. The other Romanovs were thrown down after them. When the killers heard voices from the mine, they threw in a grenade. Then, hearing voices again, they threw in a second. Rodzyanko wrote: 'When they had thrown them all into the mine they threw down hand grenades, big pieces of wood . . . and stones, and then they left the place.'

Rodzyanko added prosaic details: 'It was proved . . . that some of them had lived two hours at least, because the food they had eaten before leaving the house had been digested about six hours, and they were thrown into the mine about 9 o'clock . . . The depth of the mine was about 60 feet and on the bottom was a certain amount of water . . . The bodies were in an awful state. They were covered with bruises and many of them had wounds in the head. Some of the arms and legs were broken, and it was obvious they had suffered tremendously before dying . . .'

It is currently believed that all the victims were hit on the head before being thrown down. An axe with a wide blade was found down the mine. With all their injuries, they were said to have all died of starvation, except the Tsar's cousin, Grand Duke Sergei Mikhailovich, who was shot. Years later, Prince Philip gave a peremptory description of his great-aunt's demise: 'Ella was taken and thrown down a mineshaft in Siberia and they lobbed some hand grenades after her.'

A mystical aura around Ella's fate took hold almost immediately. Victoria wrote to Ernie: 'I have heard that it was told, by one of those who was present at her death, that she prayed: "Lord forgive them for they know not what they do"' – the same prayer that was engraved on Serge's memorial cross in Moscow.

Ella was said to have tended her fellow victims in the mine, bandaging one of the Romanovs with her veil. Peasants claimed to have heard the victims chanting prayers and singing hymns all night. Ella singing the 'Magnificat' and 'Hail Gentle Light' became an integral part of the tale.

In death, Ella was said to have had the three fingers of her right hand folded, as if making the sign of cross. In the cellar at Ekaterinburg, Alix tried but failed to make the sign of the cross before dying.

A report printed in *Romanov News*, a monthly online publication produced by the Tsar's sister Grand Duchess Olga's great-grandson, cast doubt on several of these stories.

Ella was not making the sign of the cross when she died; nor did she bandage a fellow victim. The report says: 'Both hands of Elizabeth Feodorovna were tightly clenched, fingers bent, nails sunk into the skin – this happens when a person is in severe pain. . . . The head (eyes, nose) of the nun martyr was tied with a scarf folded in four layers . . . even if she remained alive in the mine, her position and the scarf on her face, from which she did not free herself, do not correspond to the version (story) of bandaging the wounded.'

Another witness insisted he heard a struggle in water before Ella began singing: 'Save Lord Your People'. In fact, garbage had been thrown into the mine: the bodies never reached the water. Several of the more fanciful witnesses to the murders at Alapaevsk have been discredited. One, Alexander Samsonov, was said to be a brewer of moonshine.

Rodzyanko's report continued: 'The murder of these people left such an impression, even on the Bolsheviks, that they had to leave the place and one man (whose name General Dietrichs has) was so horrified at seeing the bodies moving about at the bottom of the mine that he went mad and ran away. He went back to his village and was not normal for a long time. Then one day, when he had more or less recovered, he told his wife of the horrors he had witnessed and she repeated what he had said to someone else. That is how all this was found out'.

Throughout that fateful summer of 1918, Victoria had carried on her campaign to rescue Alix, writing repeatedly to the Foreign Office as well as to the King. In July, she suggested seeking help from a neutral country, Sweden or Spain, or a royal court elsewhere. At one point she even mentioned the wife of the Bolshevik leader Lenin, then in Stockholm. The Foreign Office, through Lord Robert Cecil, was sympathetic but not helpful, suggesting that Lenin's wife might cause 'more harm than good'.

In a letter to the King, written on August 10th, Victoria referred to Ella as well as Alix: 'Just spoken to an American gentleman recently returned from Russia, who saw Ella this spring, just before she was removed from Moscow.' It was this American who had brought Ella's last, strangely worded note. 'He agrees with me in thinking she would not want to leave a country where she has created a work and interest for herself in the sisterhood . . . But for Alix and the girls it is different & he thinks it is of the utmost importance that any steps to get them out of the country should be taken quickly.'

By the time Victoria was writing this letter, Alix and Ella were already dead.

To what extent Irène fretted, at this point, about Alix and Ella is unclear. But, as sister-in-law of the Kaiser, she would have been more worried about the immediate threat to herself, Prince Henry and their sons. The Kaiser would be drummed out of power by revolutionaries within a few months.

11

'La dame des pleurs.'
Chips Channon

There were reasons the Bolsheviks maintained confusion and secrecy around the deaths of Alix and Ella. Both sisters had diehard supporters including monarchists and the whole of the White Army. Ella was a revered nun as well as a Romanov Grand Duchess.

It was not until September that the deaths of Alix and her family were confirmed.

Victoria's cousin, Princess Marie Louise of Schleswig-Holstein, took a letter containing the devastating news to Victoria, on the Isle of Wight. The Princess handed the letter – sent by the King – to Prince Louis, who then spoke to his wife.

Alix had been only six years old when their mother had died. While all three elder Princesses worried constantly about their youngest sister, Victoria had considered herself Alix's special protector. Victoria thanked the Princess for bringing the King's letter, but never mentioned its contents. The two women spent the next three weeks attending to the gardening.

She did write a heartfelt reply to King George: 'For my poor Alicky, as you say, one must be grateful that her sufferings are over, life would always have been a misery to her after Nicky & her boy were gone & though those dear girls were young enough to have recovered from the horrors they went through & happier days might have come to them, yet also there was the chance, that haunted me, of great wrong being done them.'

At this point, Victoria still believed Ella might be alive. She added: 'I hope that Ella may still be at Alapaevsk, where there are evidently people who were still kindly inclined towards the prisoners . . . Should any news of her reach you, I am sure you will let me know & I thank you once more for your affectionate & sincere sympathy with me in my distress and sorrow.'

Victoria still knew nothing of the King's decision, a few months earlier, to withdraw his offer of a refuge to the Romanovs. Her anger was directed towards their other cousin, the hated Kaiser. She wrote to King Alfonso of Spain, thanking him for his offer of a Spanish exile: 'The Sovereign who had the most direct influence on the revolutionary government in Russia, the one who had known my sister as a child, who had the same blood as her . . . deserted her . . . I shall never forget the gratitude I owe you for this.' The Kaiser had, in fact, tried several times to rescue Ella. He had also made rudimentary plans to rescue the Imperial Family.

For Victoria, the world had divided between hordes of murderous enemies and a handful of supporters who she hoped remained 'kindly inclined'. She would have been touched to hear that the people of Alapaevsk had rallied round to supply beds for Ella's ill-fated party.

Weeks after the deaths of the Imperial Family were confirmed in England, doubts persisted in Russia. The corpses of the Romanovs had not yet been found. And, as late as October 1918, the English tutor to the Romanov children, Sydney Gibbes, gave testimony in Ekaterinburg suggesting that both Hesse sisters had survived.

Gibbes had followed the Imperial Family to Ekaterinburg and entered the House of Special Purpose shortly after the killings. He made a bizarre reference to Alix's daughters' hair.

His testimony, given to the High Commissioner read: 'Since the departure of the Bolsheviks, the house in which the Imperial Family lived has been thoroughly examined and undoubted traces of murder exist, but the number of shots are not sufficient to warrant the supposition that all the persons there confined were murdered. Part were murdered and part were taken away, and as the Grand Duchesses' hair has been found, it is supposed that the Imperial children were taken away disguised.'

He continued with what he had heard of Ella: 'The Grand Duchess Serge who was also there [at Alapaevsk] is reported to have been wounded and taken away.'

Months on, Colonel Rodzyanko wrote of further mysteries surrounding the fate of Alix: 'No trace of the body [of the Tsar] however has ever been found . . . the rest of the members of the Imperial Family were taken away to an unknown destination. They are stated to have been burnt alive (their charred remains are said to have been found in a house burnt down to the ground and various articles of jewellery have been identified as belonging to them by their old servants).'

While rumours circulated about the Romanov Princes and Grand Duke at Alapaevsk, some of the Bolsheviks were afraid even to mention Ella by name. Rodzyanko continued: 'Meanwhile the Bolsheviks circulated the rumour that the Grand Dukes [sic] had escaped. To make this appear true they started firing and throwing bombs into the house. It will be noticed on the photograph attached that the windows are all broken and the state of the house looks as if some fighting had taken place there. The population believed this, so for a month or two no-one knew what had happened to the family.'

At one point, the Bolsheviks put it about that the Romanov Princes had escaped on a plane.

The Tsar's sisters vacillated between hope and despair. As late as January 1919, they seemed to have heard of the death of Ella but not of Alix. Grand Duchess Olga wrote to her sister Xenia: 'If really those devils would, in cold blood, kill all those innocent people (the Romanov Princes, Grand Duke and Ella) in Perm perhaps they have done the same with the beloved family, Nicky, Alix, etc. Oh no! no!'

A full year later, rumours were still gaining hold. On March 20th 1920, Grand Duchess Olga wrote to Xenia from Belgrade: 'Last night I met Margarita Hitrovo [a friend of Alix's eldest daughter Olga] who told me ours are all alive. She knows about them. Well we didn't lose our faith & hope this time.'

Three months after the murders at Alapaevsk, the corpses of Ella's party were unearthed from the mineshaft. It would be several further months before the Four Brothers mine was formally, and erroneously, identified, as the final burial site of Alix, the Tsar and the five children. Sydney Gibbes was among those who identified objects then retrieved from the mine, including Alix's finger: 'As I saw it lying in spirit it looked to me like Dr Botkin's finger but it was probably swollen, for medical experts have declared it to be the third finger of a lady no longer quite young, and it is held to be that of the Empress.'

The bodies of the Tsar, Tsarina, Olga, Tatiana, Anastasia and their four retainers remained stowed under the railway sleepers, where they lay undisturbed for more than 50 years. It was to be several more years before the bodies of Maria and Alexis were found buried nearby.

*

Victoria had barely recovered from the horrifying news of Alix's death before she heard that Ella's body had been found. Of her three sisters, Victoria probably regarded herself as closest to Ella. Following their mother's death, Victoria had made conscientious efforts to forge close relationships with each of her sisters, but, as they all grew up, differences became accentuated. She and Ella, though so contrasting in character, had both relished argument and discussion. Victoria would have found her other two sisters, in their different ways, too hidebound: Irène too conventional and Alix too peculiar.

She tried to console herself with thoughts of Ella's faith: 'If ever anyone has met death without fear she would have and her deep and pure faith will have upheld and supported and comforted her in all she has gone through so that the misery poor Alicky will have suffered will not have touched Ella's soul,' she wrote to her friend Nona.

Only later did she discover that Ella had in fact suffered more than Alix.

Irène had, by this time, received a photograph of the Ipatiev House at Ekaterinburg and heard stories of both sisters' deaths. She had not seen either sister since 1913; her correspondence with Alix had started to become fractious over the war-time prisoners. But there can be no doubting her anguish over her sisters in Russia. Irène and Alix had both suffered with their haemophiliac sons. The grey-robed Ella may have been viewed by some of the racier Romanovs as a killjoy, but she had been a much sought-after guest at Hemmelmark.

Nevertheless, she had little time to fret. Germany had succumbed to its own political turmoil and, in November 1918, the Kaiser was forced to abdicate. Most of the royal properties, including the 176-room Cecilienhof Palace, near Berlin, and Rheinfels Castle, overlooking the Rhine, were seized by the state. Max von Baden, whom Queen Victoria had once suggested as a suitor for Alix, released a peremptory statement on November 9th 1918: 'The Kaiser and King has decided to give up the throne.'

The Kaiser did not go quietly. 'Treachery, treachery, shameless outrageous treachery,' he raged. But his upset was apparently short-lived, for, after crossing into exile at the Dutch border and arriving at Amerongen Castle, his first words were: 'Now for a cup of real good English tea.'

As Victoria struggled to accept the deaths of Alix and Ella, Irène now feared for her own life. Following Alix's example, she set about burning her personal letters. She then fled Kiel with Prince Henry and her son

Sigismund, the last members of Germany's Royal Family to be ousted from their home. As Irène wrote later to Victoria: 'Alas! I was obliged to burn almost everything they [Ella and Alix] & you all wrote to me when we left Kiel for fear the things got in the wrong hands.'

On the journey north to Flensburg, Irène was terrified as their car, improbably festooned with red flags, was attacked by rebel German marines. Though the family arrived safely, Irène was hit in the arm and Prince Henry narrowly escaped death from a bullet that passed through his coat. The would-be assassins succeeded in injuring the chauffeur and dislodging a sailor hanging on to the footboard. On November 8th 1918, the *Schleswig VolksZeitung* bore the stark headline: 'Prince Henry Flees Kiel'.

After the proclamation of the German republic, Prince Henry and Irène were officially stripped of their titles. The postal service refused to deliver letters addressed to 'Your Royal Highness', accepting only 'Herr von Preussen' or 'Frau von Preussen'.

Victoria had already lost her titles in England. In Russia, the Tsar had faced similar slights in his last few months. Carl Fabergé's 125,000-rouble invoice for the Tsar's last two Easter eggs, in 1917, was addressed to 'Nicholas Romanov'.

As late as January 1919, Irène apparently still held out hopes for the survival of both Alix and Ella. Though she had heard the repeated accounts of the murders, she was reluctant to accept the truth. Crown Princess Cecilie wrote: 'T[ante] Irène does not believe it either, since she heard shortly before that her two sisters were well.' It was several further months before she accepted that they were dead.

*

In November 1918, the Armistice brought an official end to the Great War, but underlying hostility would take longer to dispel.

Certainly, the relationship between the two surviving Hesse sisters was irreparably damaged by their respective countries' animosity towards each other. Their sons – Victoria's George and Louis, and Irène's Sigismund – had spent years serving in opposing navies.

Just weeks after peace had been declared, on hearing of a meeting between Irène's German sister-in-law and his own son, Bertie [the future George VI], the King made his feelings clear: 'The sooner she [Irène's sister-in-law] knows the real feeling of bitterness which exists here against her country the better.'

Irène's husband, Prince Henry, once so Anglophile, was reluctant to lay down his war-time cudgels. First, he berated what he saw as his own lily-livered country, arguing for the restoration of the monarchy and the removal of 'parasitical soldiers and workers' councils'. Then he ranted against the war-mongering British, insisting that his brother, the Kaiser, had been the one trying to avoid bloodshed. He ordered the King to 'desist from any demand for the extradition of HM the Emperor William'.

Britain, he raged, had taken up arms in order to 'eliminate Germany as a troublesome competition from the world market'. Germany and her brave people, he continued, had been severely hit, but were not yet dead. 'The German spirit, which at present still lives, will one day awake to the full consciousness of the disgrace and shame which have been inflicted by its victors. It will one day demand a reckoning from its torturers, even after many years.'

Prince Henry then voiced generally held anti-Semitic views, blaming the Jews, alongside the British, for Germany's woes.

Irène tended to go along with her husband's opinions. Whether she actually agreed with him is open to question. She certainly expected Victoria to agree with her. In one garbled note to Victoria, she seemed to blame the death of their sisters on the Entente: 'All the sorrow that fell upon our dear ones originated through the net that was systematically drawn round us & Austria for years – as we now know! Europe & the world has to thank the so-called Entente for the war & all its consequences. In the end Truth! Will triumph!'

Once such a keen visitor to Britain, Irène barely ventured there again. She was, however, soon back at Hemmelmark, absorbed in those 'trifling occurrences of everyday life' so disliked by her mother-in-law. Among less trifling events were the successful marriages of both her sons to princesses. Sigismund married Charlotte Agnes of Saxe-Altenburg and Waldemar married Calixta of Lippe-Biesterfeld, both weddings being held at Hemmelmark. Irène's much-loved first grandchild, Sigismund's daughter Barbara, was born the following summer.

Perhaps it was as well that Irène was distracted by domestic matters when, in the summer of 1919, Victoria and their brother, Ernie, organised a reunion. After years at war, Victoria had to steel herself to meet Ernie and his second wife Onor. It was the first time the two siblings had seen each other in six years. Victoria felt uncomfortable about returning to Darmstadt, so the pair chose to meet at a castle in Switzerland. Tarasp Castle was in the Engadine near the Austro-Italian border and was then owned by the Hesse family. She found the meeting cathartic: 'Now the ice is broken I like meeting Ernie & Onor who are quite unchanged in character.'

The siblings avoided talking about the fates of Alix and Ella. Afterwards, Victoria wrote to Ernie: 'I have shrunk from saddening our few days together by speaking too much about our anxieties & our griefs for those dear Others in Russia.'

One of the reasons for avoiding discussions about those 'dear Others' was that Ernie, like Irène, at this point still believed that his sisters had survived. Victoria later wrote to Onor: 'If he [Ernie] like poor Aunt Minnie [the Tsar's mother] still has hope, then please do not rob him of this . . . Time will make this hope disappear in a more gentle way.' Victoria's daughter, Alice, wrote sensitively to Onor about her mother's own reluctance to mention her sisters' fate: 'It is sheer agony for her to discuss the sad Russian thing.'

Victoria shared none of Ernie's optimism. As she wrote to him obscurely in August: 'I dare not give myself up to hope, for I have fully realised since the evil days befell them the truth of saying that: "Hope deferred maketh the heart sink" & well, my good nerves are not as strong as they were.'

She gave vent to her feelings when she met Ella's stepchildren, Maria and Dmitri, in January 1919, at Kensington Palace. Dmitri found the meeting extremely harrowing: 'She cried the whole time and managed to draw various pictures for herself of the last moments of her sisters' lives. There's no doubt in her mind that Alix and Aunt Ella have been killed.'

Dmitri had long regretted his part in the murder of Rasputin. His co-conspirator, Felix Yusupov, had no such qualms and would rarely pass up an opportunity to boast about it. He proudly sported the bullet he claimed had killed Rasputin, in a ring on his finger. Months after seeing Victoria, Dmitri wrote to Yusupov expressing his remorse: 'That affair will always be a dark stain on my conscience . . . murder will always be murder'. Yusupov never read the letter; it was returned, unopened, only to be found, years later, among Dmitri's possessions.

*

For Victoria and Irène, the final confirmation of their sisters' deaths provided no resolution. There were problems, first, with the locating of the bodies, then with identifying them. Once located and identified, could they ever be transported to an appropriate place or properly laid to rest?

The monarchist White Army conducted painstaking inquiries into the deaths of both Alix and Ella. Though White soldiers had arrived at Ekaterinburg days after the murders of the Imperial Family, it was weeks before they found any remains – delays which inevitably fuelled fantasies that some or all of the victims had survived.

Ella's fate was more easily established. The White Army reached Alapaevsk three months after the killings of her party. Days later, the investigators found the bodies. Irrefutable proof of the killings reached Britain at the beginning of November 1818. The British officer, Colonel Blair, wrote from Vladivostok to the War Office: 'Photographs of the bodies which I have seen fully prove the murders at Alupaevsk.'

Further details were provided in Rodzyanko's testimony: 'When the bodies were discovered . . . [they] were carried to the Cathedral in Alapaevsk and after a funeral service, at which the Czechs and White Troops who were in Alapaevsk gave the military salute, they were buried in a vault under the Cathedral.

'They had apparently not been robbed of anything . . . A certain amount of money, letters, cigarette cases and all kinds of small things were found . . . I myself saw the clothes and things they had on them, and they were absolutely intact. I remember a wooden cross that was found [belonging to] the Grand Duchess Elizabeth, which she always wore.'

But with the return of marauding Bolskeviks, months later, the bodies of Ella and the other Romanovs were in danger of being tampered with. Rodzyanko wrote: 'A year after [the bodies were found] when Admiral Kolchak's troops were retiring, and it was absolutely obvious that the Bolsheviks were advancing and would take Alapaevsk, General Dietrichs very secretly ordered the transfer of the bodies to Chita, where they are now buried in a secret place, only three people knowing where they are.'

Ella's devoted friend Father Seraphim took it upon himself to take care of her body and that of her fellow nun, Sister Varvara. Over the course of two years, he would transfer both coffins to Peking, via Lake Baikal, later talking of marvellous cures as worshippers gathered to pray by Ella's bier.

In early 1920, Victoria received a phone call from her aunt Beatrice, who said she'd spotted an article concerning the whereabouts of Ella's coffin in the *Illustrated London News*. She sent Victoria a copy of the piece.

Victoria grew determined to fulfil Ella's wish to be buried in Jerusalem. She had lost two sisters, four nieces and a nephew to the Russian Revolution.

Six of those bodies remained missing. Victoria resolved that Ella, at least, should be properly buried. 'I could not rest thinking about the remains of our dear Ella and loyal Vari [Sister Varvara] lying in a little unprotected chapel near Peking, in the midst of a European-hating population at this time,' she wrote to Ernie's wife Onor. 'I think Ella would agree with the thought that her body should find its last resting place in this holy city, and hopefully in the church which was built in memory of Serge's mother and where she and Serge were present at the consecration.'

She joined forces with Ernie, who was by now obliged to accept the death, at least, of his sister Ella. The two siblings raised money for Father Seraphim to transport the two coffins from Peking to Port Said via Shanghai, Hong Kong and Bombay. Victoria and her husband Prince Louis joined him at Port Said, before travelling, with the two bodies, on to Jerusalem.

Though Irène doesn't seem to have taken an active role in the burial, the sisters were back in communication. A year after Prince Henry's patriotic broadsides, Irène sent her sister sympathetic letters about the death of one of her closest aunts, Grand Duchess Maria, Ella's outspoken sister-in-law. It was Maria who had complained that her stays at Windsor and Osborne were boring beyond belief. She was said to have suffered an apoplectic fit after receiving a letter demeaningly addressed to Frau Coburg.

Irène thanked Victoria for taking charge of her sister's burial; she, too, had been obliged to relinquish her hopes of Ella's survival: 'God bless you dear for the thought of bringing Ella's remains to Jerusalem & little devoted Varis [Varvara] – How I wish I could have joined you – alas! That is impossible. Perhaps some day . . . I may go and see her dear grave – for me she is always near me more so than living & yet it is so hard, so hard to believe she is gone forever.'

She asked Victoria for details of Ella's death: 'Has . . . Father Seraphim been able to tell you anything of how beloved Ella's end was? Or how it all happened? However painful his knowledge may have been one longs to know & how one would like to thank him for his faithful care of her last remains.'

Victoria passed on everything she had learnt from Father Seraphim of Ella's horrific murder. But, by this time, the monk was more concerned with Ella's body and whether or not it had decomposed. Victoria included Seraphim's speculation in a wistful note to Ernie from Port Said: 'It seemed so strange to be walking by moonlight in this out of the way town through empty streets to go & meet all that remains of our dear Ella, who had so often come to meet me after a long journey . . .

'The monk told me that the coffins were hidden for several months before they could leave Siberia. They were hidden in a convent, where they were opened, as was necessary, and our Ella's body was not decayed, only dried out.'

She spared her brother the worst details of Ella's death, writing later from Rome: 'Our Ella's body was found quite at the bottom of the mineshaft into which the party from Alapaevsk were thrown. Her skull was fractured & the doctors who examined the body said she cannot have suffered & that most likely the rush of air of the fall sufficed to stop the heart working.'

She continued in a further letter: 'It is a great comfort to me & hope it will be to you that our dear Ella's remains rest in safety now – the church lies on a beautiful & peaceful spot away from traffic and noise.'

With the wealth of grim information emerging from Ekaterinburg, Victoria could no longer indulge Ernie's hope that Alix had survived. However, writing in February 1921, she did, once again, play down the suffering of the Imperial Family: 'I fear we shall not even have the comfort of being able to do anything for the remains of our other dear ones shot at Ekaterinburg & whose bodies were burnt afterwards. Thank God . . . they were not kept in suspense having been told they must go into the basement of the house & then enter motors which were to remove them as an attack was feared. Then almost at once the men came in & shot them down at close quarters so that their end was swift!' In fact the killings had taken 20 minutes.

From Jerusalem, Victoria's husband, Prince Louis, described some of the more colourful proceedings of Ella's last journey, to Aunt Beatrice. As one of the pallbearers, Prince Louis had been obliged to step over the body of a Russian peasant woman who had fallen to the ground. The peasant had, he said, 'tripped over a stone and fallen full length. One huge lay priest, with hair like a lion's mane, was happily at the head end, but it was a relief when we reached the church safely'.

Irène was intent on building bridges between her husband and 'his old mate' Prince Louis. She may have been worrying about Prince Henry's jingoistic outbursts, as she pleaded with Victoria: 'Henry beggs [sic] me quite especially to tell you how deeply he feels for you & that I am to tell you & dear Ludwig [Louis] – that for him you both remain in his heart what you were for him before – politics are one thing but old well proved friendship another & he feels as ever that for him he is "his old mate" & sends you both his fondest love.'

Victoria and Prince Louis had once established happy foursomes with Ella and Grand Duke Serge, then with Alix and the Tsar. They may well now have been happy to forge a close relationship with Irène and Prince Henry. Sadly, it was never to be. Later that year, on September 11th 1921, Victoria's beloved husband Prince Louis died of heart failure following influenza.

With all their temperamental differences, Victoria and Prince Louis had enjoyed a happy marriage. Victoria must have particularly appreciated having Louis with her for Ella's burial. Nonetheless, she admitted that the quiet death of her husband, then aged 68, was infinitely easier to bear than the violent deaths of Ella and Alix: 'There is none of the pain that the thought of my poor sisters' last months on earth & of their death will always give me,' she wrote to the King.

Victoria's torment over her murdered sisters was both extreme and isolating. Irène could have provided support: she had always been concerned and full of suggestions. But they both knew that Victoria was the sister they all went to; she was the one who had proven unable to help.

Two weeks after her husband's death, she wrote thanking Queen Mary for a gift of money. How May intended Victoria to spend the money is unclear. But Victoria told her that it would go towards Ella's shrine in Jerusalem. The present was 'doubly welcome for I had set a sum aside to pay for the decoration of a small chapel or rather shrine under the terrace of the church in Jerusalem where Ella's body rests,' she explained.

In Darmstadt, Victoria arranged for a Russian artist to decorate the church of St Mary Magdalene. Decades before, the church had been consecrated in the presence of Grand Duke Serge and Ella. The expenses were met, this time, by Irène as well as Victoria and Ernie.

Upon her return from Jerusalem, Victoria heard that her daughter, Alice, was expecting her fifth child. The future Consort to Queen Elizabeth, Prince Philip, was born in Greece on June 10th 1921.

Alice and her husband, Andrew, had spent most of the First World War in Switzerland; they now wanted to come to Britain. They were initially thwarted in their aim by Lord Stamfordham, the King's private secretary. It was Stamfordham who had persuaded the King to withdraw his offer of an exile to the Romanovs. This time the King overrode Stamfordham, allowing Alice's family to come to Britain – although they subsequently transferred to France.

In July 1922, Victoria's younger son, Louis Mountbatten, 'Dickie', was married, in style, at St Margaret's Westminster. The wedding was attended by King George, Queen Mary and Edward VII's widow, Queen

Alexandra, and watched by a crowd of 8,000. The Prince of Wales, the future King Edward VIII, was Louis's best man.

Neither Irène nor Ernie attended the wedding. On July 31ˢᵗ 1922, Irène wrote to thank Victoria for sending the relevant newspaper cuttings. The bad weather did not escape her notice. 'Thanks so much for sending the Ill[ustrated] papers with pictures of Dickie's wedding – it pleased me so much to see them & gives one a good idea of how it was – what a pity it rained.'

In time to come, Louis Mountbatten would be characteristically outspoken about his marriage: 'Edwina and I spent all our married lives getting into other people's beds.'

The following year, Victoria's daughter Louise married the widowed Crown Prince Gustav Adolf of Sweden at the Chapel Royal. She would later be crowned Queen of Sweden. Irène and Ernie were, once again, absent, consigned to the Salon des Refusés.

*

At the beginning of the 1920s, Irène and Victoria were dusting themselves down as best they could. Now both approaching 60, did they compare their lots?

Irène may initially have felt she was stealing a march on Victoria. On January 6ᵗʰ 1923, the *Winnipeg Tribune* pronounced Victoria the 'most pathetic figure in Europe today . . . Revolution has taken a heavy toll on the Dowager Marchioness of Milford Haven for now, following the murder of her sisters—the Tsarina and the Grand Duchess Serge in Russia. Prince Andrew of Greece [Alice's husband] had been deprived of rank and banished for life.'

Irène was still proud to style herself Princess, whatever the German post office decreed. Victoria was a widow; Irène's boisterous husband was very much alive. As for their children, Victoria's two sons were both at

Irène in 1920.

large in the Navy, while Alice had settled in France and her other daughter, Louise, in Sweden. Irène's two sons lived nearby and she saw her much-loved grandchild, Sigismund's daughter, Barbara, every day: 'All the old tunes I used to play to Baby I now have for Barbara,' she cooed to Victoria, 'and she is very fond of them – she arrives at tea-time and I keep her till 6 o'clock. She is a cheerful little Body, always like a beam of sunshine.'

But Irène's moment in the sun was shortlived. First, her younger son, Sigismund, decided to emigrate. More robust than his haemophiliac brother Waldemar, Sigismund had assiduously visited his German relations, including his uncle, the exiled Kaiser, during the early 20s. But he had grown ever more intent on leaving Germany, and, in 1923, he travelled with his family to Central America, taking a job with a German firm, Schlubach, Sapper and Co. Irène's second and last grandchild would be born the following year in Guatemala, and named Alfredo or, as she preferred, Alfred.

An initial idea that the toddler, Barbara, might stay with her grandmother at Hemmelmark was abandoned. Over the next few years, Irène made increasingly forlorn attempts to persuade Sigismund and his family to return to Germany.

Writing to Victoria, however, Irène was intent on maintaining a stiff upper lip: 'Bobby's [Sigismund's] wife & little Barbara left us, on Saturday . . . & I hope are not very seasick on the Atlantic now – circumstances made it advisable that our little Sunshine should accompany her mother after all – she will I hope be a big & healthy child when we at last meet again. Bobby has hard work which he likes & much to interest him, the vegetation, the inhabitants & the mountainous scenery . . . surrounded by people with whom he harmonises.'

Then Irène faced yet more woe as she was dragged into a distressing matter that would dominate the next few years of her life.

In February 1920, a young woman came forward claiming to be Alix's fourth daughter Anastasia. The claimant was in fact a Polish peasant, with a history of mental illness, but both Victoria's and Irène's children were caught up in the furore. The sisters' grandchildren were then dragged in as court cases continued, into the 1970s, involving various legacies.

The claimant had first come to notice after apparently trying to commit suicide by throwing herself into the Landwehr Canal in Berlin. Initially refusing to say who she was, she then claimed to be Alix's second daughter, Tatiana, before 'admitting' finally that she was Anastasia.

Though many of the Hesse sisters' relations would be drawn into this bizarre case, Irène played a particularly important role: firstly, because she was based in Germany, where the drama played itself out, and secondly, because the bedraggled young woman claimed she had initially travelled to Berlin to see her 'aunt' Irène, and had got as far as the gates of the Netherlands Palace before losing heart. Convinced that Irène would not be there and that no one would recognise her, she had, she said, decided to end it all. After being pulled out of the water, she was taken to a psychiatric hospital.

Irène was tentatively helpful. She agreed that Alix's lady-in-waiting, Baroness Buxhoeveden, who was staying at Hemmelmark at the time, could visit the claimant to see if she recognised her. The mystery woman was still insisting, at this point, that she was Anastasia's willowy older sister Tatiana. The Baroness was unimpressed, declaring her too short.

Irène requested that Alix's one-time companion, Anna Vyrubova, write to the woman, now claiming to be Anastasia, with three questions:

1. Do you remember the chair which was located in your mother's room and the name which had been given it?
2. What colour was this chair?
3. It was remodelled. What was its colour afterwards?

The claimant's answers were never revealed.

The fond aunt would have last met the real Anastasia dyeing scarves and enjoying meals 'on the sofa', during her stay at Peterhof in 1913. Irène had been her godmother.

In 1922, Irène finally agreed to meet her 'niece' over an awkward supper at a police inspector's house in Berlin. 'Anastasia' was not told the identity of her visitor. After several minutes, she ran from the dining room. Her supporters claimed she fled after recognising Irène's voice. It seems more likely that she realised she was being put to the test and lost her nerve.

According to one source, Irène followed her 'niece', calling her 'dear

Anastasia' and begging her to come to Hemmelmark. Several accounts agree that Irène joined the young woman in her bedroom, where 'Anastasia' lay on a bed with her face to the wall, weeping.

Years later, the claimant, by now firmly convinced that she really was Anastasia, complained: 'I'd written to her [Irène] in 1920. She didn't answer with a single word. She permitted me to be kept for two years in a lunatic asylum, in one room, with 20 crazy people.

'And then she came. She came to me, her godchild, under a false name, she met me in a dark room . . . They said Aunt Irène loved me dearly and was ready to do everything for me. If this was true why didn't she do it?'

Irène pronounced her a fraud: 'I saw immediately that she could not be one of my nieces. Even though I had not seen them for nine years the fundamental facial characteristics could not have altered to that degree, in particular the position of the eyes, the ears and so forth.'

Curiously, Irène's letters to Victoria, through 1922, contain no reference to the claimant. Rather, she agonised over the publication of letters from Alix to the Tsar: 'An abridged extract of Alicky's letters to Nicky during the war has appeared & short notes during her imprisonment in Tobolsk and Ekaterinburg. It goes through and through – poor child what she suffered – it pains me that her innermost thoughts should be laid fallow & yet, one will judge her more fairly by this.'

She then sent Victoria bleakly comforting greetings on her second birthday without Prince Louis: 'Heartfelt good wishes from us all for your dear Birthday, may this year be a less sad one for you, though the ache at your poor heart I fear will never be overcome – may your dear ones bring you various joys & comfort and may we be able to meet in the course of the year.' In September, she gave a wistful nod to Madgie: 'Today is poor Miss Jackson's birthday. I wonder who lives in her little home now.'

In December, she commiserated with Victoria on her second Christmas as a widow: 'Xmas may perhaps not be quite as painful as last year I do hope – but nothing can fill the blank I fear which must be worse than ever at such times.'

Did Irène find the 'Anastasia' issue too painful to broach with her sister? It is hard to believe that she considered it unimportant.

She did, however, write about it to Alix's devoted lady-in-waiting, Madeleine Zanotti, who had followed her mistress from Darmstadt to St Petersburg and finally, to Tobolsk. In that letter, written, in German, on September 21st, she seemed to betray doubts about her dismissal of 'Anastasia': 'Dear Madeleine, You must have heard of my trip to Berlin on account of my false niece Anastasia . . . Just one more thing – which features are there that one can recognise?'

Years later, Irène was talking to one of her nephews, a so-called 'Anastasian', who believed the claimant, when she admitted: 'She IS similar. She IS similar. But what does that mean if it is not she?' Confused and distraught, she is said to have wept.

In the end, the affair upset Irène 'so terribly', according to one of her Prussian in-laws, that her husband forbade any conversation about it in the house. In the winter of 1924, an official at Hemmelmark wrote starkly to one of the claimant's champions, a Baron von Kleist: 'His Royal Highness . . . has requested me to inform you that he as well as his wife, after the latter's visit to your protegée, have come to the unshakable conviction that she is not a daughter of the Tsar, specifically not Grand Duchess Anastasia. Prince Henry considers the matter, as it concerns himself and his wife, cleared up and finally settled and insists that you refrain from the further sending of letters or requests to himself or the Princess.' A follow-up note requested the return of letters.

Plagued by thoughts of the fate of her sister and her family, Irène sent a plaintive inquiry to Alix's friend, Anna Vyrubova, wondering whether the gifts she had sent to Tobolsk had ever arrived. Anna Vyrubova replied: 'All the things I got through the Swedish Legation I sent to Tobolsk – all what came before June reached them.'

In 1927, Irène's husband, Prince Henry, became seriously ill. Over the next two years, he would need her full-time care; the chain-smoking Prince had suffered from angina before falling prey to bronchitis and then pneumonia. He died, aged 66, in April 1929. He was buried in the elaborate family mausoleum, alongside little Heinrich. The obituary in *The Times* included a dig at the Kaiser, saying that Prince Henry possessed 'certain English attributes of moderation, good humour and plain sense, while the Hohenzollern strain predominated in his elder brother'.

Victoria was not among the thousand mourners at Prince Henry's obsequies. Though she had visited Hemmelmark over the years, she probably felt uncomfortable attending so public an event in Germany. For all the Prince's lofty credentials as Queen Victoria's grandchild, there was virtually no British presence at his funeral.

Ernie left a poignant description of Irène's last years: 'She is alone now, but in spite of this she manages to do so much that she is sometimes completely worn out. Her only thought and concern is to find ways in which she can help people, time and time again.' Irène had taken on the mantle of her altruistic mother Alice.

She began collecting books on plants and agriculture, while adding to a collection of recipes. One of her favourite dishes was Alix's chef's cabbage soup, 'shchi'; in 1898, she had been sent the recipe, together with a drawing entitled 'Ein Lebendig Tafelaufsatz' (a Lively Table Piece). The picture, which she carefully conserved, showed the Tsar and his daughters at table: the daughters are misbehaving and the caption, in Cyrillic lettering is: '*Nyet!*'

In 1928, Victoria's elder daughter, Alice, was received into the Greek Orthodox Church. Alice had never lost her fascination with Aunt Ella's spiritual aspirations. She had been profoundly moved when she witnessed the laying of the foundations of the Martha and Mary Convent, in Moscow, in 1907.

What Aunt Ella would have made of the more outlandish aspects of her niece's religious journey is hard to tell. Alice was now insisting she had seen visions of a St Barbara, probably Ella's companion, Sister Varvara. During visits to Britain, Alice consulted Grand Duchess Xenia's mysterious companion, Mother Martha, who wore black robes and black boots, and was suspected of being a man.

Family entanglements intensified, in 1929, as the Anastasia claimant, who had by now changed her name to Anna Anderson, moved in with a relation of the Romanovs in America, Princess Xenia, a cousin of the real Anastasia, who was married to a tin-plate millionaire, Billy Leeds, and lived on Long Island. Husband and wife came to blows over the claimant and 'Anastasia' was said to have cost Billy Leeds his marriage.

Ella's stepdaughter, Maria Pavlovna, by then living in New York, was among those who refused even to meet the claimant. Maria eventually settled in Germany, where she died of pneumonia in 1958.

In 1927, the *New York Times* reported breezily that Prince Sigismund of Prussia was moving from Guatemala to Costa Rica, with his wife, Princess Charlotte, children Barbara and Alfredo, and a governess. From now on the Prince would 'engage in planting coffee and bananas'.

The planting, however, turned out to be insufficiently engaging and the Prince began devoting his energy to an altogether more delicate project: the false Anastasia. Dismissive of his mother's denunciation, unfazed by his father's earlier plea for closure, Sigismund was determined to settle the matter for himself.

By 1931, he had compiled a list of 18 questions to be put to the claimant by his brother-in-law, Prince Frederick. The questions centred on Sigismund's last meeting, aged 15, with Anastasia, during the ill-fated holiday in Spala.

Sigismund and Prince Frederick were convinced that Anna Anderson could only have known details about Spala had she actually been there. They never revealed the specific questions, fearing that they would be picked apart by the woman's opponents. Prince Frederick said in an affadavit in 1938: 'Together my brother-in-law and I had determined that this final meeting . . . had not been mentioned anywhere in the memoirs or literature of the period. I – we – stress this point because it is known how suspicious those people are who believe themselves capable of passing judgement.'

Anderson's final answers, though mulled over for a full five days, were enough to persuade Sigismund: 'This has convinced me. She is undoubtedly Anastasia of Russia.' Prince Frederick himself was so bowled over that he devoted a substantial part of the rest of his life to looking after 'Anastasia'.

*

Through the 1930s, the two surviving Hesse sisters, now well into their sixties, may have hoped to settle into a quiet widowhood. As it turned out, both continued to be buffeted by fate, facing challenges involving their six children and eleven grandchildren, not to mention an occasional brush with 'Anastasia'.

Victoria's daughter Alice's obsession with the spiritual world had developed into a form of religious mania: she now claimed to be in contact with Christ and the Buddha. Victoria had her 'involuntarily committed' to a psychiatric clinic in Switzerland. When doctors contacted Sigmund Freud about her case, he put Alice's delusions down to sexual frustration. He recommended X-raying her ovaries in order to kill off her libido.

After spells at various clinics, Alice drifted around Europe, returning briefly to the family in 1937, before basing herself finally in Athens.

Victoria and her two sons were obliged to tend to Alice's young son, Philip. His four sisters, all substantially older, had mostly begun living independent lives. The eldest, Margarita, married in 1931, when he was ten. Years later, when Gyles Brandreth was writing a biography of Prince Philip, he asked Brett Kahr, a Freudian psychologist, how a boy would be affected by having four elder sisters. Kahr's reply was crude: 'So after all those girls, here is a boy, and what do boys have that girls do not have? A penis. And the admiration and devotion of the women, especially the sisters, will have given you what might be termed a certain "phallic swagger".'

Did Philip develop a 'phallic swagger'? Whatever the case, he seems to have settled in well at Uncle George's old school, Cheam, and then at Gordonstoun.

His other uncle, Louis or 'Dickie' Mountbatten, 20 years his senior, is sometimes seen as having wielded the strongest influence over him. Philip's cousin, the future Queen of Yugoslavia recalled: 'He [Philip] talked to me with passionate excitement of Uncle Dickie's penthouse, where the lift from the street level was the fastest in London and how Uncle Dickie's study had a world map in relief on the walls, and his bedroom was like a cabin in a battle cruiser, even to the portholes.'

The historian Hugo Vickers maintains that Victoria was the most powerful influence: 'She really brought him up . . . She was the person who got his school clothes for him, and the only member of the family to visit him at Gordonstoun. When his father failed to materialise for his summer holiday, she would take him to Hemmelmark.' Victoria took a robust attitude to discipline, at one point assuring the young Louis Mountbatten that it was alright to be caned or, as she put it, 'swished'.

While Victoria struggled with her daughter Alice's mental health issues, Irène was laid low following an arduous journey to visit Sigismund in Central America. In another bid to persuade her son to return to Germany, she had set off for Costa Rica towards the end of 1933, spending four months with Sigismund, his wife Charlotte and their two children in the family's slightly rickety finca.

Irène and her husband Prince Henry had once been known for their agreeable manner; Irène now devoted herself to helping others. But her grandson, Alfredo, then aged nine, was struck by his grandmother's sternness. The atmosphere could not have been helped by Sigismund's continued refusal to bring his family home to Germany. The thorny subject of Anna Anderson created further ructions. Sigismund begged his mother to see 'Anastasia' again; she flatly refused. Sigismund's wife Charlotte told a friend that Irène would not even discuss the matter: 'She didn't want to talk about Anastasia when Sigismund mentioned her in a positive way.'

Upon her return to Germany, Irène went to Darmstadt, where she met Victoria. There had never been any let-up in the sisters' preoccupation with each other's health and Victoria was immediately concerned. 'Poor Aunt Irène arrived a week ago thin & run down & had to go to bed, where she still is, having caught a chill on her way here, which gave her bronchitis,' she wrote to her son George. 'Luckily it went no further & she is recovering steadily. She is bound to be very shaky, when she gets up. She did not stand either the food nor the climate at Costa Rica.'

Sigismund would have argued otherwise; in the interview he gave in 1976, he insisted: 'She liked it here.'

Several larger Hesse family get-togethers and celebrations gave the sisters a respite from their immediate domestic worries. In February 1931, Victoria's granddaughter, Cecilie, married Ernie's son George Donatus, and in 1936, the sisters came together again for Irène's 70th birthday at Hemmelmark. This would have been one of the last happy Hesse gatherings.

That same year, the sisters' cousin, King George V, died. Neither knew of his role in the withdrawal of the offer of a sanctuary to Alix and her family. Both were deeply upset by his death.

Victoria attended the funeral, while Irène wrote a heartfelt letter to the grieving Queen from Hemmelmark: 'My Dear May, How I feel for you that you must take up your daily life again, with that terrible heartache no one can relieve you of, that terrible yearning and loneliness. God help you through it all. What a comfort I can well imagine it must have been to you, that you both were able to celebrate your 25 years Jubilee together, and the marriage of your boys. To realize what love was given to you from your peoples in those long years and your devotion to them – and no doubt the love that surrounded you will now be redoubled for your dear self in your heartache and for David [Edward VIII].'

During the late 30s, Victoria was singled out for particular suffering. The politician and diarist Chips Channon called her 'La Dame des Pleurs'. He may have been closer to the mark than he realised.

In 1937, the sisters' beloved brother Ernie died, bringing to an end an especially precious relationship for Victoria. Since the deaths of her sisters, it had been the sensitive, cheerful Ernie, rather than Irène, in whom Victoria confided.

Weeks later, Victoria's granddaughter, Cecilie, was due to fly to London with her husband, George, and their two small sons, to attend George's brother Lu's wedding. But they never arrived. Their plane crashed into a chimney stack near Ostend, and they were all killed, along with Cecilie's unborn baby. Victoria and Irène met in Darmstadt for the family's funeral.

Reeling from the death not just of her brother, but now of her granddaughter and family too, Victoria faced the worst loss of all. In April 1938, her son George died, aged just 45, of bone marrow cancer.

Her note to Queen Mary contained one of her rare admissions of weakness: 'I am strong and my health is alright only my nerves are rather strained so that I can't control my feelings as well as I could.'

She stayed with Irène at Wolfsgarten as well as Hemmelmark, where they each apparently gleaned sisterly solace from the other. Irène wrote to her aunt, Princess Louise, from Wolfsgarten: 'It was such a comfort for me & Victoria on arriving here together yesterday for the first time in our dear old home since we lost so many of our loved ones.'

Meanwhile, the Anna Anderson saga proved unending. For several years, the main issue had been the Romanov inheritance. If Anna Anderson really was Anastasia, she would be prime legatee. In 1933, Victoria had assured her son, Louis, that the fortunes of 'poor Alix & Nicky's children should fall to the heirs according to German law . . . Aunts Xenia, Olga, Countess Brassow [the widow of the Tsar's brother Michael] & myself, Aunt Irène and Uncle Ernie.'

As the Jarndyce vs Jarndyce wrangles continued, the relatives may have asked themselves whether the fortune was worth the effort. By the time they had won one case, in January 1934, the Tsar's assets had shrunk to a modest £25,000.

When one of Anna Anderson's petitions was rejected, she launched an appeal that would not be turned down until 1957, by which time both Victoria and Irène had died.

By 1938, Victoria was sufficiently fascinated by the claimant to be reading and making note of at least three books about her. One was by a woman who had known her in her early days; another by the Romanov children's Swiss tutor, Pierre Gilliard. She also read *The Woman Who Rose Again* by Gleb Botkin, the son of Alix's Dr Botkin, who had been murdered with the Imperial Family. In brackets Victoria wrote after the title: 'Story of the so-called Gr[an]d D[uchess] Anastasia.' Gleb Botkin had, in fact, come to England to see Victoria after 'recognising' the claimant in 1927. But Victoria had, perhaps conveniently, been 'out of town'.

Victoria inevitably chatted about Anna Anderson with her friend Gloria Vanderbilt. Though she had never met the claimant, she had studied photographs. Victoria told Vanderbilt that Anna Anderson was 'an imposter of the most brazen order. After all, I was Anastasia's aunt and I know my niece when I see her. It was not as if years had intervened since she was an infant and I had lost touch with her. I visited Russia constantly and saw her up to within a year or two of the revolution.' Victoria did add that she saw a vague resemblance between the two women: 'Most certainly this was the only thing she had to pin her claim to.'

Irène may have failed to persuade Sigismund to return to Germany for good, but in 1938 he brought his family over for a visit and Irène's granddaughter, Barbara, then 18, decided to settle at Hemmelmark. Irène was delighted to welcome back her 'beam of sunshine'.

Her grandson, Alfredo, also remained in Europe for several years, though not in Germany. Following Sigismund's refusal to have his son educated by Nazis, Alfredo was sent to school in Switzerland; he spent eight years in Europe before settling in Costa Rica.

Irène and Victoria enjoyed one of their last get-togethers in May 1939, when they visited Queen Mary at Marlborough House.

*

Throughout the early 1930s, Victoria welcomed Hitler, hoping he would rout the murdering Communists and restore the Hohenzollerns to the throne. Three of her granddaughters – Cecilie, Margarita and Sophie – had married Nazis. Margarita's husband became a commander in the German Army during the war. Sophie's husband, Christoph of Hesse, was director of the Third Reich's Ministry of Air Forces. He worked for the organisation that evolved into the Gestapo, and was killed flying for the Luftwaffe. The couple named their first son Karl Adolf, after Hitler. Cecilie and her husband, George Donatus, were both members of the Nazi party when they died in the plane crash in 1937. Their funeral was attended by Hermann Göring.

In April 1933, Victoria wrote to her son Louis: 'Hitler has the true German mentality & it is his enthusiasm for a more idealistic outlook on life, which wins him the immense support he gets from the mass of people who are sick of the low ideals, money grubbing and place hunting of the Socialists . . . it remains to be seen, however, if Hitler is a big enough brain to become the German Mussolini.'

Two years later, she was still enthusing, but had become slightly worried by the Nazis' brazen attitude: 'The mass of the people still have complete confidence in Hitler & his leadership & are working hard and cheerfully – the young Nazis are less to the fore & when they have done a year's military service will have much of the swagger & conceit taken out of them,' she added to Louis.

By the time the British declared war on Germany, however, Victoria had performed a volte face and was keenly rooting for the Allies. Listening to her at the Duke of Kent's funeral, in 1942, Chips Channon noted that the garrulous Victoria was 'extremely anti-Hitler'.

Her most immediate concern had been maintaining contact with her family in Germany. She was grateful that her daughter, Louise, was in Sweden: 'Louise thank goodness is in a completely neutral country & may be able perhaps to hear from time to time how Alice's daughters & Irène are keeping,' she wrote to the Tsar's sister, Grand Duchess Xenia, now based at Hampton Court.

As the war took hold, Irène liked to stress that her Hessian relations were different from the war-mongering and rebellious Prussians: a nice point that Alix had tried to labour.

In 1940, Irène's son, Waldemar, inherited a castle in Silesia, Schloss Kamenz, from a distant cousin. He moved there with his wife and the couple were joined, at some point, by Irène. In June 1943, Victoria told

Queen Mary that she had heard reassuring news of Irène from her daughter Louise: 'Irène is well & has been to Wolfsgarten.'

But two years later, Irène suffered her worst blow since the death of little Heinrich. Waldemar was escaping the advancing Russians when he fell ill in Bavaria. He was in dire need of a blood transfusion, but medical resources had been diverted to treat concentration camp victims. He died, on May 2nd 1945, aged 46.

With the loss of an adult son, Irène shared another terrible bond with her elder sister.

Ella's stepson, Dmitri, developed TB and died in Davos, Switzerland in 1942. Throughout his later life, he had made efforts to shake off his dark links with Rasputin's murder, setting himself up as a Champagne salesman in Palm Beach, Florida. Prince Philip always remembered him fondly: 'He was around a lot when I was a boy. He was a hugely entertaining chap, I remember him with great affection.'

He married the great-aunt of novelist Edward St Aubyn. Did St Aubyn think Dmitri was haunted by Rasputin? He replies drily: 'Who knows what he was haunted by – there were so many candidates. But anyone who drinks 22 dry martinis BEFORE lunch (according to my grandfather) can't be a happy bunny. Twenty-two dry martinis after lunch is obviously totally normal, and only a nanny state would say otherwise.'

*

By the time peace was declared, in 1945, the sisters' lives were in stark contrast. Victoria's star rose ever higher, as her second son, Louis, was appointed Supreme Allied Commander South-East Asia Command. For his tireless service in the war, he was created Viscount Mountbatten of Burma.

For her part, Irène was faced with a series of humiliations. The Allies now occupied Germany and the RAF had taken over the main house at Hemmelmark. Irène and her granddaughter Barbara were obliged to move into 'the servant's wing'.

She then found herself unable to meet Victoria or her grandson, Alfredo, in Sweden, without a British travel permit. She was driven to appealing to Queen Mary: 'My Dearest May, I am in a fix as I had hoped to be able to visit Louise in Sweden accompanied by Barbara – so as to see Victoria and my grandson – before he goes to Costa Rica leaving on August 20th by sea. It seems that I cannot attain a permit from the British occupation army here in Kiel unless you kindly showed your interest in this case for our meeting to take place.

'The fact is that I have urgent family matters pertaining to inheritance to settle which Alfred must submit to Sigismund his father & also certain things to settle with Victoria which both I cannot postpone. I am already in possession of the permit from Sweden and I would be so grateful if you could help me in this case. So far we all are quite well and the Royal Airforce detachment here in Hemmelmark is leaving on July 23rd. I can only say that I am most grateful for the consideration I received during the occupation.'

The 'matters pertaining to inheritance' here probably referred to the recent death of Waldemar.

Less urgent news concerned her recent 80th birthday. She may have thought back to her happier 70th birthday celebrations with Victoria. 'On July 11 was my 80th birthday', she added grimly, 'and I am still able to work a little in the garden.' She sent a photograph of herself looking slightly woebegone amongst the shrubs.

A month later, Irène's application for a permit was formally turned down and she was reduced to writing a second beseeching letter to the Queen.

Perhaps to her own astonishment, Queen Mary tried and failed to procure the longed-for permit. Victoria now chimed in, thanking May for her efforts. She was quite philosophical, perhaps less hungry than Irène for a reunion: 'Thank you so much for your kind letter & for having enquired why Irène could not receive a visa – of course it would have been nice for us if we could have met once more, but perhaps we may have a chance to do so next year.'

By October, Irène had moved on, pleased to inform May that the RAF had finally left Hemmelmark, happier still to reminisce about 'dear Grandmama in Balmoral': 'Lu and Peg [Ernie's son and his wife] are here for a few days – a great joy to me, and it is such a comfort also to be able to hear of my dear old home and relations, the most of which are so far off. She [Peg] also gave me good news of your dear self and how grateful she was for your great kindness to her. . . . Here the British occupation, which was in the main house, has left – I go on living in the servants wing – & the Red Cross Society I have offered to take over the former as a home for old homeless nurses & such as are in need of recuperation, which seems to answer the purpose very well . . . Life is full of sadness but I like to think of old days when we were one autumn together with dear Grandmama in Balmoral especially.'

All four Princesses of Hesse had considered themselves English. But, during their last years, the two surviving sisters were kept apart by finicky British regulations. And the lives of the two sisters, now in their eighties, continued to diverge.

In Britain, the King and Queen attended the wedding of Victoria's granddaughter, Patricia. The Princesses Elizabeth and Margaret were both bridesmaids; Elizabeth and her future husband, Victoria's grandson Philip, were photographed together. The following year, in 1947, Philip would marry Princess Elizabeth: that same year Louis Mountbatten was made Viceroy of India.

Victoria was appointed godmother to Elizabeth and Philip's first child, Prince Charles. Irène had to settle for a photograph. In a thank-you note to

Queen Mary, Irène managed to point out that she was in better shape than her sister, even though she needed a hearing aid: 'I have to thank you for a delightful photo of Elisabeth [sic] Philip and their sweet baby Charles that you sent me . . . he looks such an adorable child. I am thankful to be in good health and grieve for poor Victoria who suffers so much pain from her hands and feet. I am happy to hear from you that her eyesight seems better again. At last I have found an ear-acoustic aparatus, which suits my purposes and is not very aparent [sic] which will be for my surroundings also a great boon.

'I hope you had a pleasant Xmas? The preparations are most tiring I find.'

12

'Am I still here?'
Victoria

Victoria, well into her eighties, was ailing. She expected to die daily, waking every morning with the same wry thought: 'Am I still here? I'm not supposed to be here.'

The Marchioness of Milford Haven died on September 24th, 1950, aged 87. In preparation for her death, she wrote a brave and heartfelt letter to her family: 'The bitterest grief in my life has been the loss of Georgie [her son]. You will miss me I know, but let it be a comfort to you to realize that the best part of my life & on the whole it has been a happy one, was ended when your dear father died & that I am ready & willing to enter into my rest at any time now.'

Irène was gratified to receive a warm and prompt letter of condolence from Queen Mary. 'I am deeply touched by your kind sympathy at the loss of our dear Victoria [who] we shall miss so terribly,' she replied. 'You cannot imagine what a comfort it was to Victoria – all your kindness to her – of which she so often told me and was such a comfort to her – such a dear link with old times & the happy past – it is sad when one grows so lonely in old age, even when all the many young generations are so kind to me. How kind of Bertie [King George VI] suggesting that a Destroyer should take the coffin over to Cowes so that her remains can be placed by Ludwig's, her Louis.'

Victoria and Prince Louis were buried together at St Mildred's Church, Whippingham, on the Isle of Wight.

Irène was now the sole survivor of the four Princesses of Hesse. In 1952, she adopted her beloved granddaughter Barbara as her heir. Though now in her eighties, she carried on working as Honorary Chairman of the German Red Cross.

She developed an increasingly formidable persona. One of her aristocratic neighbours recalled tense teas with the elderly 'Princess Heinrich', as she liked to be addressed. The neighbour, then aged 12, remembered being restricted to wistful gazes out of the window: 'You had to sit up and behave, you mustn't talk – or cross your legs.'

Irène insisted the English jeweller in Kiel, Hansen, import marmalade especially for her. She was particular about her scrambled eggs, insisting the egg whites rise and curve to resemble white handkerchiefs. Once, she rang a neighbour to propose a visit. Unfazed by the clumsy butler's reply – 'She says she's not in' – Irène announced that she would be over in 15 minutes.

Her former 'aimable' side was mostly reserved for her correspondence with Queen Mary. In 1951, she wrote thoughtfully concerning her son King George VI's illness: 'Just a line to tell you how much my thoughts are with you and yours in the great anxiety you are going through on your dear Bertie's account. May God preserve his life and give him a good recovery. In memory of "auld lang syne" ever your affectionate cousin Irène'. The King, in fact, died the following year.

The letter continued with philosophical musings marking May's 85th birthday: 'Many instances are impressed on my memory of long ago – which crop up more and more now as one grows older – and are quite fresh in one's memory. How strange times are nowadays, people places and things all in a perpetual move – and one can forget all around one when these memories crop up unawares. It is such a comfort to know you are there still – that one's thoughts can recall you in Marlborough House where we last met, my dear sister Victoria accompanying me to you.'

Irène, died, at Hemmelmark, on November 11ᵗʰ, 1953, at the age of 87. Her much-loved granddaughter Barbara, who had tended her through various illnesses, was beside her when she died. Perhaps it was appropriate, given her name's connotations of peace, that she died on Armistice Day.

Her correspondent, Queen Mary, had predeceased her by eight months. The German press noted with disapproval that Queen Elizabeth sent no representative to Irène's funeral, in spite of her close relationship with May. She lies in the mausoleum at Hemmelmark with her husband and little Heinrich.

*

Victoria's daughter Alice continued her erratic spiritual journey. In 1949, Alice had followed in her aunt Ella's footsteps, appointing herself Life President of her own Christian Sisterhood of Martha and Mary.

Alice attended her son's wedding in civilian clothes but, by the time of Queen Elizabeth's coronation, in 1953, she had adopted a nun's habit. Prince Philip maintained a matter-of-fact attitude towards his mother's attire: 'Wearing the habit meant she did not have to worry about clothes or getting her hair done.' But he retained a keen interest in nuns and their orders, opening discussions with: 'Which regiment?'

Victoria had maintained a sceptical attitude to Alice's spiritual pursuit, believing her daughter made a mockery of Ella's achievements: 'What can you say of a nun who smokes and plays canasta?' Queen Mary had also been critical, deeming Alice less like her aunt Ella and more like her aunt Alix: 'The trouble between Alice and Andrew [her husband] started when she became Orthodox & religion went to her head (like poor Alix of Russia). She insisted on sleeping on the floor and was too whacked for words.'

Fourteen years after the coronation, in 1967, Queen Elizabeth invited

Alice to live at Buckingham Palace. There were worries about the turmoil in Greece, where she was still living. At the palace, Alice entertained the young Prince Charles with tales of Queen Victoria, the fearsome woman she had once called 'naughty Grandmama'.

Victoria's two daughters were to die in the space of four years – Louise, by then Queen of Sweden, in 1965 and Alice in 1969.

Two years after Victoria's death, Louis Mountbatten was appointed Commander-in-Chief of the British Mediterranean Fleet and NATO Commander Allied Forces Mediterranean. From 1955 to 1959, he held the post once occupied by his father: First Sea Lord.

Though not the actual head, Mountbatten was the most prominent member of the Hesse family. It was in this capacity that he led the campaign against the claimant Anna Anderson. The real Anastasia had been his first cousin and almost an exact contemporary.

He proved a formidable opponent for Anna Anderson's supporters, the 'Anastasians'. Throughout his life, he battled with various investigators and writers, at one point admitting publicly that the controversy had cost him thousands of pounds.

It was Mountbatten who sorted out Irène's letters to his mother following Victoria's death. Did he remove references to the false Anastasia? This might explain the lack of any mention of the claimant in Irène's surviving letters from 1922, the year she met her 'niece'.

His stand against Anna Anderson put him in direct opposition to another first cousin, Irène's son, Sigismund.

For all Sigismund's strong convictions, it was a full 26 years before he actually met the claimant in 1957. One reason for the delay would have been his infrequent visits to Europe. But he may also have hesitated to pursue a meeting while his mother was alive.

Irène had been dead for four years by the time Sigismund reached

Anna Anderson's shack in the Black Forest. He was obliged to knock at the door for three days before she let him in. He was no more put out by her reluctance to see him than he was by her filthy, cat-infested home. Such obstacles served only to strengthen his conviction. In 1976, he gave a sparse account of the meeting: 'Talked of Spala – we remembered the same things . . . Spent several days at Unterlengenhardt. Stayed at house at Bad Liebenzell. Talked about Friedberg and Spala. Convinced it is she.' Friedberg was the place where the four Princesses met for the last time; Spala referred to the hunting lodge where the Tsarevich nearly died in 1912.

At around the same time that he saw 'Anastasia', he also saw a claimant posing as her eldest sister, Olga.

Louis Mountbatten was especially critical of Sigismund's decision to meet this second claimant. The even less plausible 'Olga' lived at Menaggio, on Lake Como. Both claimants insisted that the other had died at Ekaterinburg, so they were at odds with one another. Sigismund sounded faintly amused by the women's refusal to meet each other: 'She [Olga] said she saw Anastasia was finished. Anastasia said Olga was dead.'

Mountbatten was not the only relation ranged against Sigismund. Barely a year after his visit to 'Anastasia's' shack, Sigismund's own daughter, Barbara, entered the ring, when Anna Anderson tried to block her 6,000-mark inheritance and she found herself immersed in court proceedings. The result took three years to come through: 'The claim is unfounded. The plaintiff, Mrs Anderson, is defeated.'

What Sigismund thought of his daughter's opposition is unclear. Irène's great-granddaughter, Donata, the Duchess of Mecklenburg, acknowledges that the case created a 'nightmare' schism within the family. Her husband, Alexander von Solodkoff, recalls that Barbara was reluctant to discuss the affair. He adds that the family had been almost driven to sell Hemmelmark to pay for the legal costs. Irène's relations were obliged to supply photographs of the real Grand Duchess Anastasia for the trial; of particular public interest were close-ups of Anastasia's ear. These were all returned with an obtrusive stamp on the back.

Amid this surge of interest, Mountbatten was forced, at one point, to step in to prevent Anna Anderson from giving at least one major television interview.

The family historian Prince Rainer von Hessen is adamant that Anna Anderson's relentless staying power lay simply in her extraordinary facility for accruing knowledge over the years.

By the late 1960s, the last two surviving children of the Princesses of Hesse were inhabiting different worlds. Victoria's son Louis Mountbatten was installed at the palatial Broadlands, where he had lived with his wife Edwina for several decades. He had been appointed, not least, Knight Grand Cross of the Royal Victorian Order and Knight Companion of the Most Noble Order of the Garter. In uniform, he wore, alongside innumerable medals, four glittering breast stars: The Order of the Garter, The Order of the Bath, The Order of the Star of India and the Royal Victorian Order.

Such was his status that a 12-part TV series on his life had been broadcast, featuring interviews with Prince Philip and the Duke of Windsor. A royal preview at the Imperial War Museum was attended by Queen Elizabeth and Prince Philip.

On the other hand, Irène's son, Sigismund, a Prince of Prussia and great-grandson of Queen Victoria through both his parents, was living in reduced circumstances at his rather humbler finca in Costa Rica.

In October 1969, an American accountant called Greg Rittenhouse, based at the University of Washington, in Seattle, stayed overnight with Sigismund and his wife, Princess Charlotte. The Prince's four-bedroom finca, San Miguel, was clearly rundown. Their living situation seemed rather primitive,' admitted Rittenhouse. 'Everything was shabby but reasonably comfortable.'

Sigismund had once claimed to own 100 acres of land on which he grew his coffee and bananas. But Rittenhouse doubted he was growing anything, as the land surrounding the farm was hilly and covered by trees. If they had ever existed, the plantations were long gone. Sigismund later claimed, in his 1976 interview, that he owned cattle.

Rittenhouse had been invited to stay at the finca having struck up a genial correspondence with Sigismund concerning their shared faith in Anna Anderson.

Rittenhouse had met her in 1968, and in fact been rather unsettled by her behaviour. She had bawled at her eccentric fiancé and claimed to have eaten half a pound of butter in one sitting. But he sent a respectful report to Sigismund and months later received a warm reply: 'With pleasure I received the notice that you made the acquaintance of Grand Duchess Anastasia and are impressed by the humane way she treats people she meets. Yours faithfully, Sigismund, Prince of Prussia.'

Instructions for Rittenhouse's visit were elaborate. There would clearly be nothing in the way of flunkeys to help with luggage. Indeed, at one point, it looked as though he might have to do the last leg of his journey, several miles up a rough track, on foot.

At that point, anyone wishing to visit Sigismund, Prince of Prussia, had to fly from San José to Puntarenas, then get a bus to the village of Barranca. At Barranca, a driver would have to be found, willing to make the hazardous drive up various hills to the finca. 'For this purpose', Sigismund wrote, 'you must ask in a little shop which belongs to Bolivar Vargas and say that you would like to go to the house of the Prince (quiero irme a casa de Principe en la finca San Miguel)'.

In the event, a glitch arose with the driver and, in a further letter, Sigismund wrote to Rittenhouse: 'In this small village the chauffeur of the only automobile to hire refuses to go up to the finca San Miguel with you, regarding to the many stones on the way. So I beg you . . . to wait in Barranca until the man delivering this letter goes to Espartatto to fetch a car which will take you from Barranca to my house . . . Please come to an understanding with el senor Bolivar Vargas in his shop in the main street.'

After this blizzard of instructions, Rittenhouse was relieved when he was finally picked up by two men in a truck. As Rittenhouse confirmed: 'The road there was unpaved and rocky.'

It had been a challenging journey. But any difficulties were forgotten when Rittenhouse was greeted ecstatically by Princess Charlotte, who ran from the house exclaiming: 'You saw our cousin!'

Inside Sigismund's house, Rittenhouse noticed a German copy of Anna Anderson's so-called autobiography: *I Am Anastasia*. Sigismund clung to his conviction that, in her later years, his mother had changed her mind about the claimant. 'I asked about his mother's attitude to Anastasia,' wrote Rittenhouse, 'and he replied that, after receiving a letter from one of the Grand Dukes living in France, Irène had told one of Prince Frederick's aunts: "Maybe I made a mistake. Maybe it is Anastasia".'

Sigismund's skeleton staff comprised a housekeeper and an elusive manservant. Rittenhouse recalls that, after dinner, as it was getting dark, Sigismund brought a kerosene lamp into the sitting room, explaining: 'The man will be here later to turn on the electricity . . .' Towards the end of the evening, however, he made a further announcement: 'The man won't come because it is raining.'

Rittenhouse was taken aback, the following morning, to come across Princess Charlotte, then aged 70, sweeping leaves in the yard, under a boiling-hot sun.

Following the visit, Rittenhouse and Sigismund continued their correspondence, but never dropped the formalities, remaining 'Mr Rittenhouse' and 'Sigismund Prince of Prussia'. Sigismund was convinced that Anna Anderson and her outlandish tam o'shanter-wearing husband, Jack Manahan, 20 years her junior, were ready to take on the challenging journey to the Finca San Miguel, writing to Rittenhouse on Jan 20th 1970: 'I know that Anastasia and her husband intended to come to Costa Rica and that there were some difficulties about the papers of the Grand Duchess.'

On Nov 22nd 1973, Sigismund was excited after hearing about coverage of 'Anastasia' in the Philippines: 'Mr Manahan sent me an issue of the 'Woman's Home Companion', the only women's magazine published in the Philippines, about the Anastasia story, nothing new, but interesting that a publication of this matter was spread in the Far East.'

Sigismund's cousin, Louis Mountbatten, would have been less pleased to hear about the spread of the Anna Anderson story. On March 11th 1975, he wrote a terse letter from Broadlands to a Mr Woodcock-Clarke, who had written to him regarding the claimant: 'There can be no question whatever that my first cousin, the Grand Duchess Anastasia of Russia, was assassinated with the rest of her family, although in her case she did not die at once and was finished off with bayonet thrusts.

'The question gave rise to [a] long and expensive set of lawsuits but finally the Court of Appeal in Germany rules beyond all doubt that the Polish landgirl who took the name Anna Anderson was neither the Grand Duchess Anastasia nor her sister, the Grand Duchess Tatiana, as she originally claimed.'

In a repeat of his Aunt Irène's digs at the 'wavering' Tsar Nicholas, he added: 'The Emperor Nicholas II was a charming kind man but too weak to be a successful autocrat.'

Mountbatten retained powerful feelings of nostalgia for Russia. Visiting that same year, he wrote: 'I was overpowered by the emotion of going back to a country I had known fairly well as a child, where so many of my closest family had lived in such tremendous splendour and then been murdered in this ghastly way. I felt it all the way through and I was quite exhausted when I came back.'

In the summer of 1975, Victoria's grandson, Prince Philip, visited Costa Rica on the royal yacht *Britannia* and met Irène's grandson Alfredo.

The year closed with little news of Anna Anderson. Sigismund, however, paid a convoluted tribute to Rittenhouse's research into the case. His letter forms a counter to Mountbatten's rebuff of Mr Woodcock-Clarke. On October 1st 1975, he wrote: 'Al [sic] your details investigating the case of Anastasia seem to me to be very important, I admire your extensive study to search after the events occurred in the matter.'

· In one of his last letters to Rittenhouse, on August 24th 1977, Sigismund told him that he was reading a book entitled *Tutor To The Tsarevich*. Published in 1975, it was a biography of Sydney Gibbes, the English tutor to the Romanov children who had given testimony soon after the murders. He later became an Orthodox priest and, by the time he agreed to meet Anna Anderson, in 1954, he was going by the name of Father Nicholas. After meeting the claimant, the Rotherham-born Gibbes declared: 'If that woman is Anastasia, I am a Chinaman.'

Anna Anderson would outlive all 12 children of the Hesse Princesses – dying, aged 87, in Charlottesville, Virginia, in 1984.

Prince Sigismund of Prussia died, aged 81, in Puntarenas, in November 1978. After his death, his wife, Princess Charlotte, returned to Hemmelmark, where she lived with her daughter, Princess Barbara, and son-in-law, the Duke of Mecklenburg-Schwerin, until her death in 1989. Barbara died at Hemmelmark five years later.

Louis Mountbatten was the longest-surviving child of the four Hesse Princesses. In the spring of 1979, aged 78, he visited Sydney Gibbes' adopted son, George, in Oxford. He and his daughter Pamela were shown around the church set up by Gibbes, or Father Nicholas, in the late 1940s.

Stowed in the church were curious keepsakes brought back from Ekatcrinburg by Gibbes himself. Mountbatten registered the Tsar's felt boots and the chandelier from the girls' last bedroom. Years later, George Gibbes recalled: 'I showed them all that there is here. We sat in the drawing room and he said, "I have all the things of the good days of the Imperial Family and you have all the things of the sad days".'

A few months later, in August 1979, Mountbatten himself was assassinated: blown up by the IRA on a family boat trip off the Irish coast, near Mullaghmore, County Sligo.

13

*'It is done . . . but the story will go
on and on.'*
Peg, daughter-in-law of Ernie

Nearly 20 years after her death, Victoria's daughter Alice's wish to be buried with her aunt Ella in Jerusalem was granted. Her body was laid to rest in Ella's church on August 3ʳᵈ 1988. Six years later, Prince Philip visited Jerusalem to see his mother honoured as a 'righteous gentile' for protecting a Jewish family, in Greece, during the Second World War.

In the early 1990s, the Mountbatten family heard of a receipt signed by a Count Benckendorf for a 'box of diamonds and things belonging to Princess Victoria of Battenberg'. Found in a Moscow archive, the receipt referred to the jewellery left behind by Victoria as war was breaking out in 1914. Unfortunately, the lack of any further details prevented the family from ever claiming compensation.

In 1993, Prince Philip provided DNA to help identify the bones of the Romanovs. He was not inclined to blame the Russians for the murder of his relations. He later said: 'You can't condemn a whole nation for what a few extremists – fundamentalists – do or did. Even amongst the people who botched the execution, there were some – even though they were almost paralytically drunk – who decided they weren't going to take part in this.'

His DNA proved a perfect match with Alix and three of her children:

Olga, Tatiana and Anastasia. The identity of the other two children, whose bodies were separate from those of the rest of the family, has been in dispute for many years, agonised over by the Orthodox Church, and repeatedly referred to in the *Romanov News* with the curiously buoyant catchline: 'Keep Calm and Stay Tuned'.

On the 80th anniversary of the killings, in 1998, the remains of the five members of the Imperial Family were laid to rest in the Peter Paul Fortress in St Petersburg, where most of the Russian monarchs have been entombed since Peter the Great. The burial ceremony itself was controversial, with Boris Yeltsin, the Russian leader, and the Patriarch of the Orthodox Church both, at various points, refusing to attend.

There were discussions about who should represent the Queen. In the end, it was agreed that Prince Michael of Kent would attend in a private capacity. There were reports, in the British media, that monarchists had not forgiven King George V for his failure to save his cousins.

The self-appointed head of the Romanov family, Grand Duchess Maria, a descendant of Tsar Alexander II, then based in Madrid, insisted she would lead the Romanov contingent, despite several objections, not least that she, as the product of a morganatic marriage, could not possibly be the head of the family. One less generous quibble was that she did not look sufficiently regal. The other contender for leader, Prince Nicholas, a descendant of Tsar Nicholas I, who was then living in Gstaad, criticised Maria's assumption of the leading role, while gallantly defending her appearance. 'Russian ladies who do not follow prescriptions of fashion tend to be overweight,' he said.

He added that the Romanov men, too, tended to put on weight, referring, in passing, to Ella's stepson Dmitri's only child, Paul Romanov-Ilyinsky. While his father had been a martyr to his dry martinis, Paul made a success of his life, being elected Mayor of Palm Beach three times. 'I'm a portly man,' said Prince Nicholas. 'Rosty [his cousin] also portly, Paul of Palm

Beach, also portly. [Grand Duchess] Maria might not be considered regal – immaterial. In fact, she would be pleasing to the eye of the average Russian woman.'

*

In the century or more since their murders, Ella and Alix have both become cult figures, honoured with accolades, memorials and monuments.

Victoria and Irène might not have been surprised by the popular reverence for Ella. Even in their youth, Victoria recognised that her younger sister was unusually virtuous. And both sisters respected Ella's decision to become a nun.

But there was little early indication that Alix would one day be so revered. Her serious religious convictions had only become evident with her reluctance, before her marriage, to convert to Russian Orthodoxy.

The matter-of-fact Victoria and more conventional Irène had been horrified by Alix's espousal of Rasputin – and even further unsettled by her weakness for gewgaws, not least M Philippe's bell and Rasputin's comb.

The mysticism surrounding the 'Nun Martyr Ella', the 'White Angel of Moscow', began soon after her death, with allusions to Alapaevsk as Golgotha.

In an echo of the intrigues surrounding the death of Father Zossima, in Dostoyevsky's *Brothers Karamazov*, questions continued to be raised as to whether or not Ella's corpse had decomposed. Her friend, Father Seraphim, never wavered in his claim that her body remained incorrupt. When Ella's coffin had been opened in the presence of Russian clergy in Peking, they had endorsed his stance. The last Imperial ambassador to China added that, aside from a large bruise on the side of her face, Ella had not changed at all 'since the day when I, before my departure for Peking, said goodbye to her in Moscow'.

Her stepson, Dmitri, attested that, three months after her death, Ella was all too identifiable. He was in London, at the beginning of 1920, when he was shown a photograph. '[I] was told that the bodies were unrecognisable. That's not true. I recognised Elizabeth Feodorovna,' he said. 'The photographs are truly horrible and that horror remained before my eyes for a long time.'

Stories of miracles soon emerged. Some claimed that, when Ella's coffin split, clear fragrant fluid flowed from it. Her long-time admirer, Felix Yusupov, treasured a sweet-smelling piece of wood from her coffin, declaring: 'The only relics I have of the Grand Duchess Elizabeth are a few beads from her rosary and a fragment of wood from her coffin. The wood at times exudes a delicious odour of flowers.'

Ella was canonised by the Moscow Patriarchate in 1992. Six years later, a statue of her was installed as one of ten 20th-century martyrs above the West Door of Westminster Abbey. The dedication ceremony was conducted before the Queen and Prince Philip.

In Moscow, the Martha and Mary Convent holds relics, including the glove Ella dropped as she left for the last time. The schoolroom at Alapaevsk, where she was held captive, has been turned into a chapel dedicated to her memory, with a museum exhibiting photographs and documents, along with an austere-looking single bed and disquieting life-size models of nuns in habits. An additional chapel has been built near to the mineshaft where she died.

A hundred years after the revolution, in 2017, Vladimir Putin himself paid a bizarre tribute to Ella, at a memorial ceremony held alongside a recreation of the seven-metre 'forgiveness' cross she built for Grand Duke Serge. 'This extraordinary woman is worthy of special mention,' he pronounced. 'A tireless worker and well-doer she was canonised by the Russian Orthodox Church. She didn't leave the country during the years of tremendous hardships and for the rest of her life remained faithful to the ideals of Christian forgiveness and love.'

Alix and Ella were canonised by the unofficial Russian Orthodox Church Abroad in 1981. Nineteen years later, Alix was canonised as Saint Alexandra the Passion Bearer by the regular Russian Orthodox Church. Between 2,000 and 4,000 pilgrims have taken part in the annual procession from Ekaterinburg to Ganina Yama, the monastery built on the site of the Four Brothers mine, where the bodies of Alix and her family had first been stowed.

Ella and Alix are also both commemorated in the Russian chapel at their 'cosy old home', in Darmstadt. Every year, on July 17th, a liturgy is read and a procession takes place. The chapel contains a piece of Alix's embroidery and a hammer used at the time of the foundation. An annual pilgrimage is conducted between Darmstadt and the Princesses' old haunt of Wolfsgarten.

A new monument depicting Nicky and Alix with Serge and Ella was unveiled in 2020 in Primorsky Park in Alushta in the Crimea. Funds for the 18.5-million rouble statue were met by the St Basil the Great Charitable Foundation and the Double Headed Eagle Society.

Tourists may now travel a so-called Imperial Route, a train journey from Ekaterinburg to Alapaevsk. One of the train's coaches is decked out with full Imperial decor and passengers are provided with early 20th-century Imperial costumes to wear for photographs.

In the UK, the Grand Duchess Elizabeth Romanov Society, founded in 2015, has conducted innumerable tributes to both Ella and Alix. In July 2021, the society held a ceremony on the Isle of Wight to mark the 40th anniversary of the canonisation of the royal martyrs: Nicky, Alix, their five children and Ella.

During the ceremony, a plaque was installed containing soil from Ekaterinburg and Alapaevsk. In the afternoon, those who had attended the 'ceremony of the placing of soil' were invited to St Mildred's Church, Whippingham, to visit the grave of the Hesse Princesses' sister, Victoria.

These days, the society's founder, the tireless Maria Harwood, seems to be less preoccupied with Ella than with Ella's husband, Grand Duke Serge. On the subject of the Grand Duke's sexuality, she is at odds with Prince Rainer von Hessen. Over a nervous tea at the Charlotte Street Hotel in London, she emphasises: 'He was not homosexual. Sergei and Ella were very happy. Sergei was warm and loving. Sergei was an Orthodox believer . . . it was at the centre of his life. If he'd been homosexual he would have been going to hell.'

The worship of Alix and Ella shows little sign of abating. Would Victoria and Irène have felt the accolades provided any compensation for their sisters' early deaths? At the time, the heartbroken Victoria had tried to be philosophical: 'I think one is grateful to be able to look back on happy times they shared with us, so that one does not grudge them their peace or wish them back into a world that might have more sorrows in store for them.'

It is hard to know how Irène would have received one recent Russian visitor to Hemmelmark who was reported to have scooped up soil in a jar, saying he was conserving a piece of holy ground once stood on by Ella and the Imperial Family.

Irène's great-granddaughter, Duchess Donata of Mecklenburg, and her author husband, Alexander von Solodkoff, have a more worldly attitude to their ancestors. Their spruce home is yards from Irène's 90-room 'Herrenhaus', the main house at Hemmelmark. Here they have conscientiously conserved portraits, photographs, papers and letters; their collection includes an album of beautiful hand-painted envelopes sent from Russia by Alix and Ella. They are proud of the gold-domed family mausoleum nearby. But they retain an easy sense of humour and are amused by their neighbour's vivid recollections of 'Princess Heinrich' and her tea-time strictures.

Donata took her mother Barbara's side in opposing Anna Anderson, but the most she will say of the claimant is that she was 'lively'. Alexander acknowledges the pain and cost of the case; he chuckles, however, as he recalls an outing with Donata to see Kenneth MacMillan's ballet *Anastasia*, which the pair saw in London in the 90s. The ballet features the claimant's meeting with her 'aunt' Irène in Berlin. Alexander flutters his hands elaborately: 'Here was Princess Irène – dancing about!'

Alexander was with Ernie's daughter-in-law, Peg, in 1994, when she received the news that the DNA results had gone against Anna Anderson. 'It's done,' Peg announced triumphantly, before adding: 'but the story will go on and on.'

In 2010, a massive restoration programme began in the Alexander Palace. In fact, odd bits of renovation had started as early as 1994, when the Queen and Prince Philip visited. The Prince was particularly interested in the work because of the Windsor fire in 1992. The palace was reopened in August 2021 and has since received thousands of visitors.

The recreation of the Tsarina's bedchamber took two years and presented problems, not least as Ella's English manufacturers of the chintz, Charles Hindley & Sons in Welbeck Street, had closed nearly 100 years before.

Painstaking repairs followed on Alix's boudoir, the Lilac Room. Restoration experts used photographs and historic samples from the Tsarskoe Selo and Pavlovsk Museums. Around 1896, Alix had presented the original architect with an actual lilac bloom to give him an idea of the colour she wanted. Great efforts have been made to recreate all the purple fabrics, including the mauve silk on the walls. Italian specialists analysed the fibres, types of thread and the methods of weaving.

When the work was completed, the white wooden fittings and garish purple background made the room look more Sylvanian Families than Imperial. This may have brought a wry smile to the lips of Ella's forthright stepdaughter, Maria Pavlovna. She had always had mixed feelings about the decor: 'Mauve silk – the effect was frankly ugly, but comfortable and gay.' In a memoir, published in 1931, she described how the habitually awkward Alix had relished her Lilac Room: 'The Empress ordinarily sat lengthwise on the chaise longue, half reclining against cushions covered with lace. Behind her there would be a sort of glass screen, protecting her from draughts and her legs would be covered to the knees by a doubled shawl of lace lined with mauve muslin.'

After the First World War, some of the original furniture from the Lilac Room was found wrecked in the palace grounds. It included Alix's delicate writing table and an upright piano, both of which have been restored using special ivory enamel paint.

The cabinets are packed with books, drawing supplies and improving board games, including the 'flea game', *jeu de puces* (tiddly winks), that had once been thought so good for the children's eye concentration. The shelves and mantelpieces are covered with the Tsarina's favourite family photos, glass vases, porcelain figurines and handmade souvenirs.

More than a hundred years on, the Lilac Room looks eerily as it did on the fateful day when the Tsarina received Sir Henry Wilson in 1917. Sir Henry had been struck, first, by the palace's serene atmosphere, then by the prevalence of that 'bric-a-brac'.

He had taken Alix back to her childhood, evoking fond memories of joyful tennis parties in Darmstadt.

At that point in 1883, the Hesse sisters were all still unmarried. It would be several months before Victoria took her wedding vows. And Ella's fate was uncertain as she dithered pleasurably over Grand Duke Serge.

That summer, Queen Victoria was fully confident of dispatching unwelcome suitors and making perfect matches for her motherless granddaughters.

The Tsarina's mood had lifted as she remembered golden days so full of promise for her, the merry 'Princess Sunshine', and her three sisters; a time when fortune smiled on the four Princesses of Hesse.

ACKNOWLEDGEMENTS

My first thanks go to Duchess Donata of Mecklenburg and Alexander von Solodkoff, for giving me access to hundreds of unpublished letters, the majority of them written by Donata's great grandmother, Irène, to her sister, Victoria. There was also correspondence between Irène's other sisters, Alix and Ella, and letters to Irène from Tsar Nicholas II and Queen Victoria.

The collection had lain in boxes, virtually untouched, at Alexander and Donata's house, at Hemmelmark, since 1950. They generously invited me to spend several days with them, combing through the letters in their sunny drawing-room. They also introduced me to a neighbour, the late Isabella von Bethmann Hollweg, who had known Princess Irène.

Dr Rainer Maass sorted out letters and photographs for me at the Darmstadt Archive: the letters were mainly from the four Princesses to their brother, Ernie, in whom they often confided. Dr Maass printed out an article containing previously unpublished letters sent from Alix to her maid, Madeleine Zanotti, in 1918. He also located a letter from Irène to Madeleine Zanotti concerning the Polish woman claiming to be Grand Duchess Anastasia.

Julie Crocker, Senior Archivist of the Royal Archives at Windsor, was unstintingly helpful, unearthing a rich collection of letters from the Princesses, ranging from childhood notes to Queen Victoria in the 1870s to the elderly Irène's demure correspondence with Queen Mary in the 1950s. She supplied letters from diplomats in St Petersburg before the Revolution and reports from various witnesses following the murders of Alix and Ella in 1918. When the Archives were closed, during Covid, she posted copies of letters. Emily Rawlings provided material from the Hartley Library at Southampton University.

Greg Rittenhouse emailed copies of unpublished letters sent to him by Irène's son, Prince Sigismund, through the late 60s and early 70s. He gave me an account of his visit to Prince Sigismund, in Costa Rica, in 1969, and also posted me a cassette tape of an interview conducted with Sigismund in 1976. Ian Shapiro proved, as always, a rich source of photographs and documents, including handwritten cards. I also studied papers belonging to Sir Philip Preston. Thanks to all these people for their kindness.

I must also thank Prince Rainer von Hessen for taking the time and trouble to show me around the beautiful house and grounds of Wolfsgarten. Maria Harwood, the founder of the Grand Duchess Elizabeth Romanov Society, readily provided information about her society's events and work. Sue Woolmans was generous with her time and knowledge; she posted me, not least, copies of entries from several diaries kept by members of the Imperial Family.

Nicholas Underhill kindly read an early draft of the book and gave excellent advice. Aurea Carpenter was, as ever, a brilliant and encouraging first editor; Helena Sutcliffe tackled finer details with unfailing proficiency and good cheer.

I am very grateful to Hugo Vickers, who helped me at crucial stages along the way, putting me in touch with Prince Rainer von Hessen and reading an early draft. Thanks finally to my family, especially my husband Craig, who accompanied me tirelessly through the four sisters' unrelenting ups and downs – and on research trips to Hemmelmark and Darmstadt.

BIBLIOGRAPHY

Almedingen EM: An Unbroken Unity (London, The Bodley Head, 1964)

Azar Helen, Madru Amanda: 1913 Diary of Grand Duchess Maria Nikolaevna (CreateSpace Independent Publishing Platform, 2017)

Azar Helen: Maria and Anastasia: The Youngest Romanov Grand Duchesses in Their Own Words: Letters, Diaries, Postcards (CreateSpace Independent Publishing Platform, 2015)

Azar Helen: Journal of a Russian Grand Duchess: Complete Annotated 1913 Diary of Olga Romanov (CreateSpace Independent Publishing Platform, 2015)

Bernstorff Count: Memoirs (New York, Random House, 1936)

Buchanan Sir George: My Mission To Russia And Other Diplomatic Memories, Volumes 1 and 2 (London, Cassell & Co, 1923)

Buchanan Meriel: Victorian Gallery (London, Cassell & Co, 1956)

Buchanan Meriel: Ambassador's Daughter (London, Cassell & Co, 1958)

Buxhoeveden Baroness Sophie: The Life And Tragedy of Alexandra Feodorovna (London, Longmans Green and Company, 1930)

Callwell Sir CE: Field Marshal Sir Henry Wilson: His Life and Diaries (London, Cassell & Co, 1927)

Carter Miranda: Three Emperors (London, Penguin Fig Tree, 2009)

Channon Henry 'Chips': The Diaries 1938-43 and 1943-57 edited by Simon Heffer (London, Hutchinson, 2021)

Clarke William: The Lost Fortunes of the Tsars (London, Weidenfeld & Nicolson, 1994)

Crawford Rosemary and Donald: Michael & Natasha (London, Weidenfeld & Nicolson, 1997)

Duff David: Hessian Tapestry (London, Frederick Muller, 1967)

Grand Duke Mikhail Alexandrovich: The Diary & Letters Translated, edited and annotated by Stephen R de Angelis (Sunnyvale, California, Bookemon Press, 2016)

Eade Philip: Young Prince Philip: His Turbulent Early Life (London, HarperPress, 2011)

Hall Coryne: Queen Victoria and the Romanovs (Stroud, Amberley Publishing, 2020)

Hardman Robert: Queen Of Our Times, The Life of Elizabeth II (London, Macmillan, 2022)

Hawkins George: Correspondence of the Russian Grand Duchesses: Letters of the Daughters of the Last Tsar (independently published, 2020)

Hunt Violet: The Flurried Years An Autobiography (London, Hurst & Blackett, 1926)

King Greg: The Last Empress (London, Aurum Press, 1994)

Kozlov Vladimir A and Khrustalev Vladimir M: Editors of the Last Diary of the Tsaritsa Alexandra (New Haven and London, Yale University Press, 1997)

Kurth Peter: Anastasia The Life of Anna Anderson (London, Jonathan Cape, 1983)

Lownie Andrew: The Mountbattens (London, Blink Publishing, 2019)

Maria, Grand Duchess of Russia A Memoir, translated from French and Russian by Russell Lord (New York, Halcyon House, 1931)

Massie Robert K: Nicholas and Alexandra (New York, Atheneum, 1967)

Massie Robert K: The Romanovs: The Final Chapter (London, Jonathan Cape, 1995)

Maylunas Andrei and Mironenko Sergei: A Lifelong Passion Nicholas and Alexandra Their Own Story (London, Weidenfeld & Nicholson, 1996)

Mienert Dr Marion: Maria Pavlovna A Romanov Grand Duchess in Russia and in Exile. (Leonnart-Bernadotte-Stiftung, 2004)

Miller Llana D: The Four Graces (California, Kensington House Books, 2011)

Pearson John: The Selling of the Royal Family (Simon and Schuster, 1986)

Pitcher Harvey: When Miss Emmie Was in Russia (London, John Murray 1977)

Ponsonby Sir Frederick: Recollections of Three Reigns (London, Odhams Press, 1951)

Rappaport Helen: Four Sisters (London, Pan Macmillan, 2015)

Ridley Jane: George V: Never a Dull Moment (London, Chatto & Windus, 2021)

Rounding Virginia: Alex and Nicky (New York, St Martins Press, 2012)

Soroka Marina: Britain, Russia and the Road to the First World War (Farnham, Ashgate Publishing, 1988)

Stopford Bertie: The Russian Diary of an Englishman (London, William Heinemann, 1919)

Van Der Kiste John: Prince Henry of Prussia (Devon, A & F Publications, 2015)

Vickers Hugo: Alice Princess Andrew of Greece (London, Hamish Hamilton, 2000)

Von Meck Galina: As I Remember Them (London, Dennis Dobson, 1973)

Vovk Justin C: Imperial Requiem (Bloomington, Indiana, iUniverse, 2012)

Warwick Christopher: Ella Princess, Saint & Martyr (Chichester, John Wiley & Sons, 2006)

Wilson A N: Victoria: A Life (London, Atlantic, 2014)
Youssoupoff Prince: Rasputin (London, Jonathan Cape, 1927)
Youssoupoff Prince: Lost Spendour (London, Jonathan Cape, 1953)
Zeepvat Charlotte: From Cradle To Crown (Stroud, Sutton Publishing, 2006)

Other Sources

Royal Russia Annual Number 10: edited by Paul Gilbert, Ontario 2016. Elizabeth and Sergei: written by Valeria Mikhailova

Recollections of Victoria Mountbatten, Marchioness of Milford Haven, Hartley Library, University of Southampton

The Diaries of Nicholas II 1894–1896 Volume 1 and 1910–1913 Volume III. Translated, annotated and edited by Stephen R de Angelis. Powered by Bookemon

The Diaries of Grand Duke Konstantin Konstantinovich (KR) April 8 1877 – May 11 1915. Translated, annotated and edited by Stephen R de Angelis 2018 . Powered by Bookemon

Zarentage 1918–2018 Alix and Ella. Katalog der Fotoausstelling (published in German in Darmstadt 2018)

By Way Of Love, Holy Reverend Elizabeth published in Russian by the St Elizabeth Convent with text by Anna Galkova (Minsk, 2017)

Letters from Grand Duchess Maria Pawlowna to Wilhelm of Sweden included in a booklet published at Mainau

The Last Romanovs: Archival and Museum Discoveries in Great Britain and Russia. Edited by Maria Harwood, Windsor, 2017

Unpublished memoir of Prince Dmitri Romanov, property of his granddaughter, Penny Galitzine

Unpublished report written by Thomas Preston in February 1921: 'A Brief and Impartial Retrospect of Events which took place in the Urals and Siberia during 1917-1920'

Unpublished letters of Prince Sigismund of Prussia, published by kind permission of Greg Rittenhouse

Unpublished notes by Greg Rittenhouse following his meeting with Prince Sigismund in November 1969

Unpublished interview with Prince Sigismund in 1976

Royalty Digest 'The Name Irène' by Charlotte Zeepvat, September 2003 and Hemmelmark and its Mausoleum by Katrina Warne, October 2003

New York Times: articles on Prince Sigismund 21.10.23 and 22.12.27

Observer Interview with George Gibbes 14.7.85

Author interviews with Prince Nicholas Romanov and Prince Rostislav Romanov in 1998

Papers from the Personal Chancellery of the Head of the Imperial House of Russia HIH The Grand Duchess Maria Vladimirovna

German letters from Princess Irène regarding Anna Anderson; and from the Tsarina to Madeleine Zanotti published in Darmstadt's 'Archive News', translated into English by the author

Royal Archive

Chapter 1

Victoria: 'Irène is always good. I love her so much & Ella too.' RA VIC/MAIN/Z78/1

Victoria: 'we hope that he and his soldiers will return soon Victoria.' RA VIC/MAIN/Z78/26.

Ella: 'It is very foggy and we play in the corridor'. RA VIC/MAIN/Z78/39.

Victoria: 'so that she cannot write'. RA VIC/MAIN/Z78/60.

Victoria 'Papa and Mama gave us a theatre'. RA VIC/MAIN/Z78/65.

Ella: 'Victoria and I may ride together'. RA VIC/MAIN/Z78/121.

Victoria: 'We wear it alternately.' RA VIC/MAIN/Z78/131.

Victoria: 'I should very much like to be a comfort to Mama'. RA VIC/MAIN/Z78/103.

Victoria: 'we shall always think of you and dear Scotland when we wear them'. RA VIC/MAIN/Z78/158.

Ella: 'badly wounded but is much better now'. RA VIC/MAIN/Z78/166.

Chapter 4

Victoria: 'put out his hand and stroked Ella's knee'. RA VIC/MAIN/Z174/8.

Ella: 'she wishes for one.' RA VIC/MAIN/Z78/178.

Irène: 'in this dreadfully anxious time. Irène.' RA VIC/MAIN/Z174/9.

Victoria: 'I will send the hair & the flowers in a day or two'. RA VIC/MAIN/Z174/21

Alix: they are now looking down on us, Alicky.' RA VIC/MAIN/Z174/23.

Irène: 'Serge felt it also so dreadfully. Irène'. RA VIC/MAIN/Z174/32.

Irène: 'Royal Institute on Wednesday. Your very loving child Irène' RA VIC/MAIN/ Z476/84.

Ella: 'God grant health, fear worst, Ella'. RA VIC/MAIN/Z499/15

Victoria: 'I return here.' RA VIC/MAIN/Z499/21

Irène: 'Ella takes her on from frontier, am writing. Irène.' RA VIC/MAIN/Z499/24.

Ella: 'two days before us.. summer weather, Ella.' RA VIC/MAIN/Z499/38.

Alix and the Tsar: 'He gently went to sleep. Alix, Nicky.' RA VIC/MAIN/XZ499/61.

Alix: 'this morning at 10.00. Kisses Alix.' RA VIC/MAIN/Z499/74.

Ella: 'Christmas Lent makes it later impossible.' RA VIC/MAIN/Z499/89.

Ella: 'the dress is an embroidered silver cloth.' RA VIC/MAIN/Z274/25.

Ella: 'young couple looking happy, cosily established.' RA VIC/MAIN/Z499/156

Ella: 'Alix looks.. well & hardly feels her leg . . .' RA VIC/MAIN/Z274/55.

Alix: ' for have you not been as a Mother to me, since beloved Mama died . . .' RA VIC/ MAIN/Z174/57.

Chapter 5

Alix: 'Darling Ernie, Irène and Henry left late last night.' RA VIC/MAIN/Z274/49.

Irène: 'we have on the whole nice weather.' RA VIC/MAIN/174/1.

Chapter 6

Charles Hardinge: 'English gold was the doing of the Grand Duke Serge.' RA VIC/ MAIN/W/45/108.

Chapter 7

Hardinge: 'has been repeatedly warned not to drive with the Grand Duke.' RA VIC/ MAIN/W/45/111.

Chapter 8

Irène: 'Fondest love to dear May and yourself . . . cousin Irène.' RA GV/PRIV/ AA54/47.

Irène: 'God Bless from your loving cousin Irène. 'RA GV/PRIV/CC45/345. RA Queen May: 'She looks lovely still but very thin'. RA GV/PRIV/CC26/57.

Irène: 'My darling May, I must write.' RA GV/PRIV/CC45/424

Chapter 9

Colonel Blair: 'beds were furnished to them by the population of Alapaievsk.' RA PS/PSO/GV/C/M/1344A/152.

Chapter 11

Sydney Gibbes: 'Imperial children were taken away disguised.' RA PS/PSO/GV/C/M/1344A/42.

Irène: 'My dear May, how I feel for you.' RA GV/PRIV/CC45/1012.

Irène: 'grateful for the consideration I received during the occupation.' RA GV/PRIV/CC46/486

Irène: 'Alfred leaving on September 5th. Ever so much love from your affectionate Irène'. RA GV/PRIV/CC46/490.

Irène: 'Grandmama in Balmoral especially'. RA GV/PRIV/CC45/1474.

Irène: 'The preparations are most tiring I find.' RA GV/PRIV/CC45/1657.

Chapter 12

Irène: 'In memory of "auld lang syne" ever your affectionate cousin Irène'. RA GV/PRIV/CC45/1739.

IMAGE PERMISSIONS

In-text images:

The following photographs, postcards and telegrams are reproduced with the kind permission of Ian Shapiro: pages 20, 36, 52, 55, 57, 72, 111, 126, 132, 143, 159 and 178.

Page 4: Queen Victoria with Princess Victoria by Jabez Hughes, 1864 © Royal Collection Trust/HM King Charles III.

Page 118: © Frances Welch.

Page 156: Album/Alamy Stock Photo.

Page 162: © Darmstadt Archive.

Pages 165 and 172: © Duchess Donata of Mecklenburg and Alexander von Solodkoff Hemmelmark Archives (Prussia).

Page 242: © Frances Welch.

Colour Plate inset:

Page 1

Top left: Tibbut Archive/Alamy Stock Photo.

Top right: © Charlotte Zeepvat/ILN/Mary Evans Picture Library.

Bottom centre: English Heritage/Heritage Images/Getty Images.

Page 2

Full page: Royal Collection Trust/© His Majesty King Charles III 2022.

Page 3

Top: reproduced with the kind permission of Ian Shapiro.

Bottom: Duchess Donata of Mecklenburg and Alexander von Solodkoff Hemmelmark Archives (Prussia).

Page 4

Top: University of Southampton Archives and Special Collections/University of Southampton.

Bottom: reproduced with the kind permission of Ian Shapiro.

Page 5

Top: Album/Alamy Stock Photo.

Bottom: The Picture Art Collection/Alamy Stock Photo.

Page 6

Top: Sueddeutsche Zeitung Photo/Alamy Stock Photo.

Bottom: C. E. de Hahn & Co., Zarskoje Selo; Hessisches Staatsarchiv, Darmstadt/Wikipedia (CCO).

Page 7

Top: reproduced with the kind permission of Ian Shapiro.

Bottom: Archive Collection/Alamy Stock Photo.

Page 8

Top: reproduced with the kind permission of Ian Shapiro.

Bottom: © Frances Welch.

INDEX

Page numbers in *italics* refer to illustrations. The following abbreviations are used: QV Queen Victoria; AH Alexandra of Hesse; EH Elizabeth of Hesse; IH Irène of Hesse; VH Victoria of Hesse